ONE WEEK IN AMERICA

ONE WEEK IN AMERICA

The 1968 Notre Dame Literary Festival
and a Changing Nation

PATRICK PARR

CHICAGO
REVIEW
PRESS

Published by Chicago Review Press Incorporated
814 North Franklin Street
Chicago, Illinois 60610
ISBN 978-1-64160-178-8

Library of Congress Cataloging-in-Publication Data
Library of Congress Control Number: 2020950092

Typesetting: Nord Compo

Printed in the United States of America
5 4 3 2 1

The Stepan Center, the University of Notre Dame Archives. April 4, 1968.
Courtesy of University of Notre Dame Archives.

"Silver wings upon their chest
These are men, America's best
One hundred men will test today but
Only three win the Green Beret."

**—Staff Sgt. Barry Sadler
(Song: "Ballad of the Green Beret")**

"So do your duty, boys, and join with pride
Serve your country in her suicide . . .
But just before the end even treason might be worth a try
This country is too young to die."

**—Phil Ochs
(Song: "The War Is Over")**

CONTENTS

PROLOGUE

How to Create a Festival with Only $2.72

"Two choices . . . burn down the ROTC building or . . . do something constructive."

—John E. Mroz[1]

NOTRE DAME FRESHMAN JOHN EDWIN MROZ sits down with thirteen other classmates in his dormitory lounge. He's just been named the new literary festival chairman, and he has plans. First, however, he wants to gauge the tastes of his own committee. "Let's think big," he tells them.

He starts with a simple question: *Which writers would you like to see on campus?*

All the young men are between eighteen and nineteen years old. High school literature classes still loom over their minds, so a few familiar names are mentioned first. William Golding's *Lord of the Flies*—required reading. Many in the group shrug, unexcited. Another name comes up—J. D. Salinger. Some smile at the thought of the reclusive author reappearing out of the blue at their festival. All have read *Catcher in the Rye*, but some feel they've outgrown Holden Caulfield's daily irritation about phonies. Mroz agrees, but he can't help but feel motivated to contact the author. *Why not?* he thinks, jotting down "Salinger" on the list of possibilities.

John E. Mroz.
Courtesy of Karen Linehan-Mroz.

The group's thinking veers toward more extreme guests—writers with a bit of shock value. Beat author William S. Burroughs is mentioned; his *Naked Lunch,* laced with obscenities, would be an edgy, electric reading. While a few nod, Burroughs doesn't seem quite right. But what about Norman Mailer? His WWII novel, *The Naked and the Dead,* was popular among students, and his off-the-cuff personality would be sure to enthrall an audience.[2]

Mroz and the group also loft the idea of emulating the 1967 Sophomore Literary Festival. Launched by Mississippian J. Richard Rossie, the two-day festival was a salute to the life and writing of William Faulkner, who died in 1962. Scholarly and enjoyable, the festival's template would be easy to reproduce and require only a modest budget. The group entertains the idea by throwing out names such as Albert Camus, Ernest Hemingway, Franz Kafka, and James Joyce. But no one is quite convinced. Mroz hasn't accepted the position of festival chairman to simply recycle a format from the year before. All who know him know his motto: "Think big, accomplish big."[3]

While the University of Notre Dame may well be the land of Knute Rockne and George Gipp (of "win one for the Gipper" fame), Mroz wants "to show the school off in an academic way."[4] But putting on some sort of dignified, high-minded national literary event is not exactly what he has in mind either. The ever-growing shadow of the war in Vietnam hovers over the group of freshmen. In early March, President

Lyndon B. Johnson issued a nine-point plan of reform to the Selected Service system. Front and center was his adjustment to the age group who'd be targeted first—nineteen-year-olds. He reasoned that younger men can "adapt" far quicker in the military, and the potential to disrupt future life plans such as marriage, a career, or children would be minimal.[5] It was as if LBJ had pointed his finger directly at each young man in that dorm room.

At least with this group, the spirit of protest is in the air.

The brainstorming continues. Several popular authors are named. Kurt Vonnegut's *Cat's Cradle* is "an easy read . . . short," and "a book they pass around the freshman dormitory." Mroz writes Vonnegut's name down and tells the committee that he's met Vonnegut several times at a bookstore near his home in Osterville, Massachusetts. *We've got a chance.*[6]

Robert Penn Warren's *All the King's Men* is mentioned, but the group respects Warren far more as a civil rights interviewer, so Mroz jots his name down too. Ray Bradbury is also thrown onto the list. *Fahrenheit 451* continues to start conversations about censorship, and the 1966 film helped bring it back into the mainstream long after its 1953 publication.

Sometime during the conversation, *Catch-22* crops up, and the freshmen are unanimously in favor of inviting Joseph Heller to campus. They can all relate to the plight of Yossarian, fighting in a war he wants no part in. Heller's novel has edge, and committee members share that they have to stifle their "laughter in the campus library" while reading the antiwar satire.

Mroz's list of authors to contact is impressive. His aim, as he puts it, is "to balance appreciation of good literature with realities of activist things going on at the time."

There is, however, a grand dose of reality to deal with: *How* is he going to contact these authors? If he reaches them, can he convince them to come to campus for an entire week? And how will he pay them?

This last question is the most difficult. After the conclusion of the 1967 Sophomore Literary Festival, J. Richard Rossie handed John Mroz the bank account information used specifically for the event. When

Mroz checked the balance, he was far from impressed: $2.72 . . . enough for about three books of stamps.[7]

The committee needs cash.

Several weeks after the meeting, Mroz brings his author list and proposal to the Notre Dame administration and faculty. He tells them his hopes of creating a weeklong literary event, covered by the national media, featuring authors such as Vonnegut (*I can talk to him . . . he lives near my house*) and Heller (*His book is very important to our generation now*). They listen politely but won't budge. While his ambition is admirable, few believe Mroz can bring such an incredible cast of artistic talent to campus. In addition, they remind Mroz that he cannot directly appeal to Notre Dame alumni to raise funds for the event.

But one member of the committee, Father Charles Sheedy, an English professor, is sympathetic to Mroz's fantastical plan. Father Sheedy tells John about his own ongoing correspondence with Joseph Heller and offers to write a cover letter in support of the committee's invitation. The effect would be clear: *This isn't just some young man looking to throw something crazy together. I can vouch for him.*[8]

Father Sheedy and Joseph Heller go *way* back. In April 1955, Heller, then an adman with Time Inc., had been able to slide a novel excerpt of a book he'd not yet finished, titled *Catch-18*, into a relatively popular anthology called *New World Writing*. Sheedy had read the early pages and written a letter of encouragement to Heller. Sheedy's words were kind enough that Heller deemed the letter his first piece of "fan mail."

Before his freshman year ends, Mroz goes along with Sheedy's idea and sends a formal letter of invitation to Joseph Heller, accompanied by Sheedy's official cover letter. Mroz heads back to Osterville with his fingers crossed.[9]

During the lead up to the spring of 1967, Mroz (majoring in Soviet area studies) keeps an eye on the political movements occurring across the nation. Massachusetts senator Robert F. Kennedy stews on the sidelines as President Johnson vacillates between peace and force in Vietnam. Kennedy, meanwhile, drums up support for his "three-point plan" to end the war, which he had announced on March 2. His proposal defies the direction Johnson is taking the nation, and divides the party further:

Sen. Kennedy:	Pres. Johnson:
The bombing of the North would, it was hoped, reduce the flow of men and supplies from North Vietnam to the Communist forces in the South. It should be clear by now that the bombing of the North cannot bring an end to the war in the South; that, indeed, it may well be prolonging that war.	The bombing of the North . . . is an integral part of our total policy which aims not to destroy North Vietnam but to force Hanoi to end its aggression so that the people of South Vietnam can determine their own future without coercion.[10]

On April 4, Rev. Martin Luther King Jr. delivers a fiery speech at Riverside Church in New York City calling for an end to an immoral war. After the speech, King urges all young Americans to declare themselves conscientious objectors. Answering a questioner in the audience, King expresses deep concerns about the country's direction: "I feel we are wrong in Vietnam, but if there are not some changes in our national direction and character, we are going to be in several more wars like this. . . . College students have already started responding with the kind of disenchantment and . . . dismay that causes many to say that they will go to jail . . . before they will fight in an unjust war."[11]

On April 15, many witness one of the largest antiwar protest movements in American history, with gatherings occurring simultaneously in San Francisco and New York. Dr. King is one of several leaders who help lead the New York City movement, titled the National Mobilization Committee to End the War in Vietnam. As many as five hundred thousand march in New York alone, coincidentally around the same number of American soldiers currently fighting in Vietnam. Streets and sidewalks are jammed throughout the march's two-mile stretch between Sheep Meadow in Central Park and the UN Secretariat Building in midtown. On television, news programs show protesters holding signs that say WOULD NAPALM CONVERT YOU TO DEMOCRACY? and NO VIETNAMESE EVER CALLED ME NIGGER. One couple holds a poster of an American flag with the stars swapped out with swastikas and question marks.[12]

Around this time, former vice president Richard Nixon tells reporters that North Vietnam's capital, Hanoi, "believes that if they just hang on they will win in Washington," thanks to the antiwar movement undercutting military confidence. General William Westmoreland tells Congress that "our Achilles heel is our resolve." In the eyes of John Mroz and many other young Americans, the nation seems split into rival camps: one camp would die in support of the government, right or wrong, while the other would die to assert its right to hold the government accountable.[13]

Television news coverage is personalizing the war to an uncomfortable degree, with on-the-ground reporting by journalists in Vietnam keeping worried families up at night. The experience of one Mrs. Morrow is commonplace. As she sits in the living room of her LaGrange, Georgia, home on April 30, 1967, watching the eleven o'clock news on Channel 2, the camera hones in on an unidentified wounded private. Mrs. Morrow looks closer at the television screen and then shouts at her husband in the other room, "Come quick, Landon!" For a few seconds—seconds Morrow says she'll never forget—Channel 2 shows her injured son, Spec. 4 Albert Landon Morrow Jr.[14]

———————————

For Mroz, the summer in Osterville means directing his disenchantment with Vietnam into a project he can believe in. Through the mail, Mroz receives his first bit of good news. Thanks to Father Sheedy's cover letter, Heller has accepted the offer, but with one condition: Heller's seven-year-old son is an intense Fighting Irish fan, and Heller wants an autographed football. It's an easy condition for Mroz to make good on. Just like that, one slot of the festival is filled.

Heller also delivers valuable advice to Mroz about contacting other authors: write personal letters and show very clearly that the author's work was deeply considered and would be given the utmost respect. With this in mind, and with Heller now committed to the event, Mroz fires off invitations to, among others, Ray Bradbury, Eudora Welty, Robert Penn Warren, Taylor Caldwell, and a Hail Mary to J. D. Salinger.[15]

Despite having Heller's strong written commitment, Mroz wants to make more of an impact on the author—to show that this festival is a serious operation with dedicated staff. So on June 27, Mroz meets up at Penn Station with George Ovitt Jr., a fellow committee member, aspiring writer, and New Jersey resident. From there, they take a taxi to Heller's New York apartment. Ovitt is wearing his only suit, a gift from his father; it's acrylic, in "a color we now describe as 'wheat.'" As they step out of the taxi, Ovitt takes a few deep breaths, straightens out his suit, and prepares to meet an author whose book he'd "devoured . . . in one sitting." Unfortunately, as they walk into the building, a pigeon drops a load on his suit. Heller opens his door and immediately sees the long whitish-brown stain. Already nervous, Ovitt can't help but be embarrassed. Heller's wife, Shirley Held, guides him and Mroz into Heller's study to help wipe off the splatter. Ovitt gushes to Heller for a few minutes about how much he loves *Catch-22*. He sees Heller as "young and handsome, and warm, and not even a tiny bit patronizing . . . the first writer I'd ever met in the flesh."[16]

As Ovitt sits rapt with awe, Mroz tries to keep the meeting professional. During the conversation, Heller mentions a few other authors who might consider attending. One is already on Mroz's list: Kurt Vonnegut, who Heller had mainly been following from a distance at that point. Ralph Ellison, author of the 1952 instant classic *Invisible Man*, also enters the conversation. While Mroz jots down names and strategies, Ovitt hands Heller his Modern Library edition of *Catch-22*. Heller signs it. (Fifty years later Ovitt would still treasure that autographed copy sitting on his library shelf.)

Mroz's home in Osterville, Massachusetts, is but a stone's throw from the homes of several other authors. As he awaits responses to his letters, Mroz shifts his attention toward securing another author high on his list: Norman Mailer. One of the committee members is friends with Michael Ellis, a New York producer who mentioned that Mailer lived in the Brooklyn Heights neighborhood. Perhaps for a moment, Mroz considers first writing a personal letter. But he decides to be more direct. With a few other fellow committee members, Mroz travels to Brooklyn Heights and hopes to introduce himself to Mailer face-to-face.[17]

Mroz walks around the area in search of Mailer, creeping up and down sidewalks and streets. Eventually, the police come over and ask him what he's doing there. Mroz doesn't try to explain himself and decides to abandon the idea.

Mroz heads back to Osterville disappointed, but upon arriving home, he learns a bit of good news. It turns out that Mailer has a house in Provincetown, on the water. Provincetown is located about one hour away from Mroz's home and rests on the clenched-fist coastal arm of Massachusetts. Dressed in suits and looking more like up-and-coming businessmen than nomadic soon-to-be college sophomores, Mroz and a couple of other committee members tentatively knock on Mailer's door. Norman's wife, Beverly, answers. Mroz is direct: "We came to talk to Norman Mailer."

Their timing, and the general all-are-welcome vibe of P-Town, is fortunate for the group; 1967 Provincetown is filled with carpenters, fishermen, and artists looking for an extra level of focus or dimension to their work. Nobody would bat an eye at a bunch of rebel sophomores tracking down a famous author.

Beverly tells the young group that Norman has been planning a walk through the famous sand dunes nearby. It's Mailer's way of clearing his head. Undeterred, the group decides to wait it out.

Upon his return, Norman can't help but chuckle at the sight of the suited young men. "Look at you guys," he says. "Why don't you go and change into something human and we can go for a walk."[18]

Mroz and company take him up on his suggestion and return later in the afternoon for a walk through the sand dunes.

At this stage in his career, Mailer has been bouncing from one genre to another. He's written an off-Broadway play, *The Deer Park*, based on his 1955 novel, and a collection of his short fiction has recently been released. But now Mailer has his attention fixed on something else.

Actors Rip Torn and Eddie Bonetti join the group on the hike through the dunes. The conversations range from the logistics of the weeklong festival to unidentified flying objects, a natural-enough topic of discussion in the Martian landscape of the dunes. Eventually, Mailer shares his current ambitions with Mroz and the gang. He's in the process of self-financing two independent films and hopes to make his mark as a director. Although nothing is set in stone, Mailer, Torn, and Bonetti all feel that perhaps something could be done at the festival.

For Mroz, it's as if he's caught lightning. *We officially have a festival.* He drives back to Osterville with the commitment of two leading authors and the confidence to rope in others. While Mailer's commitment is hardly set in stone—the sand dunes conversation may have just been a thinking-out-loud moment—the afternoon they had spent together is enough to breathe new life into the chairman's dream of putting on a festival worthy of national attention.

On July 24, Mroz gets a reply in the mail from Ray Bradbury. It's not a *no*, but it's not a *yes* either. Bradbury wants another two months to make his decision. At the moment, he is at his home in California overseeing the film adaptation of *The Illustrated Man*.[19]

One week later, Mroz receives another letter, this time from Robert Penn Warren. Writing from France, Warren all but shuts the door on attending. "The dates ruin it for me." But he leaves open a glimmer of hope; maybe "an evening or afternoon thing" would be possible.[20]

There is one final author for Mroz to visit before he returns to Notre Dame—a tall, quirky, perpetually depressed middle-aged man living in Osterville, and then West Barnstable, for over a decade. To Mroz, Kurt Vonnegut is "practically a next-door neighbor." He decides to head over to Vonnegut's home with a cadre of committee support . . . and suits, of course.

Upon arriving, Mroz sees Vonnegut "wood-paneling a new party house next to his home overlooking a lake—his mouth was full of nails, he was swinging a hammer, the air filled with sawdust." They talk for two easygoing hours, and Vonnegut says he'll come to their festival. The author is "especially pleased to see the festival being undertaken by *sophomores*." The next day, Vonnegut, working on his "Dresden book" at the time, invites the sophomore committee to dinner.[21]

By the end of the summer, Mroz has three authors verbally committed to the festival, and two authors he'd check in on again. Driving back to campus, Mroz knows he'll be having a different conversation with the Notre Dame higher-ups than the one he had in the spring. Yes, it's great that he has these big names, but he knows there is the matter of a budget to attend to, and $2.72 is still staring him in the face.[22]

> "We did about anything we could that was legal to raise money."
>
> —John Mroz[23]

In the early fall of his sophomore year, Mroz goes before the Notre Dame administration committees and pleads his case for more funding. Compared to the previous spring, his confidence is soaring. Not only have Mailer, Heller, and Vonnegut agreed to come, Mroz and the committee actually met with them, face-to-face. The promise is real. *They'll come, and we need to be ready for them.* Mroz may have even dangled the possibility of Ray Bradbury's attendance. *We're still working that out.*

A sophomore negotiating terms with Ray Bradbury, and "checking back in" with Mr. Robert Penn Warren—one summer had turned Mroz into a major literary player.

The administration committee feels reassured by the involvement of Father Charles Sheedy and agrees to support the festival. Suddenly, $2.72 becomes $2,002.72. Several faculty departments also pitch in undisclosed amounts. The English Department is among them, backing up Professor Sheedy's assistance with cash—after all, besides the obvious connection of literature being the heartbeat of the festival, four of Mroz's cohorts are English majors.

Having several thousand dollars to work with relieves Mroz, but it's not nearly enough to fulfill his vision. In the summer he'd talked with Mailer about creating some kind of film event, a spectacle that would gain national attention. While Mroz isn't sure if Mailer will deliver, he wants to have the money ready just in case.[24]

To raise funds, Mroz and the sophomore committee begin to plan a small film series starting in January 1968, after the football season has ended. They also offer their fellow undergraduate students a chance to be a patron of the festival for only one dollar. Flyers are pinned to boards around campus, and notices in the school newspaper become regular.[25]

Now that he has a small stream of financing and a trio of big-name authors to trumpet, Mroz follows up with Ray Bradbury.

On October 12 Bradbury replies, but "with deep regret" he tells Mroz his schedule won't allow it. Owing to the popularity of his books with the committee, losing Bradbury is a tough blow. On November 3, Robert Penn Warren also sends a rejection, writing that he is "toward the end of a book, and I must be stern with myself and decline even the most attractive distraction."

With Warren and Bradbury bowing out, and with no response (as expected) from J. D. Salinger, Mroz pivots his attention toward Heller-recommended author Ralph Ellison, who in the fall of 1967 is delivering lectures in Chicago and Detroit about the experience of being a Black American. Ellison had been making headlines for his refusal to take sides in the complex arguments of Black separatism versus integration facing the civil rights movement at the time: "I don't see a bunch of people who hate themselves. . . . I don't care what Dr. Martin Luther King says. On the human level there are many sources for self-regard and they exist within the Negro community."[26]

Having grown up in predominantly White communities, Mroz is a bit intimidated by Ellison at first. His freshman roommate, Marty Kress, recalls a moment in those early fall months, when everyone was getting used to each other in Breen-Phillips Hall. There was a Black student who lived on the same floor. Kress had been looking for Mroz, and when John came back about an hour later, Kress asked where he'd been. It seemed as if John's mind had been altered in some way. "That's the first time I've ever had a conversation with an African American," Kress recalls John saying. One year later, here he is, corresponding with Ralph Ellison, offering the author a chance to speak at a Mroz-orchestrated festival.[27]

On November 5, Mroz receives a brief reply from Ellison, pointing the young chairman toward a secretary of a speakers' bureau. "She will inform you of free dates and . . . under what arrangements."

Not exactly hopeful, and the letter implies that if Ellison does come, they'll need to pay up. Nevertheless, Mroz is determined to diversify the lineup of writers, even if no one around thinks they can get Ellison to attend.

By the middle of November, Mroz and the committee can see that as long as they continue pushing themselves and sending personal invitations, they *will* end up with an unprecedented event worthy of national attention. But therein lies the rub. Being *worthy* of national attention is one thing, but actually getting it is another thing entirely. Though well known to the general reading public, Joseph Heller isn't a journalist. Heller and the other attendees aren't going to write a detailed report of the festival. These men are writers, not contracted reporters.

The sophomore committee wants as close to a guarantee of media attention as they can get, and that means adding a literary critic to their lineup. Father Charles Sheedy recommends one of the most respected critics in the country, Granville Hicks, who for nearly a decade has been contributing a popular monthly column for the *Saturday Review* called Literary Horizons. Hicks has also been a judge for the National Book Award, and his book reviews hold influence over other critics across the country. At sixty-six, Hicks has experienced the highs and lows of the twentieth century—joining and leaving the Communist Party in the 1930s and later writing humanistic, even-handed critiques. His presence would provide the festival a chance to be fairly represented by a neutral observer.

But Mroz can't simply ask Hicks to "write about our literary festival!" Such a blunt request would be, well, sophomoric. Nor does Mroz have the means of resorting to underhanded tactics like "buying" a positive review—assuming, that is, Hicks could even be bought. After doing a bit of background research on Hicks, Mroz sits down at his typewriter and focuses on creating a *personal* connection between the writer and the committee:

> My dear Mr. Hicks,
> It is indeed my most distinct pleasure to write to you on behalf of the students of Notre Dame. As you might have heard, the Sophomore Class at Notre Dame is sponsoring the 1968 National Literary Festival entitled: "Minds and Motivations: A Symposium of Great American Writers." The Festival will take place April 1–6, 1968 with a most impressive list of writers.
>   We definitely wanted you to be here for the Festival in April to deliver and hopefully participate in the final panel of discussion. Then, one of the distinguished members of our English department suggested that Granville Hicks should not only give a lecture, but that he should be Master of Ceremonies for as many days as he could possibly stay (hopefully, Wednesday afternoon to Saturday afternoon). We are all quite familiar with your outstanding background and there is a unanimous belief that only Granville Hicks can be our Master of Ceremonies. Now that I've let the cat out of the bag, we can only hope that you are already saying "yes", or at least "possibly"!
>   . . . We feel a particular pride in this Festival because it is a student orientated and organized (and financed) event. There is so much talk of the grubby and uninterested college student. We're tired of such talk, and we stake our case on this Festival. It's the students who want the Festival . . . the students who want you, Mr. Hicks. I only can say that I hope you will not consider this just another invitation—but rather as a please from the hearts of thousands of interested students. We will all be anxiously awaiting to hear from you. Thank you so very much for your time. Please give us your deepest consideration—your reply means a lot to many of us.
>   Most sincerely,
>   John E. Mroz[28]

It's in the second paragraph where Mroz shows his persuasive abilities. Requesting a lecture as well as a panel discussion isn't too outstanding, but asking Hicks to be *master of ceremonies*—a malleable, glittery title—shows how serious Mroz's offer is. The seriousness is doubled by mentioning the recommendation of a "distinguished" faculty member who "suggested" the MC idea in the first place. The subtext is clear: *If you don't believe us college students, believe a Notre Dame professor!*

It only takes five days for Hicks to reply. Yes, he'll come, but the title master of ceremonies is far too gaudy. He prefers "keynote speaker." He also recommends that the committee invite author Wright Morris to the festival. Morris and Hicks are friends, and the implication to Mroz is clear: *If you can get Wright Morris, I'll definitely enjoy myself a lot more, and you know what that might mean.*

Mroz makes plans to write to Morris as soon as possible. There is just one problem. Who *is* Wright Morris?

By late 1967, Morris has written fourteen novels, one of them a National Book Award winner. He's become a beloved professor at San Francisco State University but writes with a Nebraskan's soul. Most of his books encapsulate the Midwestern experience but have escaped the interest of the mainstream. In short, he is a critic's darling, churning out nuanced, mid-American material on an annual basis, all under the commercial radar. In 1963, fully aware that his work had not been able to capture a wide audience, Morris shrugged off the problem: "No book of mine can be read under a hair dryer, while bolting a hamburger or half-watching TV . . . everything is not for everybody."[29]

Before writing to Morris, Mroz makes sure to give his full attention to the author's 1957 National Book Award winner, *The Field of Vision*, a revolving-door narrative of Nebraskan characters on a trip to see a Mexican bullfight. Once the young chairman understands enough of Morris's voice, he types up his letter, lifting a bit of his own wording from his correspondence with Hicks.[30]

Mroz pops it in the mail and waits.

By this point in late November, Mroz is receiving correspondence almost daily from authors or their representatives. The momentum continues with a reply (*finally!*) from Norman Mailer. Well . . . from Mailer's secretary, Sandy Smith. Even though Mroz and other members of the committee had enjoyed a day in P-Town with him, bonding over films and UFOs, Mailer hadn't sealed his acceptance in writing.

It stays this way. Mailer communicates that he is still "slightly tempted" to come, and it's enough for Mroz to go ahead and refocus on fundraising. Small donations are coming primarily from faculty, administration, and an ever-increasing subculture of the student body.

Mroz and company scrape for every dollar they can get in late 1967. The university is beginning to rally around their effort, but with Notre Dame football every Saturday, the challenge of redirecting students' thoughts away from supporting their sacred team is an uphill battle. Until January, after the college football season, the only thing the sophomore committee can do is build their lineup, and that means securing as many big-name authors as possible.

George Ovitt understands the sophomore committee's struggle for student attention. To him, the literary festival exists on the fringes of campus life, what one might call the "other Notre Dame," a subset of "young men who hung out in the library and who attended the student-faculty coffee hour," and are "also the most likely to be seen at protests against the Dow Chemical Corporation, . . . the ROTC, or the continuation of Jim Crowism from Montgomery to Chicago." These young men have "long hair," wear "peacoats," and listen to protest singer "Phil Ochs." They drink "sparingly" and smoke "a bit of pot." They "love 'cinema' and read nonstop."[31]

Even without long hair, John Mroz is a proud member of the "other" Notre Dame, and his motivation for putting on a literary festival isn't only for his own personal gain. A greater, perhaps impossible goal is to have the event, for one blip of time, overshadow the football program and the military romance between Notre Dame and ROTC.

On December 4, Mroz hears back from Wright Morris. It's a *yes*, with conditions. His wife will come, and he wants travel expenses paid for, but he won't travel by plane, stating, "Since I plan to be the last man in space I shall take the train."[32]

It's not a problem. If bringing Morris into the fold guarantees a fully invested Granville Hicks, Mroz believes it's worth it, even with Morris's travel expense request.

Mroz writes to Granville Hicks, letting him know that, even though details are being worked out, Wright Morris and his wife will be attending the event. Writing from Athens, Ohio, on December 12, Hicks delivers his guarantee but asks, "Shouldn't we have an understanding with regard to the stipend?"

Ah, yes, the stipend. Mroz has batted around a baseline rate with other committee members, but without knowing the final numbers from their fundraising efforts, Mroz is reluctant to offer anything soaring. Besides, without knowing what Norman Mailer has planned, spectacle-wise, Mroz can't even begin to mention a figure without potentially offending the man who will be the "keynote speaker."

In order to settle this confusion, Mroz decides to visit New York City over the break, in the hopes of persuading Ralph Ellison and Norman Mailer.

But around December 20, just before his trip to New York City, Mroz receives an exciting letter from Sandy Smith. It's filled with details of Mailer's film project and, most important, confirmation that he wants to premiere the movie at Notre Dame. The film will have a bit of obscene language, but with "seven Irishmen" in the cast, Mailer believes that's enough to justify having the premiere at a university with an Irish Catholic background. Sandy ends the letter, "Let us know how this sounds to you."

Soon after the letter comes a phone call directly from Mr. Mailer. He wants Mroz to watch the film before it premieres, to make sure the "controversial segments" will be allowed. Mroz isn't too worried. The campus film series he and the committee have lined up to help with fundraising will also be controversial—an aspect they hope will help generate more interest in the festival.

With Mailer now on board for a two-night stay, the sophomore committee lasers in on two other names: Wright Morris and Ralph Ellison. Since several young men on the committee live on the West Coast, they decide to split up into teams. One group travels to San Francisco to make sure Morris will attend, while Mroz and others use their connection to Joseph Heller to see if they can greet Ralph Ellison in person.

In San Francisco, Morris is very impressed by the well-dressed committee's determination and respect. Morris says that he and his wife will indeed attend for the entire week, via train and bus.

In New York City, Mroz first visits a creatively overwhelmed Mailer, who shows Mroz nearly seven hours of unedited footage for his film, titled *Beyond the Law*. Mroz thinks a few of the obscenities in the film could cause Notre Dame administration some discomfort, but he isn't too concerned about it, saying later that the film can "still be shown on campus without the danger of . . . scandal erupting." The scandal Mroz is referring would stem from Notre Dame's conservative approach toward any and all artistic expression on campus. But Mroz is determined to push the boundaries President Theodore Hesburgh has established.[33]

Later, the committee meets Ralph Ellison rather quickly, thanks to Heller, who aids a few of the sophomores in finding Ellison's home. Confronted by the team of suits knocking on his door, Ellison is understandably flummoxed. After referring them to the speakers bureau, he has informed the group "no by letter" and even "no by phone," but "here you are at my door in New York!"

But the at-your-door-tactic is hard for the authors to resist. It takes a long conversation, but Ellison lowers his shield and agrees to come. Mroz is spellbound by Ellison's mind, calling him "one of the most intellectually stimulating, pleasant, entertaining men" he's ever spoken with.[34]

With the frenzy of college football finally fading from view, the committee seizes its chance to grab the spotlight. Ads and flyers go up again all over campus. In January, the *Notre Dame Observer* includes a notice for the literary festival, along with an impressive lineup of authors. The committee has only enough space in the paper to "sell" each of the writers with one short phrase:

Ralph Ellison	**Joseph Heller**
("*Invisible Man*")	("*Catch-22*")
Norman Mailer	**Wright Morris**
("*The Naked and the Dead*")	(Pulitzer Prize, 1957)*
Kurt Vonnegut Jr.	**Granville Hicks**
("As featured in *Playboy*")	(Editor, *Sat. Review*)[35]

In late January 1968, Mroz hears that the Student Union Academic Commission has been able to secure conservative writer and *Firing Line* television host William F. Buckley Jr. for a night at the beginning of

---

* Morris actually won the National Book Award (not the Pulitzer) in 1957, for his novel *The Field of Vision*.

April. The sophomore committee takes one quick look at their strongly left-leaning lineup and realizes they could use a better balance in voices. They also could use a piece of the revenue that the SUAC would rake in after selling out the Stepan Center. And it wouldn't hurt to have another big name. By early February, the SUAC and the sophomore committee make a deal. They will cosponsor the event. Both organizations will split the cost of Buckley's stipend, and in exchange the sophomore committee gets a cut of ticket sales.

Mroz respects Buckley but isn't much of a fan. Still, he appreciates the fact that a variety of perspectives will now be represented. *The more the merrier.*

By the end of February, the twelve sophomores have a fundraising operation on multiple levels. Two thousand undergraduates decide to become patrons and plunk down a buck each—their direct reward being their name in the festival program. In addition, the committee finds six hundred other "special patrons" who willingly hand over five dollars.[36]

Their biggest coup comes from their film series, however. The committee chooses three films to show on campus, one for each month.* The three movies altogether bring in another $4,000. All told, and including estimated totals of advance ticket sales for the Mailer premiere and the Buckley lecture, the sophomore committee raises $22,000 . . . to go with the $2.72, of course.[37]

In the middle of March, the committee makes sure to contact every major news outlet in the country—ABC, CBS, NBC—to let them know that something special is about to happen at Notre Dame.

With their extra pile of dough, Mroz also makes sure to spare no expense for Mailer's world premiere. The sophomore committee is still working out of their "dorm room office" at this point. Marty Kress calls sponsors and authors on the phone. In Breen-Phillips Hall, there are only two pay phones, "one on the first floor and one on the fourth floor. When your three minutes are up, you get a recording." If you need it, you can "get an extra minute if you put more coins in."[38] In March, days are filled arranging hourly schedules for the authors, calling hotels, and, for Mroz, getting one last gift for the author who has helped them from the beginning:

---

* Films shown: *The Collector*, *Lord of the Flies*, and *The Pawnbroker*, in that order.

a symposium of
great American writers

University of Notre Dame
April 1 - 6, 1968

The front cover of the program given to all literary festival attendees. Cover art by Edward Suzuki, a friend of John Mroz's who lived on the third floor of Breen-Phillips Hall. *Courtesy of Edward Suzuki.*

March 17, 1968

Dear John:

Autographed football arrived yesterday and was an immediate and fantastic sensation. To celebrate, we went to the NIT games at Madison Square Garden, rooted for Notre Dame, and saw the team upset Army. Thanks, from both of us.

The plane tickets have not arrived yet; should they have? I enjoyed the writeup in the school magazine.

When I arrive on campus, I will be wearing—if it will not embarrass you—a "McCarthy for President" button. If there is a campus, or local, organization participating in McCarthy's Indiana campaign, and there probably is, I would not mind spending some time with some of the members and being of any use to them I can. I therefore would not mind if you passed this message along, if you can do so conveniently, along with my address if there was some reason to get in touch with me now.

I am looking forward to my trip and hope everything is going well.

Sincerely,

Joseph Heller

From son: *"Thank you"* [signed] *Joe Heller*[39]

As the sophomore committee puts everything together, a storm of political activity has begun to overtake the campus. Televised dead bodies from the Tet Offensive have reelectrified the Vietnam conversation. The draft lottery is coming, and college students feel the need to take sides. Multiple reports in the *Observer* document political factions forming on campus. When Robert F. Kennedy announces on March 16 that he will be attempting a run at the presidency, Mroz is hopeful and soon tries to rouse support around campus. Before RFK's entry into the race, most of the committee had been fans of Eugene McCarthy, though a couple of them had kept their support private. Pretty soon the campus has five independent student-run political organizations: Nixon, Rockefeller, McCarthy, Kennedy, and even one for President Johnson—"to offset increasing support for Kennedy and McCarthy," says one student reporter.[40]

By late March, the committee realizes that politics will inevitably be woven into their scheduled events. With the Indiana primary on May 7, both Robert Kennedy and Eugene McCarthy plan to have rallies on or around Notre Dame's campus.

John Mroz can see it approaching—an intersection of politics and literature, all coming to Notre Dame. And it will all have to be organized by a nineteen-year-old sophomore who can't even vote, with the help of a committee Mroz describes as "a small band of desperados" who are "gutsy and maybe a little nuts."[41]

But what Mroz can't see is a week so chaotic across the country that it will cause the publisher of the *South Bend Tribune* to declare on April 7, "If any week in 1968 lays special claim to an important page in tomorrow's history books, it surely will be the week that has just passed."[42]

The Week That Was: March 31–April 6, 1968

Students listen to Robert Kennedy's talk inside the Stepan Center, April 4, 1968. *Courtesy of the University of Notre Dame Archives.*

The 1968 Notre Dame Sophomore Literary Festival Schedule— And Other National Events

March 31	April 1	April 2	April 3	April 4	April 5	April 6
Granville Hicks, 8:00 PM *A Bad Time* Library Auditorium	Wright Morris, 4:00 PM *Life and Literature* Library Auditorium	Norman Mailer, 8:00 PM World Movie Premiere: *Beyond the Law* Stepan Center	William F. Buckley, Jr. 8:00 PM *An Evening with William F. Buckley* Stepan Center *(Cosponsored)*	Joseph Heller, 8:00 PM *Readings and Comments from Catch-22* Washington Hall	Kurt Vonnegut Jr. 4:00 PM *Teaching Writers to Write* Library Auditorium	*Banquet & Symposium* Hicks, Vonnegut, Heller, Ellison, (Morris) *Reality is a Crutch* 2:00 PM Center for Continuing Education Building
President Lyndon B. Johnson announces that he will not seek reelection.	Norman Mailer 8:00 PM Topic: *Norman Mailer in Lecture* Stepan Center		Sen. Eugene McCarthy visits South Bend in the afternoon.	Sen. Robert Kennedy visits campus. Dr. Martin Luther King Jr. is assassinated.	Ralph Ellison, 8:00 PM *The Function of the Novel in American Democracy* Washington Hall	*Eugene McCarthy Fundraiser* Heller and Vonnegut 4:00 PM

1

SUNDAY, MARCH 31, 1968

A White Flag of Celebration

The view from Lyndon B. Johnson's seat, March 31, 1968. *LBJ Library photo by Yoichi Okamoto.*

"World War II, begun in a graveyard of sinking ships, ended with atomic bombs that should never have been dropped, destroying Hiroshima and Nagasaki. The cold war spawned Senator [Joseph] McCarthy, who turned men into cowards the length and breadth of this nation, and we're not done yet with the fear he engendered. A young American President had the back of his head shot off into the hands of his wife. And now, in Vietnam, a small, gentle-faced people, caught between two armies, have become living torches."

—Bernard Malamud[1]

It Begins with a King

At 10:00 AM, an interracial congregation of four thousand has jam-packed the Neo-Gothic Washington National Cathedral to listen to Rev. Martin Luther King Jr. speak from behind the Canterbury Pulpit. The WNC is only three and a half miles away from the White House, and despite receiving letters of protest demanding King not be allowed to "stir up more racial tension & anxiety which can only lead to disaster," WNC officials go ahead with the event. The turnout is massive, five times more than a typical WNC Sunday morning service. At its maximum, the cathedral can seat three thousand, but for today's special guest many sit on the steps and lawn just outside the doors.[2]

King's sermon is titled "Remaining Awake Through a Great Revolution," and he starts with an anecdote he has been recycling as far back as 1959, the cautionary tale of author Washington Irving's *Rip Van Winkle*, and how Rip "slept through a revolution," never fully understanding how his country had changed. King fears that the somnolence of the general public, its ability to ignore what is hard to confront, will lead the country toward a darker version of its current self.

Most of the address is a pastiche of vignettes he's used in sermons for years, but when it comes to the issue of poverty, King lets his listeners into his heart by recounting his visits to regions of the country in desperate need of relief:

In our own nation there are about forty million people who are poverty-stricken. I have seen them here and there. I have seen them in the ghettos of the North; I have seen them in the rural areas of the South; I have seen them in Appalachia. I have just been in the process of touring many areas of our country and I must confess that in some situations I have literally found myself crying.

I was in Marks, Mississippi, the other day, which is in Quit-man County, the poorest county in the United States. I tell you, I saw hundreds of little black boys and black girls walking the streets with no shoes to wear. I saw their mothers and fathers trying to carry on a little Head Start program, but they had no money. The federal government hadn't funded them, but they were trying to carry on. They raised a little money here and there; trying to get a little food to feed the children; trying to teach them a little something.[3]

The congregation listens closely as Dr. King's confident baritone voice echoes off the walls of the cathedral, but there is a quiet dejection to his voice. He is bone-tired, and a close friend with him that day can't recall ever seeing King so "discouraged and depressed." Still, he has enough fight in him to say that the Vietnam War "is one of the most unjust wars that has ever been fought in the history of the world."[4]

Ever since publicly denouncing the war in Vietnam on April 4, 1967, King has been scrutinized for his antiwar stance, especially by President Johnson. Now that an ever-growing faction of America has awakened to see the war in all its horror, King is comfortable with his own outlook, and feels free enough to push back against a president who can't seem to stop committing financial resources toward a war that doesn't need to be fought:

One day a newsman came to me and said, "Dr. King, don't you think you're going to have to stop, now, opposing the war and move more in line with the administration's policy? As I under-stand it, it has hurt the budget of your organization, and people who once respected you have lost respect for you. Don't you feel that you've really got to change your position?" I looked at him and I had to say, "Sir, I'm sorry you don't know me. I'm not a consensus leader. I do not determine what is right and wrong by looking at the budget of the Southern Christian Leadership Conference. I've not taken a sort of Gallup Poll of the majority opinion." Ultimately a genuine leader is not a searcher for consensus, but a molder of consensus.[5]

He ends his sermon in a melancholic tone of voice, even though his words are designed to be sent soaring: "God grant that we will be participants in this newness and this magnificent development. If we will but do it, we will bring about a new day of justice and brotherhood and peace. And that day the morning stars will sing together and the sons of God will shout for joy. God bless you."

During a press conference after his sermon, King removes his robe and makes clear his opinion of LBJ. While the president and King have a shared history of passing landmark legislation such as the 1964 Civil Rights Act and the 1965 Voting Rights Act, the war in Vietnam causes King to step away from supporting him for reelection: "I see an alternative in Mr. [Robert] Kennedy and Mr. [Eugene] McCarthy . . . both [are] very competent, both understand urban problems."

King doesn't see the importance in choosing between the two "peace candidates," though he prefers Kennedy, a man who at the very least has attempted to recognize the dire state of poverty and income inequality. Of greater concern to King, before flying back to Memphis to support a sanitation worker's strike, is communicating his feelings on the American condition. Referring to the 1966–1967 summer race riots in cities such as Chicago and Detroit, where African Americans had grown fed up with issues such as police brutality and marginalization, King is "convinced we cannot stand two more summers like last. . . . [Further violence] will bring only a rightist takeover of the government and eventually a fascist state in America."[6]

Soon after the press conference, King flies home to Atlanta. He arrives at his house at night and chats with his wife, Coretta, and their two sons and two daughters. They turn on the television and soon see President Johnson staring at them as he sits behind his desk in the Oval Office.

As Johnson speaks, they listen closely to what he has to say. Less than an hour later, they are stunned. The president's announcement that he will not run for reelection is unexpected and rejuvenates King, who hopes Johnson's action will "bring us closer to peace among nations."[7]

LBJ's Political Sacrifice

On Sunday, January 14, 1968, President Lyndon B. Johnson and speechwriter Horace Busby were talking in the White House presidential bedroom. Johnson was in his bed, and Busby had a pad in his hands, ready to take notes about the upcoming State of the Union address on Wednesday. Johnson had known Busby for decades and trusted him deeply. From one friend to another, the president said bluntly, "I didn't get you down here to waste your time on the State of the Union."

Busby paused, somewhat in shock, and went numb when Johnson informed him that "I have made up my mind. I can't get peace in Vietnam and be president, too." Johnson, still in his bed but with pillows bolstering him, vented to Busby about how both "Southeast Asia" and "Capitol Hill" won't let him accomplish what he wants. He's being pulled in two different directions, soon to be torn in half.

Johnson lifted himself out of bed to tell Busby his dramatic plan not to seek reelection. He would deliver his standard State of the Union speech, take in the applause coming from the House and Senate, and pull from his inside jacket pocket a folded two-page document that only he and "Buzz" would know about. He pantomimed the grandness of the moment to Busby in a hushed tone: "I have come before you to announce that in this year of nineteen and sixty-eight, I will not, under any circumstances, be a candidate for reelection of the President of the United States."

Johnson seemed at peace with his vision, but Busby was floored. "That ought to surprise the living hell out of them," Johnson told his frozen friend.[8]

They began creating a point-by-point outline, but all progress came to a halt once they came to the topic of the war in Vietnam. The conflict had overwhelmed Johnson. "This war," he said, massaging his forehead, ". . . this goddamn war."

Busby decided to let a silence fill the room. There wasn't much to say. The war had split the nation and, at least as of the middle of January 1968, Johnson would still have a bit of support from his own party. "The name of this game is to quit while you're ahead," the president said. "I've always prayed I'd have some sense enough to get out when the time came, before they had to carry me out."

For the next hour, Johnson skewered his own presidential qualities. He was too "personal . . . intimate." He had the wrong accent, and his overall style didn't fit the times. For a longtime friend to hear another friend mentally immolate himself, let alone as a US president, was too much. After enduring long enough to write something down, Busby left, sullenly saying, "Mr. President, we'll have to think about this."

Several days later, Busby watched the State of the Union address. With a sharp eye, he checked as Johnson finished the last part of his speech. *Will he reach into his pocket?* Busby was relieved to watch his old friend do nothing. "I concluded," Busby would later write, "that my visit to the White House on the previous Sunday must have been for purposes of therapy."[9]

The two friends didn't speak to each other again for ten weeks. During this time, the North Vietnamese coordinated the Tet Offensive, targeting over a hundred cities in the south. They began the attack on January 31, and soon televisions across America were reporting death and losses on a nightly basis—232 American soldiers in two days. The negative press devastated a section of the general public, and soon President Johnson's approval ratings began to plummet. Johnson watched steadfast and trusted news anchor Walter Cronkite tell America, "To say we are mired in a stalemate seems the most realistic and unsatisfactory conclusion." For Johnson, it was yet another sign of how disconnected he felt from his own country: "If I've lost Walter Cronkite, I've lost Middle America."[10]

On March 16, Robert Kennedy announced that he would seek to unseat President Johnson at the Democratic National Convention. In light of this, on top of Minnesota senator Eugene McCarthy's ongoing peace campaign and near New Hampshire primary victory, the Tet Offensive nightmare, and his own lingering personal doubts,

Johnson summons Busby back to the White House around midnight on March 31.* At six in the morning, Busby checks the *Washington Post* and sees a revelatory piece of data in the Gallup Poll; the support for the war in Vietnam has dipped below 50 percent within the Democratic Party—a first. Knowing Johnson's affinity for Gallup Polls, Busby feels this may be a sign of the reason for his White House invitation. It's time for LBJ's final bow, and he wants a trusted friend to write the words to his curtain call.

At 9:00 AM on March 31, Busby walks into the presidential bedroom and sees a dozen staffers hovering around Johnson. The president stands by the bed and squats down to play with his grandson, who charges toward him with a smile, only to surrender after the president pokes him in the stomach. The mood in the bedroom is too jubilant for Busby to believe a letter of withdrawal from the presidential nomination is set to be written. Soon he realizes that most of the staff only know of one bombshell piece of news: LBJ has announced a bombing halt in Vietnam in order to create a chance for peace talks. To make matters even clearer, Johnson gives Busby a "shh" gesture from across the room.

Busby and Johnson move to a more private setting, a West Hall sitting room on the second floor of the White House. It's past 10:00 AM, and Johnson, after unloading an emotional monologue about sacrifice, clears his mind and asks that he and Busby look at their matter objectively. Johnson asks his friend for a bit of trust: "You and I are the only two people who will ever believe that I won't know whether I'm going to do this or not until I get to the last line of my speech on the TelePrompTer." Then, after a moment of reflection, he says, "These days, you never know what might happen somewhere in the world between now and tonight."[11]

The president goes point by point as Busby's pencil burns the notepad. Johnson mentions his move as a potential way to expedite peace in Vietnam, but he knows that is far from certain. He also mentions money,

---

* The nightmare was even worse than Johnson realized: on March 16—the same day that Kennedy officially entered the presidential race—407 Vietnamese men, women and children were brutally executed by American soldiers over a four-hour span in what became known as the My Lai Massacre. This heinous war crime would be kept secret and would only be revealed a year later, with President Nixon then in office.

and that it'd cost millions of dollars just to be nominated again—a debt he would owe shadow donors for the rest of his career.

To Busby, it all sounds methodical and case building. But this is a heartfelt moment between two Texan friends who can say anything at any tone and still maintain a balance. Johnson leans in close to Busby and lets a bit of raw emotion slip out: "I want out of this cage."

He thanks God for getting him to such an exalted position, having come from so little, but, as only Busby can understand, "Sometime before I go, I want to be able to go down to that ranch and sit by that river and look out over the hills and be a human being."[12]

At noon in the green-walled Treaty Room, Johnson uses an intricately designed wooden Victorian desk to read Busby's handwritten final pages. The president places them in a horizontal line, his 6'3" frame hovering over the words. He stands pensively, but soon Busby hears LBJ jingling coins in his pocket. The speechwriter takes it as a good sign that what he's written has passed . . . for now.

With the idea of dropping out growing stronger by the moment, the president leaves Busby behind and tracks down Hubert Humphrey. The vice president has just finished attending a church service, and Johnson lets him know that he's decided to call it quits. Tears begin to flow, and Humphrey confides in Johnson that he doesn't think he can take on Robert Kennedy and win what may end up feeling like a popularity contest.

For Johnson, it's exactly what he doesn't want to hear at the moment. Senator Kennedy's holier-than-thou attitude has always been able to make his blood boil, but public pressure keeps Johnson's anger at bay. By the time he returns to Busby, LBJ's mood has darkened, and it's almost impossible to concentrate on anything other than the thought that his presidential replacement may very well be a man he'd like to punch in the face. "Humphrey," Johnson says, "doesn't know whether he even wants to try" to compete against Kennedy. Instead of saying the name "Kennedy" or "Bobby," Johnson chooses "that fellow."[13]

Thankfully, ol' Buzz is there to talk Johnson away from the ledge. He tells the president that Humphrey will have an incredible amount of support, and an infrastructure already in place to campaign across the country. "Humphrey will have more money and more support than he ever thought possible because he'll be the man to stop Kennedy."

It's enough to lift Johnson's spirits. He grabs a pen and sits down at the table with tonight's national speech awaiting his edits. One line—or one word, to be exact—irks him: "I shall not seek and will not accept the nomination of my party."

Johnson crosses out "will" and instead writes "would." To the president, it sounds too presumptuous, and he tells Buzz that "they haven't offered me any nomination yet." Buzz tries to hold firm to his original word choice, telling Johnson that it needs to "be firm and unequivocal." He warns the president that "the press will nitpick every word in that sentence, looking for an escape clause."

Johnson doesn't care. "Well let 'em, dammit, let 'em. I am still not going to reject something that hasn't been offered to me, and that's final."

After the editing has finished, Johnson leaves Buzz and the speech behind for a moment, but summons Buzz again in less than an hour, this time for lunch with seven other people within the president's inner circle—his wife, daughter, and secretary, to name a few. Buzz is already known as the "drop-out guy." If he's around, that means the president is talking about throwing in the towel. Soon, Buzz realizes why he's been invited: lunch will be a verbal firing squad, everyone aiming their words at the time-to-call-it-quits speechwriter.

The onslaught of disagreements goes on as Buzz tries his best to tiptoe around feelings, but he stands his ground as he sees the president nodding his head. *If he doesn't do it now, he might not ever have another chance to make a difference in Vietnam.* The conversation causes everyone to lose their appetites, and soon Johnson swoops in and takes Buzz to the presidential bedroom.

He closes the door and says to Buzz, "Did any of that swerve you any?"

Despite the emotional pleas, Buzz stands his ground. "No, sir, I still feel the same."[14]

Like coconspirators, they stand together behind the closed door and eavesdrop on the conversations out in the hallway. In six hours, three networks will simultaneously broadcast the address to over a hundred million viewers. As they wait for a lull in the office gossip, the two stand ready to jolt an already-frenzied country.

Notre Dame Hears the News

> *"What disturbs me and disturbs millions of people is that the administration seems simply to have blundered into a war that it need not have fought and cannot win."*
>
> —Granville Hicks[15]

Six hundred miles away, as Johnson and Busby deal with their own roller-coaster decision and Reverend King defends his plans for a Poor People's Campaign, sixty-six-year-old literary critic Granville Hicks and his wife, Dorothy, step off a plane at the St. Joseph County Airport. John Mroz and three other Notre Dame sophomores stand nearby, ready to greet tonight's keynote speaker, and drive the couple to their hotel. In Hick's luggage is a typed copy of his nine-thousand-word speech, a doom-filled yet wisdom-tinged collage of thoughts titled "A Bad Time."

Granville Hicks sitting next to Wright Morris's wife, Josephine, at the University of Notre Dame, April 1968. *Photo taken by John Mroz.*

Granville Hicks has witnessed his share of history, most of it with Dorothy by his side. As a poor teenager during World War I, Granville listened with pride as a local band at an armory near his home played "The Star-Spangled Banner" "every morning and evening as the flag was raised and lowered." At seventeen, Granville and Dorothy shared their first kiss on November 11, 1918, after watching fireworks light up a night sky, a celebration of the end of the war. It sounds romantic, but the always-self-effacing Hicks said he fumbled the smooch. "I'll do better next time," he'd told Dorothy, full blush.[16]

Soon after, his love for books gave him a greater sense of confidence. Like the young sophomore literary festival committee members, Hicks allowed certain novels to frame his perspective on society. One of the dozens that affected him was F. Scott Fitzgerald's romantic debut novel: "I remember well enough reading *This Side of Paradise*, for it excited me as it did thousands of my college generation, to whom, mild as it now seems, it came as a declaration of independence." Every Wednesday, he watched plays from "the second balconies" around Boston, and soon an assortment of actors, English professors, and authors was seducing him toward a life in the arts.[17]

It's a thirty-minute drive from the airport to the on-campus Morris Inn, and the sophomores have planned out Mr. Hicks's schedule to the hour. John Mroz knows that every moment of Hicks's trip matters, since the critic will be writing about the festival for the nationally distributed *Saturday Review*. The day's hits, Simon and Garfunkel's "Mrs. Robinson," from the film *The Graduate*, or Aretha Franklin's "Since You've Been Gone" await them on the radio, but it's unlikely Mr. Hicks would have cared for sound, having declared his "extensive ignorance" of modern music decades ago. Around 3:30 PM, the sophomores check Mr. and Mrs. Hicks into their hotel and go over the schedule before giving tonight's speaker some time to settle in.[18]

Currently speaking at the library auditorium, where Hicks will give his talk, is Paul Boutelle, a thirty-three-year-old firebrand running as the vice-presidential nominee of the ever-evolving Socialist Workers Party. Heavily influenced by Malcolm X, Boutelle introduces himself and his platform to a predominantly White audience, firing off statements meant to spark outrage. He tells his listeners that "a total of seventy-six white families possess as much wealth as the entire negro population in America." Knowing most of his audience has their minds set on the draft lottery, he's direct with anyone on the fence: "If you're for the war in Vietnam, why aren't you over there fighting?"[19]

Boutelle has nothing to lose. At thirty-three, he's too young to accept the vice presidency. His talks across the country are meant to establish the SWP as an antiwar, pro-union, and pro–Black nationalism movement. He accuses senators Eugene McCarthy and Robert Kennedy of being hypocrites and proclaims that the US government "is the enemy of all people of freedom anywhere." Naturally, the audience connects him to what in the last several decades has become a dirty word: communist. But Boutelle, who was invited to speak by Notre Dame's Student Academic Commission wants to challenge the stigma attached to the word: "We are not pro-violence, we are not pro-sabotage, we are not anti-America, we are not financed by Peking, we are Communists."[20]

If there is one man on campus who can appreciate Paul Boutelle's position, it's Granville Hicks. In 1934, nearing thirty-three years old, Hicks was writing for the *New Masses*, a Marxist magazine, his voice a megaphone of outrage. Addressing himself to the magazine's diverse body of potential contributors, Hicks had gone so far as to assert:

> Every one of us believes that the capitalist system must be destroyed by the power of the proletariat, in alliance with the exploited farmers, the ruined middle class, and the aroused intellectual and professional class. Every one is determined to fight such manifestations of capitalism as war and Fascism. Every one is resolved to support the workers and poor farmers of America wherever they are struggling against injustice, starvation, and oppression.[21]

Hicks has seen America at various states of desperation. Driving around New York City with Dorothy in the early 1930s during the Great Depression, Hicks stared "with dismay at the Hooverville that had grown up by the tracks, wondering what life could be like in those shacks made of packing boxes and hunks of corrugated iron and odds and ends of cardboard and cloth." Even worse, when the couple had decided to live in rural Grafton, New York, they saw a quality of life that was "more depressing than anything I had seen in New York City." Hicks couldn't take the "tarpaper shacks, with skinny ragged children staring at our roadster." Life in the country had been briefly abandoned, in favor of the roaring city culture, but "the depression, instead of glutting the market with cheap farms, was sending people back from the cities to take up the farms they or their parents had abandoned or to build shacks on the family property."[22]

But the committee hasn't brought Hicks to Notre Dame (and paid a $500 stipend) just to reflect on the 1930s. Hicks knows to keep his speech in the present moment, the current "bad time." Hicks sees the country struggling mightily in two ways: the domestic economy and foreign policy, the latter keeping the former from reaching its potential. He still sees the same thorns in America's side that have been around for decades: income inequality and an irrational fear of communism. To Hicks, America's shadows are cyclical.[23]

After dinner at the Morris Inn with John Mroz and other sophomore committee members, Dorothy and Granville Hicks walk across campus to the library auditorium, where an audience of five hundred awaits his words.

––––––––––––––

As of March 31, 1968, Notre Dame campus culture stands as a fractured set of political opinions and a microcosm of '60s White America. To start with, there is the 219-member ROTC, in which many support the war in Vietnam and desire a stronger commander in chief who is not afraid to up the stakes. For many members of the ROTC, football team, and conservative-leaning university administration, that means Nixon is their guy. As George Ovitt puts it, "The majority of my fellow Domers in 1968 had short hair, went to Mass every Sunday, studied business or engineering, supported the War, hated hippies, and preferred beer—oceans of beer—to pot. The most important annual event wasn't the [sophomore] literary or the film festival, but Mardi Gras."

A sketch in the *Notre Dame Observer* just after RFK entered the Democratic primary race. *Sketch by W. Maloney.*

Set apart from this dominating presence are young men who have "come not for the gridiron but for the library, the world-class instructors, and what they call, without irony, 'the life of the mind.'"[24] Within this small but vocal faction stand young men who have thrown their support behind Senator Eugene McCarthy, but as of March 16 find themselves splintered now that Robert Kennedy has entered the race. Sketches such as the one here, appearing in the *Notre Dame Observer* on March 18, show how many in the McCarthy camp feel about Kennedy's late entry. Yet at the same time, the name Kennedy has an undeniable glow to many across the country, and young men begin to slide over to Bobby's camp; owing to his nationwide name recognition, they consider him their best bet for ending the war.[25]

It is this politically fragmented audience that applauds Granville Hicks at 8:00 PM. It's evident from the start that the literary critic will not try to be as caustic or provocative as, say, Norman Mailer, nor can he speak with the intellectual eloquence of Ralph Ellison. With Hicks, it's a strong dose of earthbound honesty:

> In a world in which nationalism is more rampant than ever before, the danger of an atomic holocaust is always present, but it becomes more and probable if there is a decline of statesmanship in the government of one of the great powers. Moreover, there has been a great loss of American prestige in almost every part of the world.[26]

On paper, the speech reads like a forty-five-minute apocalyptic thunderstorm, and if a more dynamic speaker were delivering it, there's no telling how much of an impact it may have had on the audience. TNT, dead lakes, history repeating itself—it is Hicks expressing himself without needing to carefully calibrate every word for column space in a consumer magazine. It is a rare chance to broadly review the state of the nation, and not to sound "WASPy," as Norman Mailer once stated about him. And make no mistake, Hicks wants his message to reach *everyone*, as evidenced by this one sadly timeless statement: "Much has been written about the alienation of the intellectuals, but millions of people are alienated who never heard the word. They don't write books about their alienation; they shoot people."

Sophomore committee member Tito Trevino remembers Hicks as "shy . . . dry and quiet." Trevino is seated next to Kurt Vonnegut, who'd arrived in the afternoon, and it's Trevino's responsibility to escort the author of *Cat's Cradle* around campus. After Hicks's speech ends around 10:00 PM, he walks out with Vonnegut by his side. A crowd of people are momentarily jammed in the lobby when someone shouts, "Johnson's not running again!"

According to Trevino, "Everyone cheers!" Vonnegut, a Eugene McCarthy supporter, is thrilled and smiles. He joins the cheering and says, "Finally, we're making some progress!"[27]

Hicks, while standing offstage, hears "a gasp of astonishment." Within moments, a university student runs into the backstage waiting room and tells Hicks the stunning news.

Hicks is surprised, but he's more preoccupied with how his words will be remembered. Now that his speech has been eclipsed by LBJ's announcement, he knows "no one [will recall] what I said." Still, he's relieved that news of LBJ not seeking reelection was only reported after his talk. If it had been before, "no one would have listened."[28]

"I shall not seek, and I will not accept, the nomination of my party for another term as your president."

—Lyndon B. Johnson

In the end, Johnson takes Busby's word-choice suggestion. He firmly states that he "will not" accept the nomination of his party. At 9:41 PM, LBJ rises from his chair and places his microphone in a case. The teleprompter that rolled the transcript of his speech has stilled, and as he begins to walk away from the camera, his wife, Lady Bird, is there to greet him with a warm hug and kiss. Also there are their daughters, nineteen-year-old Luci and twenty-year-old newlywed Lynda, who found a way to be there for her father despite taking a red-eye from California and arriving at the White House in the early morning after seeing her marine husband, Captain Charles Robb, board a plane bound for Vietnam.

Moments after the speech, Johnson and his family, along with Busby, decompress a bit by having a late-night buffet-style meal on the second-floor of the White House. Lady Bird has mixed feelings about her husband's decision. Ever since LBJ's 1960 heart attack scare, she has been worried about his level of stress. But she has also seen the love of her life push through federal programs such as Medicare and the National Endowment of the Arts and Humanities. Yet despite his many successes, the shadow of Vietnam looms so completely over him that he's become defined by it—a potential one-issue legacy. "We have done a lot," Lady Bird tells the press an hour later. "And there is a lot left to do in the remaining months. Maybe this is the only way to get it done."[29]

Indeed, the Johnson family understands history well enough to know that the only way the president can escape a negative portrayal is to end the war, and in this way LBJ has decided to take a different kind of bullet, killing his own political career in the hopes of ending a war that risks tearing the nation in two. It's a war he has perpetuated, and it has taken on a life of its own.

From a media standpoint, the announcement creates a ripple effect across the country. Besides the literary festival, concerts and sporting events are interrupted immediately by the news. Telephone lines become overwhelmed, services in major cities shutting down from the overload.

In the San Francisco Bay area, a frenzy of joy peppers the campuses immediately after LBJ's telecast. At Stanford, a large group of "boys and girls embraced in ecstatic disbelief" as writers for the student newspaper try and describe how their "blue and white McCarthy button" seems bigger, and how their "black and white draft card" now appears smaller in some way. On the San Francisco State College campus, where literary festival author Wright Morris currently teaches creative writing, "about 50 men and women students" have chosen to watch LBJ's speech in a dormitory lounge. As soon as the speech ends, they react with "alternate laughter and tears which spread through the dormitory buildings" as they spread the message.[30]

Within two hours of the announcement, a celebratory march occurs in downtown Boston. At least two thousand university students walk en masse from Cambridge's Harvard Square "up Beacon Street to converge on the state house steps." So often the marches have been organized to criticize policy, but the president's decision has given activists a jolt. At around eleven at night their newly adapted chant can be heard blocks away. "Hey, hey, what do you say! LBJ gave up today!" Independently, around six hundred students march from the University of Pennsylvania campus in Philadelphia and end up at Independence Hall. Their chant is more direct than the one in Boston. "The hawk is dead! The hawk is dead!" they say, amid cheers.[31]

The celebrations and demonstrations may grab the spotlight, but the middle of America feels differently, and most of them don't believe it's necessary to make a show of their beliefs. In eastern Kansas, *Emporia Gazette* editor William Lindsay White begins typing a front-page editorial that many of his thirty-five thousand readers would agree with:

> Down [President Johnson] goes, under the stabs of opportunists within his own party. We Republicans may thank God and Richard Nixon that we share no blame in this tragedy, for Mr. Nixon has always been careful not to criticize the President's Vietnam policies, not to make political capital out of our country's misfortune, not to stir up our youth to the point of treason.[32]

The Candidates Respond

That night in Waukesha, Wisconsin, Senator Eugene McCarthy hears the LBJ news while onstage during a campaign rally at Carroll College. He has just completed his speech and been given a rousing three-minute applause. Just before the question-and-answer period starts, a young man far in the back of the crowd shouts, "He's not running!" It takes a few moments for the crowd to register the statement, but once they do, pandemonium sets in—shouting, whistling, red-white-and-blue hats sent airborne.

At first, McCarthy is stunned, but soon a smile forms. He hears the details of the speech, then tries to process the bombshell. "This is a surprise to me—I hope this will be reflected in the Wisconsin primary on Tuesday." He attempts to remain composed onstage, but concludes his rally with this comment: "[Johnson's decision has] changed the entire political picture. . . . I don't think it's the time now to answer questions."[33]

After the initial shock has worn off, McCarthy's able to look at the announcement from Johnson's perspective: "I look upon this as a personally sad and difficult moment for a man who has given so many years to the service of his country."[34]

In a way, Johnson's decision is bittersweet for McCarthy. By completing a primary victory over a sitting president, McCarthy would have been able to show the nation the legitimacy of his campaign, but now that the president has chosen to wave a white flag, an expected McCarthy victory in Wisconsin will carry less weight.

At JFK Airport, Robert Kennedy runs into a group of reporters, as well as nearly a hundred teenage supporters who have gathered at the gate with signs. Some of them shout, "It's Bobby all the way!" and "The president's pulled out!" The reporters ask Kennedy to comment on the news, but Kennedy stays mum. "I have nothing to say." The New York senator tells everyone he'll talk about it at a 10:00 AM press conference tomorrow.[35]

Meanwhile, Richard Nixon and his team land at La Guardia after flying from a campaign rally in Milwaukee. Nixon has plenty to say. "[Johnson's decision] may have strengthened his hand in the [Democratic] party and made it possible for him to name his successor."

Nixon has been enjoying the month of March. It started with his main competition, Michigan governor George Romney, dropping out of the race months after saying during a television interview that he'd been "brainwashed" or manipulated by army generals into thinking that the Vietnam War was winnable during his visit there in 1965. His stance may have won him a few antiwar moderate Democrats, but his Republican base couldn't stomach Romney's new views. With McCarthy's strong March 12 showing in New Hampshire and Robert Kennedy's entry into the race, all Nixon has to do is watch the Democratic Party tumble over itself. Now that LBJ has decided to leave it all behind, Nixon tells the newsmen surrounding him at the airport, "This seems to be the year of the dropout."[36]

Notre Dame and the Vietnam Blues

Back on the Notre Dame campus, John Mroz takes Granville Hicks over to English professor Andrew Thomas Smithberger's house for a night of drinks. Smithberger, sixty-four at the time, specializes in teaching the Romantic poets—Coleridge, Blake, and Wordsworth, to name a few. But LBJ's announcement takes precedence over poetry, tonight.[37]

For Mroz and the sophomore literary committee, nearly everything revolves around Vietnam. It's not that Eugene McCarthy is such an outstanding man; it's that he has vowed to end the war in Vietnam, thus *protecting* the lives of young men across the nation from getting drafted. The same is true of Robert Kennedy, although with RFK they see a more realistic chance of victory owing to his name and place in the popular consciousness. With Nixon, they see a man with the potential for that dreaded word batted around on television: *escalation*.[38]

In the *Notre Dame Observer*, there have been plenty of articles discussing the state of the country, even reports from the local airport about what soldiers coming back from Vietnam were saying to outgoing soldiers who'd yet to see combat. According to a piece written by student reporter Chris Jarabek for the March 29 issue of the *Observer*, one exchange between an outgoing twenty-year-old private from Oklahoma named Tom and two returning privates went like this:

> **Tom:** Where are you stationed? Guess I'll be in Vietnam soon. I suspect I'll be sent to Saigon.
>
> **Returning Private:** Oh no, baby, it won't be Saigon. There's nothing left there. I know. I'm just back from 'nam. We'[re] pulling out of Saigon as fast as we can go. The Tet offensive did it. There's nothing left for us there. We're pullin' out to a place about 30 miles north.
>
> **Tom:** But that can't be. I know I'll be sent to Saigon.
>
> **Returning Private:** Look baby, take my word for it. You won't be. That's a military secret right now, but what the hell. You just won't be there.

Confused, Tom manages to find another returning GI.

> **Tom:** When did you get back? What's it like?
>
> **Returning GI:** Well, don't believe everything you read about the war. Maybe one quarter to one half of it is true. Like I mean, Saigon is destroyed as far as we're concerned and we're withdrawing to another stronghold.
>
> **Tom:** You mean the entire city is destroyed and we don't know it?
>
> **Returning GI:** No, I mean, the city is destroyed as far as our forces are concerned. Some of the civilian areas are fine, but our headquarters were demolished. They aren't reporting it but it's true. And besides, the South Vietnamese don't want us in Saigon anyway, because we're wrecking the city's economy with American dollars. It's too inflationary. So we have pressure there not to rebuild."

Tom: What about Khe Sanh?

Returning GI: Well, like I told you, you can't believe what you read. We flew 400 guys in last week and 13 of them came back. I was with a helicopter crew and I know. But you won't read that. The reports will be spread out over a week.

Tom: Thirteen? Surely not all of them died. You just mean casualties, don't you—I mean wounded?

Returning GI: No, as far as we know they all died.[39]

One very recent campus drama helps to illuminate just how all-encompassing the Vietnam drama has become. It revolves around "parietal hours," or a college-enforced curfew. The Notre Dame rule states that women are not allowed to be in a male-only dormitory after a certain time, but when four young men were caught last week having girls in their rooms overnight, President Father Theodore Hesburgh chose to suspend them. The student body government was enraged, and soon the story took over the front page of the student newspaper. Accusations such as a lack of due process—*Why weren't the students given a chance to explain themselves!*—to the triviality of parietal hours, found their way into campus conversations. The incoming student body president was "doing everything in his power" to get the students reinstated. Meanwhile, the young men attempted to explain themselves: *The girls were just waiting in our rooms. They were uninvited and ran away from home!*[40]

This seems like a minor campus conflict, but a closer look reveals how the war affects even the smallest controversies. To be a full-time undergraduate student in 1968 means an important protection from being drafted. Students who take fifteen credits a semester and remain in good standing are classified by the selective service as 2-A. As long as the student remains on track to graduate in four years, he will at least be guaranteed to have one barrier of protection from joining other soldiers in Saigon.

But if a student is, say, suspended from school and unable to return, eventually his university would report the changed circumstances to the draft board. Soon enough, his status would be changed to 1-A, and, depending on the number of recruits needed that month, a notification to report to camp may come in the mail.[41]

These were the underlying circumstances surrounding the four young men. A suspension from school meant a newfound availability to be ordered to kill people in another country far from home.

Fortunately for them, Father Hesburgh had a change of heart after an off-the-record conversation with one of the students. On April 1, all four students were reinstated and attending classes, protected once more from the claw of the Vietnam draft. In the student newspaper on April 1 is a pencil sketch of a larger-than-life Father Hesburgh holding the four young men in his hands, three words scrawled underneath—*you may live.*[42]

This sketch showing students being reinstated shows the importance of staying enrolled as a full-time college student in Vietnam.
Photo from the Notre Dame Observer,
April 1, 1968, by W. Maloney

The Road to Vietnam

General Lewis Blaine Hershey and the selective service have asked for forty-eight thousand men to be sent to Vietnam in April. This number is divided among the more than three thousand counties across the country, then made specific based on, among other factors, population density. For St. Joseph County, where the University of Notre Dame is located, the magic number for April is seventy-one.[43]

Even this number is divided. In St. Joseph County, there are seven draft boards assigned to "specific geographical areas." The draft boards are made up of five volunteers from their local area. Apart from this quintet of judgment stand an appeals agent, an associate agent, and a medical adviser.[44]

Imagine for a moment that John Mroz, for some reason, has been kicked out of college and receives a notice from the draft board that his new classification is 1-A. Naturally, Mroz is now a prime candidate for the draft. Fearing that dreaded moment of escalation, Mroz chooses to declare himself a conscientious objector. This sounds harmless, but the 1-O designation does have potential consequences. If, for example, Mroz's parents are conservative and politically active, having a son declare himself a CO risks family embarrassment and one extra hurdle for Mroz as he applies for jobs.

In addition, Mroz does not have a religious background. If he'd applied as a Mennonite or Quaker, or especially a Jehovah's Witness, he'd be able to defend his stance against violence by declaring himself a pacifist on the grounds of faith. Those without such an excuse faced further scrutiny.

After applying as a CO, the next step is writing an essay that convinces the draft board of your stance against fighting in Vietnam. This can be done many ways. Mroz might describe his opposition to violence or his opinion that the United States is fighting an immoral war.

The essay, however, is not the end. No matter how powerful Mroz's words are, the next step is a question-and-answer interview with the draft board, in person. The five draft board members (the majority being older White veterans who'd fought in prior wars) would then ask Mroz questions to weaken his position: *Would you have fought in World War*

II? What if the fight came to American soil? Wouldn't you want to protect your family?

If Mroz survives the gauntlet of quizzical challenges and they accept his stance, he still will need to serve for two years as a noncombatant at a location one hundred miles or farther from his home. If he is rejected, he is conscripted into the armed forces. The alternative is a two-year prison sentence. At this point, the only other options Mroz has are extreme: move to Canada, saw off the tip of his trigger finger, or live the life of a drifter and gamble on not getting caught.[45]

It's these thoughts that swirl in the minds of John Mroz and his friends and fellow classmates. Yes, tonight President Johnson has made a valiant gesture toward peace with his announcement not to seek a second term. But Mroz is far more concerned with the war itself. *That's* what matters, not Johnson's legacy. Will Johnson's bombing halt help bring peace before he graduates? Or will the war escalate to the point that even full-time undergraduates are called to serve?

These questions won't go away. But Mroz can see that the literary festival he has put together this week will now become even more political than he'd previously imagined. And for the young man who dares to dream big, this is just fine.

2

MONDAY, APRIL 1, 1968

The Loner and the Noisemaker

Norman Mailer and John Mroz just after Mailer's flight arrives, April 1, 1968. *Photo courtesy of Marty Kress.*

LBJ Hears a Strange Sound—Applause

Around 11:00 AM, Lyndon Johnson rests inside Air Force One. He's headed to Chicago for the National Association of Broadcasters conference. Surrounding him are morning editions of newspapers from across the country. Horace Busby, invited along at the last minute, is baffled at how staff have been able to retrieve copies as far away as Miami, even Omaha. Reports from over two dozen cities give Johnson a clear glimpse into his country's pulse. With "wonderment and occasional disbelief," the president is taken aback by the accounts. He reads a few of them out loud to nearby staff as Air Force One enters Midwestern skies. Stunned, the president takes a break in the plane's lounge area: "I didn't think there would be this much interest."[1]

After Johnson lands at Chicago's O'Hare Field, his motorcade heads to the convention hotel. The visit has been scheduled for weeks, according to Busby, but hasn't been announced nationally, so when he arrives at the hotel entrance, no one is around to greet (or heckle) him. Busby does notice a few "photographers, police and a handful of local dignitaries," but besides them, the area is deserted. Johnson has just read about the nationwide fever-pitch reaction to his decision. Maybe Chicago will react differently.

Inside the hotel, Johnson walks up a staircase behind a human blockade of Secret Service agents, oblivious to a slowly appearing hotel lobby below him that "is jammed from wall to wall."[2]

Busby's eyes widen at a flood of people standing and looking at the president. Soon, applause, but it is not a sound of jubilation or victory. It's more controlled, yet positive, and Busby, standing back behind Johnson, interprets the applause as "a rare quality of awe and respectfulness."

Eventually, Johnson slows down his hunched yet methodical ascent up the steps and turns to acknowledge the admiring crowd. He seems uncomfortable, and Busby hones in on the president's hands, "moving hesitantly and nervously, touching along the edge of his coat, rising chest high, then falling back to his sides, where he held them stiffly, clenching and unclenching his fists uncomfortably."

Such moments of unabashed positivity have been rare for Johnson, especially in the last several years. Protest chants along Pennsylvania Avenue of "Hey, hey, LBJ, how many kids did you kill today?" haunt his thoughts, and his daughter Luci sees the conflict in Vietnam "lancing his gut" through "sleepless nights."[3] So now, after sacrificing his job, he hears that unfamiliar sound of hope coming his way. "Poor man," says a secretary close to Busby as they watch Johnson fidget, "he doesn't remember what a friendly crowd sounds like."[4] Johnson briefly waves his hand at the applauding crowd then races toward the stage.

His speech to the convention room full of broadcasters must have felt cathartic, and for twenty-seven minutes, barring a few comedic asides, his soaring tone approaches the orbit of a Southern Baptist preacher. Twelve hours earlier he'd been stuck in a tar pit of his own creation, but here he is, free to insert jokes about last night's media bombshell. "Some of you might have thought from what I said last night that I had been taking elocution lessons from [midcentury radio announcer] Lowell Thomas," he quips. This morning, free from the tonal restraint of someone speaking to a diverse national audience, Johnson has returned to his natural Texan drawl, and now that he is halfway out the door, he can be honest with how he feels about television's ever-increasing power: "Well, there is no denying it. You of the broadcast industry have enormous power in your hands. You have the power to clarify and you have the power to confuse. Men in public life cannot remotely rival your opportunity—day after day, night after night, hour after hour on the hour—and the half hour, sometimes—you shape the nation's dialogue."[5]

Johnson is well aware how television's coverage of Vietnam has helped create a division in the country. Only two months ago, during the Tet Offensive, NBC aired the bullet-to-the-head execution of Vietcong prisoner Nguyen Van Lem by South Vietnam general (and American ally) Nguyen Ngoc Loan. The moment is immortalized by photographer Eddie Adams, and the disturbing image of a man milliseconds from death helped to deepen the stewing moral outrage. *How can we allow this to happen?*

In this room, Johnson reaches back into history, wondering how other wars would have been received had they been given "prime time":

> As I sat in my office last evening, waiting to speak, I thought
> of the many times each week when television brings the war
> into the American home. No one can say exactly what effect

those vivid scenes have on American opinion. Historians must only guess at the effect that television would have had during earlier conflicts on the future of this Nation: during the Korean war, for example, at that time when our forces were pushed back there to Pusan. Or World War II, the Battle of the Bulge, or when our men were slugging it out in Europe or when most of our air force was shot down that day in June 1942 off Australia.[6]

Throughout his speech, Johnson vacillates between praising broadcast coverage and cautioning its potential for abuse, but near the end, Johnson implores the media to remain as transparent as it can:

> You are the keepers of a trust. You must be just. You must guard, and you must defend your media against the spirit of faction, against the works of divisiveness and bigotry, against the corrupting evils of partisanship in any guise. For America's press, as for the American presidency, the integrity and the responsibility and the freedom—the freedom to know the truth and let the truth make us free—must never be compromised or *diluted* or destroyed. The defense of our media is your responsibility. Government cannot and must not and never will—as long as I have anything to do about it—intervene in that role.

The room applauds. In this sense, Johnson has remained true to his word. He shakes a determined fist on the words "never will." Even though he faces the bitter truth that the media's reporting on the war cemented his unpopularity, Johnson still believes in the authority of a free press, as long as it remains objective.[7]

MLK Grapples with American Poverty

> *"I choose to identify with the underprivileged. I choose to identify with the poor. I choose to give my life for the hungry. I choose to give my life for those who have been left out. . . . This is the way I'm going. If it means suffering*

*a little bit, I'm going that way. . . . If it means dying for
them, I'm going that way, because I heard a voice saying,
'Do something for others.'"*

—Martin Luther King Jr.[8]

While President Johnson talks to the media in Chicago about its responsibility to never be compromised, Martin Luther King Jr. and the Southern Christian Leadership Conference (SCLC) are devising ways to make sure the media focuses on their Poor People's Campaign march, the first stage of three to begin on April 22. The SCLC previously used the media to their advantage in 1963 Birmingham, thanks in large part to police chief Bull Connor's decision to use high-powered fire hoses and attack dogs to intimidate teenage demonstrators. The brutal effect of news programs televising such a brazen display of racial brutality rejuvenated the civil rights movement, and now, on a late April 1 morning, King sits in a meeting near his home in Atlanta, Georgia, hoping to galvanize underrepresented groups across the country. Their plan is simple—to nonviolently disrupt the American power structure by organizing a united march of hundreds of thousands of people who live below the poverty line.

Around King are representatives from across the country. Grace Mora Newman has come to speak for Puerto Ricans living in New York City, and she tells the group that she "has been exposed to the system's corruption" while growing up in Harlem, and she implores the SCLC to "work more directly with Puerto Ricans and against the power structure to achieve what we all want." She will do her "best" to send out a hundred thousand Spanish-language leaflets to get the word out about the campaign, and also set up "street meetings."

Clifton Johnson speaks for "white Appalachia." His message to the group is direct and urgent: "Me and my people, we're fighting the local politicians. I'm here to find out what we can do. I'm after information." Johnson mentions that he's "been working with poor people about two years."

As King alluded to yesterday morning while speaking in the Washington National Cathedral, he has seen firsthand the Appalachian region's financial and borderline third-world woes. Another representative at the meeting mentions Mercer County in West Virginia: "Eighty-seven percent of the people of the county are on welfare." Their grim living situation prompts King to bring his voice into the meeting: "I want to ask brother Johnson . . . How long do you think it would take to set up meetings with staff SCLC people to talk to the people in that part of the country?"

Johnson doesn't think it will be a problem, but he's blunt with King: "For God's sake, send someone intelligent. Not someone who's going to stir up trouble between colored people and white. He's got to have an understanding that it's in the interest of all these people. Colored and white . . . we got one thing in common: they're all poor . . . the power structure would like nothing better than to have us fall out among ourselves."[9]

A representative from the "northern cities" chimes in about their progress in "organizing *all* poor people. Poor whites, Puerto Ricans, Mexicans."

The firecracker in the meeting is activist Reies Tijerina, representing the Federal Alliance of New Mexico. Most of the people in the meeting, including King, had met each other for the first time on March 4, but this second meeting feels different—as if the momentum of the campaign is gaining speed. Today, Tijerina's energy reflects the growing optimism: "Super-strategy, super-wisdom is needed to develop justice in this country! The power structure, our enemy, is worse than a snake!"

Many in the room agree with Tijerina, laughing at his mix of truth and dynamism. The comment appears to wake up a still-fatigued King, who replies to Tijerina that, indeed, the enemy's "weapons can bring down empires." Tijerina is very excited about what many in the room feel is an unprecedented moment of unity among disenfranchised sections of the country. "I have a great desire to see a great coalition. Especially if we can put leadership in the hands of the most competent and proper leaders." Tijerina also reemphasizes King's original concept for the march. In order to attract the media's attention, "we are advising people to come as poor, with patches and poor clothes. There is great need for dramatizing."

Next is Tillie Fay Walker, a Native American activist who grew up on a reservation and helped create the United Scholarship Service, a nonprofit devoted to aiding young Native Americans in their attempts to gain admission to elite preparatory schools. Today she tells King that a few weeks ago she had asked a tribal council in North Dakota to join the march. The vote was unanimous, and their motivation to take part is tremendous, since 85 percent of the 2,700 living on the reservation are currently unemployed and the "poverty program on our reservation will be cut."[10]

King is "amazed to hear that the percentage is as high as 85 percent." Walker then lets twenty-five-year-old Native American activist Hank Adams report on his progress discussing the rights of American Indian fishermen in western Washington state. Adams alludes to complications he's having with the Bureau of Indian Affairs. Since the Poor People's Campaign was King's original idea, most of the uninformed feel as if the rights of Black people will be prioritized over other groups. Andrew Young dismisses that notion and reminds those in the meeting that "in the (old) South . . . there was real interest [in uniting] between slaves and Indians. Indians were the ones that would take in the escaped slaves . . . even into the tribes."

Tillie Walker jumps back into the conversation, saying that "our reservations are surrounded by white people. Our relations have been with white people."

Adrian Foote takes note the of the frustration Adams and Walker have been having in dealing with White authority and offers a quick anecdote. "My grandfather said: 'When the white man shakes your hand, it's the one behind his back that you have to watch for!'" Foote can see, as many others do, one commonality among everyone at this meeting. "We have one problem . . . POVERTY."

Newman nods in agreement. "People are NOT politically aware. We don't understand each other, there is no communication between the various groups. It's the system—the whole damn system—that's responsible."

It is a meeting rich in communication and unity. Other representatives are mentioned as well, such as mothers on welfare in Washington,

DC. Etta Horn proclaims Washington as "really a slave city," and tells the committee that "we've been threatened" by governmental organizations. "If we participate, the mothers don't receive their checks."

King and others are entirely aware of the negative editorials in newspapers regarding their Poor People's march. Many see an inevitability of violence taking place when thousands of people decide to disrupt traffic and sit-in around the nation's capital. But Andrew Young only has to remind the group about the fickle nature of public opinion by mentioning how many felt about the Vietnam War one year ago, when King spoke out fearlessly against the war's immorality. "Dr. King attacked the war; they attacked *him*." Now, here Dr. King sits, while the president is set to leave office largely because of how he handled Vietnam.[11]

The meeting runs long and, appropriately, King ends it with a final statement before returning to his home. "We have gotten into the main substance, and the great need now is to translate what we have. This campaign is where the poor people are demanding their rights. We are going to Washington to make the invisible visible. This campaign is not just for the black, but for all of the poverty stricken in the world."[12]

The "First Gentleman" of Alabama Would Like Some Privacy

"And I want to tell the good people of this state, as a judge of the Third Judicial Circuit, if I didn't have what it took to treat a man fair, regardless of his color, then I don't have what it takes to be the governor of your great state."

—George Wallace, 1958[13]

Twelve hours after Lyndon Johnson's announcement, presidential candidate George Wallace holds a press conference at a downtown Montgomery hotel. It's to be short, since his wife of twenty-four years and the current governor of Alabama, Lurleen Burns Wallace, is recovering from cancer treatment at St. Margaret's Hospital a few blocks away. Wallace tells the press that he was with her in the morning and plans to go back right after the press conference.[14]

On LBJ's announcement, Wallace says that he is "more interested in peace in Southeast Asia than I am in who brings it about, but he will "certainly wish him well when he retires from government."[15]

It's been ten years since George Wallace first attempted to become governor of Alabama. In 1958 he ran as a moderate judge only mildly in favor of segregation and was known by African American lawyers as one of the first White Alabama judges to respectfully address them as *Mr.* in the courtroom. But after being "out-niggered" in the Democratic primary by Ku Klux Klan–supported John M. Patterson, Wallace ignored the endorsement he received by the NAACP and devised a new strategy to become governor using segregation as his platform. The loss to Patterson pained Wallace to no end. He began to drink and cheated on Lurleen, who considered divorce.[16]

In 1959, still a circuit judge, George Wallace's identity began to change. He attempted to generate headlines for himself by refusing to turn over voting records to federal judge (and former college buddy) Frank Johnson, who was reviewing claims of discrimination. By publicly defying Johnson, Wallace was then seen by the Alabama segregationists as a man fighting to maintain the current systems within the state. Although he ended up giving the records to Johnson, Wallace was able to manipulate the local press into believing that he had defied federal officials and declared himself a winner in the ongoing struggle against integration.

Race-fueled rhetoric followed, and Wallace delivered his statements the way boxers throw jabs. His language was punchy and abrasive, and White Alabamians, feeling embarrassed and disrespected nationally by the ever-growing civil rights movement and the sympathetic national media, found in the voice of George Wallace a frustrated sense of pride in their state's traditions. By the time the next governor's election came around in 1963, Wallace had had several years to refine his message and outspoken delivery. He won easily.

Soon after his victory, however, Wallace grew somewhat bored. He seemed to enjoy the competition of politics more than its administration.

On June 11, 1963, Wallace, only five months into his first term, con-cocted his Stand in the Schoolhouse Door to demonstrate his toughness on segregation, attempting to keep newly enrolled Black students Vivian Malone and Jimmy Hood from entering the University of Alabama. The spectacle gave Wallace nationwide notoriety, and he began traveling the country and speaking to crowds who waved the Confederate flag. "I remember speaking at Harvard," Wallace boasted at a rally. "I made 'em the best speech they ever heard."[17]

Wallace, quickly recognizing integration as inevitable, changed his language to "state's rights." The following year his name grew even more after testing out a presidential run in the Democratic primaries, nearly taking Maryland, but also being booed, heckled, and serenaded by "We Shall Overcome" at the University of Notre Dame.

In 1968, Wallace decided to run for president as the American Inde-pendent Party's nominee. His strategy is simple—take enough electoral votes to force the decision to go to the House of Representatives. So if, say, Nixon, Kennedy, McCarthy, or Humphrey can't reach the 270 mark, Wallace would suddenly find himself "in an enviable position." As stated in his "George C. Wallace **Can** Be Elected President" paper, "with the two existing major parties stymied, he could win the electoral votes needed to win. But even if he didn't win, he would be in a position to bargain for concessions by the other parties."[18]

So, on April 1, this is the Wallace strategy. But as the press ask him questions about Johnson's withdrawal, Wallace begins to retreat from his "House of Representatives strategy," claiming he never said such a thing, even though it's in his campaign papers. He tells the media today that it's the national press who have perpetuated the theory.

The step back is, like everything else, a strategy. He wants to be considered a *major* presidential contender, and not simply the third choice hoping for a miracle. With Johnson out, Wallace has a chance to be taken seriously.[19]

But with Lurleen in the hospital, Wallace's campaigning has been halted. He tells the press that she is very sick and he "is going to be with her" until her health improves. Indeed, Wallace returns to the hospital after the news conference. He owes his wife every ounce of attention he can give her, especially since she agreed to help keep him front and center by running for governor. As she attempts to recover, and with LBJ exiting the race, Wallace puts his best professional foot forward.

The Beginning of the Beginning of Ethnic Studies in Academia

Meanwhile, at San Francisco State College, where Wright Morris has taught creative writing for the previous six years, the campus YMCA has been taken over by the Third World Liberation Front (TWLF), a newly formed student coalition of four minority organizations—the "Black Student Union, the Latin American Student Organization, the Filipino-American Student Organization and the Mexican-American Students Group."

The confrontation officially began on March 22, when fifteen TWLF members entered the Quonset hut YMCA and told the only paid SFSC employee there, an executive secretary named Connie Dubner, that "we're taking over this space. You've got ten minutes to get out." Dubner, stunned, attempted to negotiate. "Can't we talk this thing over?"[20]

On that day, talk was cheap. "You've now got nine and a half minutes to get out."

After Dubner exited, the TWLF disconnected the main phone lines and electricity, and occupied the YMCA for the next week, until the SFSC president threatened them with legal action.

Their motivation stemmed from the treatment of their faculty adviser, Juan R. Martinez, an SFSC professor who hoped to teach Mexican American history and other ethnic studies courses in order to counterbalance the largely Anglo-Saxon narrative. The department chair didn't share his vision and told Martinez that they would be replacing him. Sensing discrimination, Martinez and the TWLF chose the YMCA to publicize the matter. They occupied the Y for one week.

But today, a security guard enters the building only to find that it has been vacated. The TWLF have left, avoiding a court battle with the president of the school, but this minor confrontation will soon snowball into a successful five-month strike on campus between students and faculty against the administration, starting on November 6, 1968, and ending on March 20, 1969, with their very own College of Ethnic Studies, as other universities across the country follow their lead.[21]

As for Professor Martinez, he will begin accepting invitations to speak on behalf of the students at SFSU. During one speech in Colorado, Martinez tries to be clear and direct: "People ask 'What do the browns and the blacks want?' and the answer is 'More.' They want more of everything. They want more education, more health care, more housing. They want what the rest of America has. They only want their share. . . . America is not at a crossroads. It is past that. It is going one way. It must now meet its commitments or meet its doom."[22]

Wright Morris and the Ignored Middle-American Writer

It was Christmas Eve, 1920, in Omaha, Nebraska, and a ten-year-old Wright Morris was staying with the Mulligans, a family who had gladly taken him in; his mother had passed six days after he was born, and his father was a drifter who couldn't seem to hold down a steady job, leaving him for months at a time. Wright knew his father wouldn't be sending him a gift—either out of thoughtlessness or because he lacked income—so instead he saved the coins he'd been earning as a newspaper carrier and bought a "gold watch in a pawnshop." It was all part of a master plan. First, he gathered a few boxes of incremental size and placed the watch in the smallest one. Then, he did a Russian doll routine and wrapped the box in a box that went into another box, and so on. He put the nested boxes in a package and addressed it "From Dad, To Wright."

On Christmas Day, the package now under the Mulligan tree, and Wright opened the boxes one by one. *Gee, Dad has a great sense of humor, doesn't he?* Finally, he pulled out the gold watch and put it on his wrist. Perfect fit. He showed it to the Mulligans with a smile. *You see . . . I told you he wouldn't forget.*[23]

Wright Morris with Granville Hicks's wife, Dorothy, on the Notre Dame campus in April 1968. *Photo taken by John Mroz.*

After sixteen books, a 1957 National Book Award, and critical acclaim from national voices such as Granville Hicks and Ralph Ellison, Wright Morris may very well be the most unread writer at the literary festival. But, here he stands at 4:00 PM inside the modestly sized library auditorium, preparing to talk to students, many of whom have yet to pick up anything he's written.

Morris knows full well why he has been given the library auditorium; tonight's special attraction, Norman Mailer, is preparing for a much larger audience in Washington Hall. Perhaps it's best if Morris tells you how he really feels about Mailer, from his newly released book of essays, titled *A Bill of Rites, A Bill of Wrongs, A Bill of Goods*, on bookshelves as of March 13. "Mr. Norman Mailer speaks with the clearest voice and with the least calculation, since he speaks for himself. It is his talent, and it is a large one, that he speaks out for two generations of rebels who have not grown up." You see, Wright Morris is a writer's writer. He *has* grown up, and the East Coast blare of Sir Norman is simply noise for the sake of noise. "Mr. Mailer's art may well represent what can be done with a writer's frustration, a child's disenchantment, and a man's sense of his impotent rage. It is surely a subject for talent, but talent will not transform it into a great subject."[24]

In a Wright Morris novel, unlike Mailer, you will find little to no violence, sex, and murder. Instead, what greets you is a heartbreaking sense of loss and isolation, underlined by a comic sweetness. For most of Morris's childhood, he lived *around* people—but not *with* them. Unable to register a real memory of his mother, Wright spent most of his childhood imagining the personalities of both his parents. He had a phantomlike fascination for their passion and energy. His father, as Wright's sad Christmas story describes, was a wanderer, a man who took odd jobs, started and failed businesses, and left his son alone to cobble a life out of fragments—poor and half-orphaned, a Huck Finn without the Mississippi River to navigate.

This sense of alienation is never more apparent than in his 1952 novel, *The Works of Love*, which begins:

> In the dry places, men begin to dream. Where the rivers run sand, there is something in man that begins to flow. West of the 98th Meridian—where it sometimes rains and it sometimes doesn't—towns, like weeds, spring up when it rains, dry up when it stops. But in a dry climate the husk of the plant remains. The stranger might find, as if preserved in amber, something of the green life that was once lived there, and the ghosts of men who have gone on to a better place. The withered towns are empty, but not uninhabited. Faces sometimes peer out from the broken windows, or whisper from the sagging balconies, as if this place—now that it is dead—had come to life. As if empty it is forever occupied. One of these towns, so the story would have it, was Indian Bow.[25]

While it's possible that not one student in the library auditorium crowd today has read Morris, Ralph Ellison, who grew up in Oklahoma and lost his father at the age of three, adored *The Works of Love*; for anyone who has experienced significant loss or perceived the absence of some *thing*, its plaintive prose has the power to penetrate the heart like a cool, melancholy breeze. In a 1952 *New York Times* article, Ellison went so far as to identify it as a book he wished he'd written.* "In its sheer writing artistry," he wrote, "and its command and fulfilment of its stylistic and formal commitments, I found it one of the most completely achieved of recent American novels."[26]

From any perspective, Morris's art is a tough sell for the current college campus. He doesn't have the anarchic wit of Mailer or Heller's antiwar laugh riot *Catch-22*, or Vonnegut's imaginative rings of fire.** Ellison has a classic novel read by millions and a position as a leading voice of the minority, and even good ol' Granville Hicks emanates a critical importance the same way a dusty tenured professor commands respect at a lecture. Today's talk will start as an uphill battle.

But Morris is ready.

Bill of Rites is filled with contemporary issues, and Morris stands ready to push his opinions out into the public sphere. Living with his wife, Josephine, near San Francisco—the nexus of hippiedom—Morris has had a first-row seat to the counterculture's heartbeat. Morris had written, "Hippies share some knowledge of where they have been, but no demonstrable insight into where they are going. . . . What they share is a condition, not a direction. The condition is that of adolescent rebellion, a stage in the normal development of the species."

When it comes to Lyndon Johnson, Morris has issues, and it starts with a sense of betrayal he has been feeling ever since Johnson was given four more years in 1964. Back then, Johnson hoped to focus his policies on the development of a Great Society—or a domestic-driven agenda based around eradicating racial prejudice and poverty. But as Vietnam's shadow grew ever larger, Johnson redirected his efforts (and the budget) toward a controversial war. Morris and the nation watched as Johnson's "face value" dropped and declared his previous agenda dead. "The Great

---

* Ellison's kind words may have been a bit of a favor in return, since earlier that year Morris had written an off-the-charts laudatory book review of Ellison's *Invisible Man* for the *New York Times*, two weeks after its release.

** *Publishers Weekly* top five fiction bestsellers for this week: *Topaz* by Leon Uris, *The Confessions of Nat Turner* by William Styron, *Vanished* by Fletcher Knebel, *Christy* by Catherine Marshall, and *Myra Breckinridge* by Gore Vidal.

Society," Morris wrote, "is a concrete urn with the cremated ashes of our Great Expectations." As for Johnson himself, "The crisis of the nation is not in Vietnam, or in Watts or in Selma, or the fire next time, but in the profound and disquieting realization of the people that their face-value judgment of Lyndon Johnson was wrong. His face value is out. We have no idea what value is in. There are many who feel that they have been the victims of a gigantic hoax."[27]

Morris's talk today is titled "Life and Literature," and he tells the audience that the global landscape is "obviously shrinking," but the "consciousness of man" is "pleasurably expanding." Today, people are simply "seeing *more*"—a gift and a curse. "Our torment [as writers] lies in that we see more, rather than less. . . . And much of what we see we do not like."

For Morris, the torment of watching the nightly news coverage of Vietnam is hard to take, and as a fiction writer he feels bombarded by visual facts. "Who needs fiction?" he wrote in *Bill of Rites*. "What could be stranger than the news on the hour?"

What could be stranger? He answered his own question—the government not providing the general public accurate information:

> The war is already covered by the networks better than the war department; the participating audience covers the war for itself. Thousands fight it. Numberless millions sit in on it. As a continuing serial, war goes far toward solving the networks' major programming problems. A story without end. A cast of millions. An international theatre in the round. Seen as a game, the game of war need not wait for weekend billing. It gets prime time. We can predict its appearance on the late, late show. There is always something playing in the theatre of war.[28]

Even so, as Morris tells the audience, just because television is airing more violence and adult programming doesn't mean fiction writers should follow suit. Perhaps alluding to Norman Mailer's sensationalistic tendencies, Morris believes more and more novelists are falling into a trap of trying to "tell it like it is," giving the momentary spasms of reality far more pages than they deserve. "When the author tries to make sex a lure and a sideshow it is a sign of panic," Morris tells the audience.[29]

But Morris worries about the younger generation in front of him. Seeing the dark heart of war through a television screen has caused the population to become both "fire and ice"—reacting extremely to extreme news with immense rage or calculated indifference.

Notre Dame professor John Matthias enjoys Morris's lecture and his "dignified presence," and Granville Hicks watches as "a score or more" of university students follow Morris "into the anteroom" of the library auditorium, "some with copies of *In Orbit* and *A Bill of Rites* to be autographed, more with questions."[30]

George Ovitt is one of the students. As a member of the sophomore committee and a creative writer, he's enjoyed Morris's "wonderful" talk and has bought a brand-new copy of *The Field of Vision* for Morris to sign. Ovitt is intimidated by Morris's place in the literary community. Aside from Ralph Ellison's exalted presence, Ovitt regards Morris as the most important speaker in attendance. Nonetheless, Ovitt can't shake the feeling that Morris doesn't seem "entirely happy—as if the circus surrounding Mailer and the fame of the others" makes him "uncomfortable."

Ovitt moves through the line and eventually reaches the front and hands Morris his copy. As Ovitt gulps, the author examines the pristine, untouched book. Then he looks at Ovitt and, in a "rather stern voice," asks, "Did you read it?" Ovitt had, but Morris's insecurity toward his readership, reflected in his declining sales, will be an issue for the remainder of his career.[31]

Still, Morris wouldn't for a second trade his above-average, under-the-radar fame with tonight's novelist and provocateur. Morris, like the rest of America, has watched Norman Mailer's literary high-wire act from a distance, and "Mailer's remarkable antics are those of a mountaineer trapped on the summit. After *The Naked and the Dead*, what next? His public exhort him to rise to heaven; his enemies confidently anticipate his pratfall. It is no contest. Pratfalls carry the day. There is a limit to what can be done on the flying trapeze."[32]

With his wife and the Hickses sitting next to him, Morris will have a front-row seat to Mailer mania, part one.

Fan Mailer to her son Norman Mailer, June 1941:

> How is the writing coming along, honey? Put all the feeling
> you possess into it and it has to be good. When you were a tiny
> infant every time I nursed you, I would whisper a little prayer in
> your ear, "Please God, make him a great man some day." This
> is a secret between you and me, sonny. Take care of yourself.
> Love, Mother.

Norman Mailer to first wife, Beatrice Silverman, circa 1944:

> We go back to finish the raspberry ice, and you straddle me in the
> chair and my hot hard pride slips into your lubricious embrace.
> We fuck very gently, and finish the ice, and light cigarettes, and
> drink more wine, until we glow and become tumescent so that
> I must lay you out on the divan, and fuck the shit out of you.
> Do you like my French mind, darling? Do you love the thought
> of alternating food nibbles and love nibbles? Am I heating your
> snatch from 10,000 miles?[33]

Mailer's three-hundred-thousand-word first novel, *The Naked and
the Dead*, a work he had been piecing together ever since joining the
military during World War II, was an attempt at writing *the* great
American novel. He sent letters home to his wife, Beatrice, filled with
descriptions of soldiers, the geography of the island he was stationed
on, and after being discharged in 1946 he spent "four days a week, five
hours a day, producing about thirty typed pages a week." He read *Anna
Karenina* in the mornings to rev up his voice, and in the afternoons
had, according to his biographer J. Michael Lennon, "a can of beer."
He paid a friend $150 to type a cleaned-up version of the manuscript.
Then, in October 1947, he sent it off to Rinehart—a publishing house
whose editor, Ted Amussen, had reached out to Mailer back in 1941
after he'd won a national short story competition for college students.
Mailer then left for Paris, where he had always hoped to follow in the
footsteps of Ernest Hemingway and Dos Passos and the Lost Generation of expatriates.[34]

Around May 1948, Norman and Beatrice were still sightseeing around Europe. What awaited them back in America was the beginning of a media blast that Norman was in no way prepared for. "I dread the return to America," Mailer wrote in his journal, "where every word I say will have too much importance, too much misinterpretation. And of course I am sensitive to the hatreds my name is going to evoke."[35]

On May 1 *The Naked and the Dead* received a cautiously positive review by Mailer's Long Branch, New Jersey, hometown newspaper, the *Daily Record*, which noted his "keen ear for sound effects, a sharp eye for the looks of a jungle or a firing line, and the ability to paint a scene in vivid colors." But the literary critic couldn't help "the feeling . . . that you've been to Anopopei before, and that the author, for all he is a born writer, keeps you there longer than you want to stay."[36]

Far more glowing reviews followed in droves, however, thanks to Rinehart's strategy of placing the book in the hands of numerous media outlets, and soon Mailer found himself inundated with heaps of praise. But Mailer, writing to his adoring mother on May 12 after receiving the most mail "ever in my life," felt "more empty than I ever have, and to fill the vacuum, to prime the motor, I need praise. Each good review gives fuel, each warm letter, but as time goes by I need more and more for less and less effect."[37]

He labeled this need "praise-opium," and in June, while on a nice road trip with his wife and younger sister, he'd reach max addiction to it. Norman walked out of a post office in Rome with a pile of mail that had been forwarded to him by his father back in New York. His wife and younger sister sat inside a "small Peugeot," and they started going through rave reviews, admiring letters, and offers. Then, Norman, in a surrealist state, flipped to a page in a newspaper. There he was, at the top. He stared at the line, then said with a small voice, "Gee, I'm first on the bestseller list."[38]

John Mroz was only five days old when *The Naked and the Dead* entered bookstores, but over the past twenty years Norman Mailer's antiestablishment voice has been a part of his upbringing. Instead of becoming a traditional novelist in the vein of his heroes Ernest Hemingway and John Dos Passos, Mailer instead, after two novels failed to sate his cravings for praise-opium, transformed into a public figure who, from afar, Mroz sees as "pugnacious, loud, and rude."[39]

Mroz knows that Norman Mailer is the flashiest name in the literary festival lineup, and he has no problem giving the author two consecutive nights to share his visions with the public. While standing outside tonight's event, Mroz senses an "atmosphere of electricity" and observes "lines of people waiting outside Washington Hall." He takes a moment and feels a great sense of pride. For so much of the school year, Notre Dame is dominated by its sports culture, but in bringing a literary treasure to campus, he believes that Mailer is good for the university and the student body.[40]

What makes tonight even more electric is that Mroz has coincidentally brought one of the sharpest political commentators onto campus less than twenty-four hours after one of the decade's most shocking political moments. The timing can't be better, and a man of Mailer's creative impulsivity won't need much time to turn his talk into a headline.

If Mroz could have known in advance that LBJ would be making such an enormous announcement, he may have tried to move Mailer into the larger Stepan Center. Instead, after Mroz introduces him as "America's most exciting and controversial author," Mailer walks up to the podium and stares out at a standing-room-only audience eager to hear a blitz of opinions.

There's a loud ovation, and the forty-five-year-old Mailer draws a deep breath and in his best LBJ-Texan drawl says, "Well, Gawd damn Vietnam."

The students love it, perhaps even more because of Notre Dame's Catholic backbone, highlighted by several unsmiling nuns sitting in the audience. Mailer is quick to make fun of himself—"My wife tells me I sound more like Bobby Kennedy"—and moves through his commentary, as Granville Hicks notes, "without text or even notes," enthralling the audience. Hicks, sitting near the front, senses that many of the students see the "pudgy, disheveled" Mailer as a "valued symbol of rebellion."[41]

Mailer mentions a newfound appreciation for President Johnson. Of his announcement not to seek reelection, Mailer declares it "a splendid, awesome, and breathtaking thing that proved we were all wrong about him." He proclaims, "If Lyndon Johnson is a better man than I thought he was, then this country is a better country than I thought it was yesterday."[42]

Mailer's not sure if LBJ is being honest or deceptive, but to him the fact remains that "he is nonetheless splendid." Ever an admirer of audacity, Mailer tells the young crowd that it's "better to have a president who is a large and evil man than one who is small and ignoble."[43]

He goes on: "And the reason for that is . . . there is no condition more intolerable to man than to live in some form of social servitude to a tyrant who is small." Mailer takes a beat, then gives Notre Dame's religious roots a backhanded compliment, "which is one of the reasons for the well-continuing love of the Church over all these centuries."[44]

When discussing what will be next for America, Mailer can only offer the extremes he's most familiar with. "We have no idea what our future is. Will it be magnificent or debased?" Perhaps both, but Mailer is most concerned with the damage the current government may bring upon the country. "[America] is founded on literature, [but] it may founder on politics."[45]

South Bend Tribune journalist Patricia Koval views Mailer as a combination of the menacing eyes and intelligence of the American lawyer Daniel Webster mixed with the anarchic wit of Irish poet Brendan Behan. But it's wholly Mailer's "gusty delivery" that captivates the audience for the next two hours, and the provocative author can't help but throw a few right hooks at the religious overtones of Notre Dame.

Far from being a Catholic, Mailer, with disapproving nuns looking on, begins to wonder aloud about the "common ground occupied by existentialism and Catholicism," receiving a "fluctuating combination of appreciative laughter and nervous giggles." He prefaces his ideas by proudly saying that he speaks with the "extraordinary presumption of a non-Christian" before volunteering a thought that perplexes him—the schizophrenic nature of American belief. To Mailer, the country seems to be able to live with the juxtaposed ideas of "the love of mystery of Christ versus the love of no mystery whatever."

He's losing the crowd, so he pushes away his random thought circles and tells the audience that he'll be reading an excerpt from his forthcoming book, *The Armies of the Night.* Just before digging into the reading, he gives the audience a way out. OK, he warns, if there is anyone here who just "came to see what I look like," you can leave now—I won't hold it against you.

Several nuns, dressed in full habit, stand up and walk out, as do others. Everyone notices, and the laughter is strong since Mailer seems to have brought it upon himself. Still, a surprised Mailer calls out in sympathy, "I made a mistake!" but it's too late.[46]

With the mood now less rowdy, Mailer brings the focus back to his book. One passage, rich with metaphor, stands out from the rest, given the state of the times:

> America, once a beauty of magnificence unparalleled, now a beauty with a leprous skin. She is heavy with child—no one knows if legitimate—and languishes in a dungeon whose walls are never seen. Now the first contractions of her fearsome labor begin—it will go on: no doctor exists to tell the hour. It is only known that false labor is not likely on her now, no, she will probably give birth, and to what?—the most fearsome totalitarianism the world has ever known? Or can she, poor giant, tormented lovely girl, deliver a babe of a new world brave and tender, artful and wild?[47]

Mailer has always been in love with the maddening contradictions of America, and the chaotic mix within *The Armies of the Night* seems to exemplify Mailer's own artistic torment. Granville Hicks enjoys the reading, calling it "one of his finest pieces of prose," but the wise literary critic knows never to be too enthralled by Mailer, whose canon of work after *The Naked and the Dead* seems to take one step forward and two steps back. When Hicks reviewed Mailer's 1967 novel *Why*

Norman Mailer speaking in Notre Dame's Washington Hall on April 1, 1968.
Photo courtesy of the University of Notre Dame Archives.

Are We in Vietnam? he called it more a "lark" than a story, and wondered, "How much of this we are supposed to take seriously I haven't the slightest idea.[48]"*

So, yes, today Hicks is impressed with Mailer and his genuine warmth toward the Notre Dame students, but he has to wonder "what kind of Mailer will appear tomorrow night."[49]

After his reading, Mailer allows for a quick question-and-answer period. He wants "provocative questions," such as, jokingly, "Mailer, is this the way you make your living?"

The first question asked is about Richard Nixon. "How do you feel about him?"

Mailer reads the air. He can tell his young audience is looking for a punchline. "I'd feel sorry for Richard Nixon if he is elected president of the United States because he will discover that hell that is reserved for actors who are without . . . charisma." The crowd loves it.

The next question is about a recent remark by folk singer Joan Baez, who said that "the only way to stop killing is to stop killing." *What are your thoughts on that?*

Here again, Mailer has one ready. "It gives one pleasure that Bob Dylan doesn't make political speeches if Joan Baez's speeches are indications of what to expect from him."

Proud of himself for reining in his bad language tonight, Mailer warns the crowd that tomorrow night's film will have plenty of it. "This [night], as 24 hours will prove, is a masterpiece of understatement."[50]

Mailer later joins Mroz and several other professors and sophomore committee members back at the Morris Inn for a bit of bourbon and conversation. Mailer mainly nurses his glass, careful not to become too inebriated since he has a big day ahead of him tomorrow. But he enjoys

---

* Hicks (along with John Updike and Josephine Herbst) was one of the three National Book Award fiction judges in 1968. *Why Are We in Vietnam* was a finalist, along with *The Confessions of Nat Turner* by William Styron, *Eighth Day* by Thornton Wilder, *A Garden of Earthly Delights* by Joyce Carol Oates, and *The Chosen* by Chaim Potok. Wilder's *The Eighth Day* took the prize, announced on March 5, 1968. It's unknown if Mailer held any kind of grudge toward Hicks, who, judging from his review, wouldn't have recommended Mailer's novel for the prize. Betty Tyler, *The Bridgeport Post*, "Wilder Outdistances Styron For Book Award in Fiction," March 10, 1968, 7.

talking with the sophomores, and as the night progresses, Mailer's car-
ousel of accents—twirling around Ireland, New York, and to yet another
LBJ Texan impression—finally settles on a "dry and ironic" Harvard
sound. There just might not be *one* true Norman Mailer, and for the
sophomore committee eager to grow themselves, that is quite all right.[51]

3

TUESDAY, APRIL 2, 1968

A World Premiere in Middle America

Norman Mailer surveying the setup inside the Stepan Center on April 2, 1968. Marty Kress is in the background setting up chairs for the world premiere of Mailer's film *Beyond the Law*. *Photo courtesy of Marty Kress.*

Lyndon Johnson Is Misunderstood . . .

On Tuesday morning, Lyndon Johnson sits in a White House conference room, breakfast in front of him. It's his weekly meeting with Democratic legislative leaders and the agenda is filled to the brim:

What "political implications" should we consider now that you're withdrawing?

How should we gauge the reaction coming out of North Vietnam regarding peace talks?

At the meeting is Vice President Hubert Humphrey. He mentions to those in attendance his willingness to enter the race if he receives broad-based support. Humphrey is Johnson's man, but allegiances have already been made—some toward Robert Kennedy and others to Eugene McCarthy—and congressional leaders are not about to set aside their promises until Humphrey begins campaigning.

For the now-unshackled president, the political nomination process may feel a bit exhausting to think about, and he conveys this to the people around him. Perhaps in response to a Democratic leader urging Johnson to trumpet his support for Humphrey before the August convention, Johnson says he's "tired of begging anyone for anything." He then begins to reflect. "I had a partnership with Jack Kennedy, and when he died I felt it was my duty to look after the family of stockholders and employees of my partner. I did not fire anyone. The divisions are so deep within the party that I could not reconcile them. I'm not going to influence the [August] convention . . . Probably won't even go." Then he lets loose a statement that reflects his open mood. "Much to everyone's disbelief, I never wanted to be president to begin with. I'm leaving without any bitterness."[1]

Perhaps he is leaving behind the Democratic primary nomination circus without bitterness, but Vietnam is another story. On Tuesday morning, direct quotes from North Vietnamese leaders begin to be picked up by the American press. In the *Quan Doi Nhan Dan*, a North Vietnamese newspaper run by its army, one quote is taken by China's Radio Peking then translated to English: "The Johnson clique, although it has openly declared its intention to overhaul the strategy of its war of aggression in Vietnam, is still looking for ways and means of misleading public opinion and does not agree to stop the bombing and other military actions finally and unconditionally throughout the Democratic Republic of Vietnam."[2] Another pro-Communist newspaper, the *Nhan Dan*, accuses the United States of *increasing* their bombing runs, perhaps around the demilitarized zone, where official reports document at least two navy bomber strikes, one of which occurred four hours after Johnson's Sunday night speech.

The *Nhan Dan* then restates its hope for an unconditional halt to all bombing. "Our people want peace," writes the *Nhan Dan*, "but real peace must go with genuine independence and freedom. As long as our beloved homeland is overshadowed by American aggression, our country will not have genuine freedom and independence."

President Johnson can see that his sincerity is being questioned. His official orders to the armed forces in Vietnam were to halt bombing everywhere except "a small area immediately north of the demilitarized zone." In his Sunday night speech, Johnson had in a previous draft a more specific location to mention—the twentieth parallel—but had opted against telling the general public because of advisers pushing for "military security." By not mentioning an exact, definitive location, the public is left to believe that the bombing would stop at the boundary line dividing North and South Vietnam—the seventeenth parallel.

The miscommunication may seem minor, but from a diplomatic point of view, the repercussions send ripples of doubt as to how serious Johnson's promises are.

Senate majority leader Mike Mansfield can't help but rib the text of Johnson's Sunday night speech to a *Los Angeles Times* staff writer: "May I suggest that the next time a speech of this significance is written it would be better if a word artist were used who can write English as it should be and not fuzzy sentences that can be interpreted several different ways."[3]

Somewhere, Horace Busby grits his teeth.

MLK's Bittersweet Day Off

While Johnson scrambles to bring North Vietnam into proper peace talks, Reverend King arrives home after a standard SCLC meeting at 234 Sunset Avenue in Vine City, an Atlanta neighborhood, with Coretta and their four children. It is a rare, much-needed moment of downtime.

Recently, whenever King enters his home, he is greeted by Bernice ("Bunny"), their youngest at four years old. Bunny runs up to him to "swing into his arms," and King, now carrying her, meets her eyes and says, "Give me some good old sugar." Bunny gives him a quick smooch on the mouth. Then he says, "I bet you don't know where Yoki's sugar is." Bunny doesn't need time to think. She's played the "kissing game" before, and she plants one on the right side of King's mouth. Then he says, "Where's Dexter's sugar?" Sure enough, Bunny finds the spot on King's right cheek. And finally, "I know you don't know where Marty's sugar is." Bunny smiles. "Yes I do!" She puts down one more smack on King's cheek.[4]

Coretta and the children are happy to have him for the day. The oldest, Yolanda ("Yoki"), is twelve. Her lifespan covers her family's part in the civil rights movement. She was a newborn during the early stages of the Montgomery Bus Boycott, and King often "came home from the stress and turmoil that he was suddenly plunged into" and would find Yoki in her crib, "cooing and cuddly and trustful and loving." Nearly three weeks old when Rosa Parks was arrested for not moving from her seat, Yoki helped lighten the ever-increasing load King had started to carry.

Even at a young age, Yoki learned how to defend her father and support the cause. At six years old, Yoki was once confronted by a White classmate. The White girl had clearly been told by her parents that Reverend King was not a good example to follow. The girl then said to Yoki, "Oh, your daddy is always going to jail." Precocious for a six-year-old, Yoki stood her ground. "Yes, he goes to jail to help people." A year later, Yoki had grown tired of being given special treatment simply because she was Reverend King's daughter. With the teacher temporarily outside the classroom, Yoki managed to get the class's attention and said "Look, all I want is just to be treated like a normal child."[5]

Their second oldest at ten, Martin Luther King III ("Marty") has difficulties at school as well. After switching schools two years earlier, one White classmate came up to him and asked what his father's name was. Marty told him, and the eight-year-old White student replied, "Oh! Your father's that famous nigger." It's a word Marty already knew should not be spoken, especially by someone White. "The word is 'Negro,'" he replied.[6]

Still feeling dispirited about a March 28 Memphis march that started out nonviolent but eventually led to 150 arrests and the murder of sixteen-year-old Larry Payne by a policeman named Leslie Dean Jones,* King phones Ralph Abernathy and asks him to reschedule their flight to 7:00 AM Wednesday morning. They are scheduled to leave Tuesday night for Memphis, but King chooses to stay one more night with the family. Perhaps he wants to throw a football to Marty, or head down to the Ollie Street Y with Dexter and go for a swim. Or, perhaps he simply wants to enjoy a nice home-cooked meal without worrying about how much time he has left.

Regardless, the children, especially seven-year-old Dexter, have a nagging feeling about their father once again returning to Memphis. Something is "off," but Dexter can't explain it. None of the children can. All they feel is that "something bad was going to happen."[7]

Their father may be feeling it more than they realize, but he's not about to let it stop him from going back. As he sits with his family, he's well aware that in Memphis the tragic funeral of Larry Payne is being attended by hundreds of Black Memphis residents, and no matter the unwarranted brutality of the police department, it will be King who is blamed by a majority of the general public for the teenager's death. Unless he can conduct a nonviolent march without an incident, Payne will have died in vain.

---

* According to historian Michael Honey's account, Larry Payne stole a television and was being chased on foot by Officer Jones. Payne went into a basement stairwell and closed the door. Officer Jones "banged on the door" but Payne "wouldn't come out." When Payne finally did with his hands up (claimed by over a dozen eyewitnesses) Officer Jones stuck a twelve-gauge shotgun "into Payne's stomach and pulled the trigger." Jones would not receive punishment, later stating that Payne had drawn "the biggest knife I ever saw . . . [I'm] very sorry it happened. I didn't want to kill him." Last quote from Charles Rond, *Times*, "Memphis Youth's Wake Worries Police, Guards," April 2, 1968, 24. See Michael Honey, *Going Down Jericho Road*, 359.

Richard Nixon Stays on Message in Cincinnati

*"If people looking at me say that's a new Nixon, then all
that I can say is, maybe you didn't know the old Nixon."*

—Richard Nixon, February 1968[8]

As Robert Kennedy and Eugene McCarthy continue to bump each
other out of the way, Republican presidential candidate Richard M.
Nixon appears to have everything under control. On the morning of
April 2, he's in Cincinnati speaking at an Ohio Republican Women's
Federation luncheon at the Convention Exposition Center, his skin
tanned after a brief vacation in Florida. One Ohio councilman views
Nixon as a candidate with enough time and freedom that it's as if he's
"waving a finger in the wind to determine whether to be more hawk
or more dove."[9]

Yes, Nixon has room to stretch his legs. His main competition,
Governor Nelson "Rocky" Rockefeller, is currently in a state of political waffling, and his indecision about entering the race has pushed away
potential supporters. Coupled with Michigan governor George Romney's
withdrawal from the race a month ago, Nixon appears to be in complete
control of the Republican nomination.

Ever since starting his campaign in early February, Nixon has chosen to run on a centrist message, standing in as a potential fulcrum
between two explosive sides. This is not easy to do. The art of speaking
middle-lane political-ese takes decades of experience, but Nixon has
them—having been active in politics for the last twenty years, most
prominently as Dwight Eisenhower's vice president, and also narrowly
losing the 1960 presidential election to John F. Kennedy.

Today, Nixon, in a dark blue suit, stands at the podium speaking
to around two thousand predominantly Republican women, and he's
confident. "I believe we are going to win because a divided Democratic
party cannot furnish the leadership."[10]

He receives bursts of applause, and continues rolling his bowling
ball down the middle, no-spin, emphasizing the need to "restore the
nation's military strength so that we may negotiate from strength." Also,
he invokes fear and urgency by saying that "in the next four years the

threat to peace, in terms of world war, will be the greatest in our life-time. . . . Russia will soon surpass the United States in nuclear capabil-ity, and Red China is coming up." To manage relations with these two countries, Nixon proposes (as he would have in a national television spot on Sunday that he canceled because of LBJ's bombshell) "continu-ing discussions" in a "series of summit conferences between the United States and Soviet Union to tackle Vietnam." Nixon need not bring up the three-day June 1967 Glassboro Summit in New Jersey between Presi-dent Johnson and Russia premier Alexei Kosygin, where the Vietnam War was briefly discussed.

Nixon doesn't give the press much to use. The knockout punches being thrown are coming from Kennedy and McCarthy, but now that Johnson has agreed to stand aside, all Nixon has to do is redeliver him-self to the American public as a kinder, wiser, and gentler Nixon—a fifty-five-year-old man with a sense of humor.

Starting in New Hampshire in February, Nixon began grabbing any chance to make a joke or two about his past losses, especially his poor television debate against Kennedy. "There has been a lot of criti-cism of President Johnson, some of it justified, much of it petty and unjustified," he said to a crowd in Concord, New Hampshire. "There are those that don't like his accent. There are those who don't like his style. And there are others that don't think he comes off too well on TV. . . . [*Laughter*] I know how he feels [*more laughter*]. . . . But my friends, the issue of 1968 is not the Johnson personality, but the Johnson policies."[11]

His 1968 campaign will stretch across six months. To illustrate Nix-on's ability to stay on message, two paragraphs are provided below. The first is from one of his first speeches as a Republican contender. The next is Nixon's nationally televised speech at the Republican National Convention, delivered six months later after he was officially given the nomination. Nixon recycles the same material, altering only key phrases.

February 3, 1968, Highway Hotel, Concord, New Hampshire

When the strongest nation in the world can be tied down for four years in a war against a fourth-rate military power* in Vietnam with no end in sight, when the richest nation in the world cannot manage its own economy, when the nation with the greatest tradition of the rule of law is torn apart by lawlessness, when a nation which has been the symbol of equality and opportunity is torn apart by racial strife, when the president of the United States cannot travel at home or abroad without fear of a hostile demonstration—then I say** it's time for new leadership in the United States of America.

August 8, 1968, Republican National Convention, Miami, Florida

When the strongest nation in the world can be tied down for four years in a war in Vietnam with no end in sight, when the richest nation in the world can't manage its own economy, when the nation with the greatest tradition of the rule of law is plagued by unprecedented lawlessness,*** when a nation which has been known for a century for equality and opportunity is torn by unprecedented racial violence,**** and when the President of the United States cannot travel abroad or to any major city at home***** without fear of a hostile demonstration—then it's time for new leadership for the United States of America.

---

* *Against a fourth-rate military power*: Nixon may have omitted this phrase for the convention because of the potentially offensive tone toward the American military. *Why can't our boys beat a fourth-rate military power?* In New Hampshire, however, his audience was looking for more of an edge.

** *Then I say*: As LBJ's "shall not seek and will not accept" decision shows, conviction matters. At the RNC, Nixon needed to show tremendous confidence in his abilities. "I say" would sound weaker, as if he is only speaking for himself and not for the party as a whole.

*** *Plagued by unprecedented lawlessness*: Owing to continued protests and demonstrations across the nation, many Republicans believe that not enough respect and compliance has been given to the nation's institutions. The word "unprecedented" has a strong, dangerous ring to it as well.

**** *Unprecedented racial violence*: As you'll read in this book, the nationwide racial violence after MLK's assassination will be unprecedented, whereas before King's death it was viewed more as *strife*, or a troublesome disagreement.

***** *To any major city at home*: Despite LBJ's jump in approval after his March 31 speech, young protesters in New York City and other major cities continued to show their disapproval for the ongoing war. It would also be well known by August 8 that heated protests were planned at the Democratic National Convention in Chicago, a potential melee Nixon

Despite his extensive experience, Richard Nixon's "face value" has echoes of an average Joe who would love to sell you an Oldsmobile. During a campaign stop in Green Bay, Wisconsin, he makes fun of his infamous nose by offering up a brief anecdote about the first time he met fellow large-noser Bob Hope in 1952. "Boy," Nixon remembers Hope saying, "when we get our noses together, what a wonderful ad for Sun Valley."[12]

This "new Nixon" convinces commentators and writers enough to write how much less of a phony he seems. Norman Mailer will later write of Nixon that he's "less phony now. . . . He had moved from a position of total ambition and total alienation from his own person . . . to a place now where he was halfway conciliated with his own self."[13]

One wonders how Nixon is now able to come off as a sincerely kind man. From a personal standpoint, his mother, whom he loved dearly, passed away on September 30, 1967, and the loss affected Nixon deeply as he sobbed in the arms of Billy Graham during the funeral. Perhaps losing his "saint" brought from within him a groundedness to talk to people with less of an agenda and more from his heart.

Regardless, as Nixon finishes his Cincinnati speech, he's aware that thousands of voters are at poll booths for today's Wisconsin primary—a race so noncompetitive that Nixon doesn't feel the need to spend the entire day there. By day's end, Nixon will end up winning four hundred thousand votes, or around 80 percent of the vote, with a not actively campaigning Ronald Reagan earning 11 percent. The finish line is near, and all Nixon needs to do is drive straight through the madness with a genuine smile on his face.

---

wouldn't mind seeing, and would eventually capitalize on by taking a motorcade down the same Chicago street a few days later as thousands cheered him on. Furthermore, the reference to "major cities" was Nixon's way of flattering rural America by leaving it out of the conflict. He knew his voters.

L'Enfant Terrible Brings a World Premiere to Notre Dame

"The picture attempts to deal for the first time with the relations between police and criminals as a matter which is primarily human, existential, even spiritual, rather than legal or sociological."

—Norman Mailer[14]

Chicago Tribune film critic Clifford Terry will write that he has come to the world premiere of Norman Mailer's *Beyond the Law* so he can hear the author "say something dirty." *South Bend Tribune* reporter Patricia Koval will later comment that the only thing missing is popcorn. *Saturday Review* literary critic Granville Hicks will later remark that the "gala occasion," at least to him, shows the author "at his worst," while Joseph Haas of the *Chicago Daily News* notices that "only a few walk out."

Mroz's April 2 starts early. Along with Marty Kress and a few other sophomore committee members, he begins setting up 3,800 "Hertz Rent-All wooden chairs" across the circular Stepan Center floor. They also roll out a rented red carpet down the center aisle and out the entrance, since many of the film's cast members are flying in later. Mroz also checks on the two rented klieg lights by phone to make sure they'll be ready to go.[15]

Mroz, Kress, *Chicago Daily News* critic Joseph Haas, and Notre Dame professor Richard Bizot and his son are all on hand to greet a late-to-rise Norman Mailer at 1:00 PM.

"This is the only copy of the movie," Mailer tells one of the already-sweaty projectionists as they very carefully "mount the giant reel on the projector," observes Haas. The next step, however, will be far more stressful. In order to achieve sound, they need to "synchronize the film with the independent, tape recorded soundtrack."

A setback. After a few tries, the film plays, but without sound. Mailer takes a nervous breath, perhaps realizing how far from New York City he actually is. He tells the projectionists he needs to call someone. But before he leaves the team eases his mind. "I think we've got it now, Mr. Mailer." With everything set, they click it into place and, voilà, a kablam of sound blares from the overhead quad of speakers.[16]

Mailer can't help but show his relief. "Boy, my heart was up in my throat for a while there. You know, anything can go wrong with films." But as the sound continues, the group can hear a disturbing reverberation when the volume is loud. Mailer chooses to ignore it. "When we get people in the hall tonight we should get a better sound." The young men look at each other and then nod. *Yes . . . yes, of course.*

Richard Bizot's son is nearby, and Mailer asks how old he is. "Four, eh?" Mailer says, squatting next to young Rick. "That's the age of my oldest son." Mailer knows just what to do. He makes a fist and holds it out between the two and points to a specific spot on his hand. "Press there." The moment Rick presses the imaginary button, Mailer's hand becomes a gun. "Boop!" he says, shooting Rick as the boy laughs.[17]

Mailer smiles. "Want to try it again?" With Joseph Haas looking on, the boy goes for it. "Press, pistol, 'boop!'"

Around ten cast members arrive at the airport on the same flight, and Mailer heads over to greet them. Rip Torn, Lee Roscoe, Mara Lynn, Buzz Farbar, Mary Wilson Price, Eddie Bonetti, and others greet their film general. To Haas, they appear to be a "little band of bored sophisticates, so New York-ish."

By the time the entourage reaches the Stepan Center, Armand's Searchlight Service has brought one of the klieg lights, and a few members of a college swing band arrive and pull out their instruments.

Lee Roscoe, standing out in her peekaboo blouse, nearly has a conniption when she sees the students. "Oh, my gawd . . . They're *not* having a band! Oh, I can't stand it!"[18]

Mailer claps his hands twice and says, "All right everybody . . . We're going to rehearse the entrance." They organize single file and walk along the rented red carpet with Mroz looking on, thinking it all a bit surreal as they take their front-row seats. *This is happening.*

Norman Mailer's *Beyond the Law* world premiere in Notre Dame's Stepan Center, just before 8:00 PM on April 2, 1968. *Photo courtesy of the University of Notre Dame Archives.*

Ticket holders start filing into the Stepan Center around 7:00 PM. Finished in 1962, the Stepan Center's geodesic dome structure allows for the main floor to be pillar-free, with zero obstructions. Still, the space-age look of the building from the outside causes one attendee to imagine it being constructed "of Buckminster Fuller Saran Wrap cubes" and the perfect place "to watch a roller derby."[19]

By 7:00 PM the sky is almost dark, and the two rented klieg lights on the left and right sides of the building are switched on. Soon enough, residents of South Bend driving home from work see two beams of light swaying back and forth across the moon. It's a Hollywood moment in small-town America.

A Stepan Center–record 3,800 tickets are sold, and by night's end the committee will have made $11,000 from the event, minus the $6,000 it cost to put it on, including local advertising and chair and klieg light rentals.[20]

Chicago Tribune film critic Clifford Terry is given a program and led to his seat by a "white-blazered St. Mary's usherette," one of dozens of volunteers from the neighboring all-female college. Forty minutes before the premiere, Terry rests in his wooden chair as a few members of the Notre Dame student orchestra begin playing Elmer Bernstein's energetic theme song to the Western film *The Magnificent Seven.* The music will play until the film begins, and Terry can tell that the band members begin running out of material. Soon he can't tell if they want to sound like "the Jimi Hendrix Experience or Raymond Scott and His Lucky Strike Orchestra."[21] Terry, in his twenties, takes in the predominantly young audience, many of them wearing presidential-spoof buttons supporting NORMAN MAILER FOR SHERIFF. They don't seem to mind the genre-hopping song selection—perhaps he shouldn't either.

At just before 8:00 PM, John Mroz walks over to the podium and checks the microphone. Since every author at the literary festival needs to be introduced, Mroz has purposely assigned those duties to others on the committees, or to other Notre Dame professors. But this night is his, and he deserves it. Mroz is the one who has already seen a much longer and uncut version of *Beyond the Law* after being invited by Mailer to his home over the Christmas holidays. Coupled with the summer dunes walk, Mroz feels closely connected to the world premiere, and its success represents the crowning achievement of his first nineteen years of life.

Mroz, "every mother's dream son," grabs the crowd's attention and goes through the schedule for the rest of the week. It's also a way to gauge which writers are strongly supported. "Tomorrow night, William F. Buckley will be here." Mroz pauses as the crowd returns a jolting mix of boos and cheers. "On Thursday, Joseph Heller will be speaking." Cheers all around; *Catch-22* has found its way into the hands of many of the students. "On Friday, Kurt Vonnegut and Ralph Ellison will be speaking." Clifford Terry notices the cheers are much louder for these two.

Mroz proceeds to introduce the film. "The world premiere of Mr. Mailer's movie, *Beyond the Law,* is what we consider one of the greatest events ever to have occurred at Notre Dame . . . or, in fact, anywhere!"[22]

And then down an aisle walk almost the entire cast of *Beyond the Law.* They take their seats close to the screen as the lights dim.

According to Joseph Haas, the nearly two-hour *Beyond the Law* was "filmed entirely in four nights at two New York City locales, a rented floor of an office building and in the Butcher Shop, a saloon, where Mailer hangs out." Famed Bob Dylan documentarian D. A. Pennebaker shot the film with a hand-held 16mm camera, employing his cinema vérité style.

As for the script, well . . .

Here's how Mailer puts it: "We used no script at all. I don't think this sort of thing, this attempt to capture reality, can be done with a script. As soon as you bring in a script, you must bring in all of those elegant Hollywood processes, and the processes take over. What we ask of the audience, of course, is that they suffer with us a little more than an average Hollywood movie. This is not as comfortable as a Hollywood movie, but at its best it can be more exciting. It just might capture the feeling of reality."[23]

Unfortunately, there are sound issues. Despite the earlier sound tests, the dialogue can't be heard clearly. This is due in part to the Stepan Center's aluminum-coated ceiling. Whenever Mailer's character, a police detective named Francis X. Pope, begins shouting in a confluence of accents, most of the words plunk off the tinny ceiling like the *mwa-mwa-mwa* of Charlie Brown's teacher.

For some in the audience, the experience is unbearable. Keynote speaker and curmudgeon Granville Hicks finds the film "amateurish in the most painful way" and complains the speaker volume is "calculated to deafen the audience." He would later write that "home movies, God be praised, are usually short, but this occupied 115 endless minutes."[24]

Other younger critics find a few aspects to appreciate. Clifford Terry is surprised by Mailer's performance, calling him "not a bad actor (professionally speaking) . . . and at times seems to be imitating Marlon Brando, Colonel Sanders, Barry Fitzgerald, Jack Webb, and Jack Kennedy." Patricia Koval finds the film "a completely engrossing portrayal of the complexities and degrees of corruption present in and around men saddled with a dirty, difficult job." Joseph Haas comments that "technically, the film won't win any prizes . . . the language is as brutal as anything Mailer has ever used in any of his novels. Surely, there are students in this audience who are hearing words screamed and shouted repetitively that they probably have never before heard in their lives."[25]

But as the film abruptly cuts off (its "The End" title card to be added later), criticism takes a backseat to the excitement of the moment itself. Mroz and the packed-like-sardines crowd of nearly four thousand "burst into tremendous and prolonged applause." Mailer, happy to hear it, jumps up to the podium and basks in his fix of praise-opium. He mans the mic and tells the cheering crowd that "we're fortunate to have ten actors in South Bend tonight." The crowd lets out "a large laugh," perhaps because many of the actors have "never performed professionally before."[26]

A rapid-fire press conference backstage, behind the projection screen, occurs right after, and a jovial Mailer fireballs potential meanings he's thought of during the making of the film. "The problem is how to maintain order in a world that is chaotic; I didn't make the picture as an anarchist." *Why spend a fortune making a film?* "It's like a . . . No, it's not a hobby. It isn't a hobby when a poor man owns a yacht, it's too expensive to enjoy as recreation. I guess I do it because it's new, and so it's fun in a way writing cannot be. But I'm not going to quit writing."

With the press fulfillment complete, Mailer and the cast head out by car into downtown South Bend and stop at Roma's Cocktail Lounge. The night is still young, and Mroz has handed out tickets to a large but select group of people who have helped with the festival, officially calling the get-together a "Cocktail Party and Social Hour."[27] So joining Mailer and the cast are Notre Dame professors, members of the sophomore committee, and a few other journalists curious to see if Mailer will make some kind of scene.

Granville Hicks begs off, perhaps on account of a noise headache, but leaves torn about Mailer as an artist. Hicks can see that Mailer considers "himself as a kind of superman and that he" is "incapable of applying his intellectual powers, of which he'd given an impressive demonstration the night before, to the critical examination of his own work." Hicks surrenders to the thought that this '60s rebel will always have a side he can never relate to. "The badness of *Why Are We in Vietnam?*" is now "easier to understand."[28]

Mary Wilson Price,* April 2, 1968. *Photo taken by John Mroz. Permission courtesy of Martin Kress.*

Mara Lynn,** April 2, 1968. *Photo taken by John Mroz. Permission courtesy of Martin Kress.*

---

* Price would go on to marry Irish writer J. P. Donleavy, author of the bestselling novel *The Ginger Man.*

** Lynn, an experienced actress in 1950s musicals, once gave Marilyn Monroe acting lessons.

The party at Roma's (a "glorified pizza parlor") is enlivened by the same band that played at the premiere—the Mag 7, a diverse group of undergraduates (usually more than seven) who play a variety of genres throughout the night, including the sounds of Otis Redding, Eddie Floyd, and James Brown. The group plays at a volume that "makes shouting essential for conversation."[29]

Actors and actresses take their turns mesmerizing onlookers with their moves. Lee Roscoe has changed into a "shimmering, clinging two-piece white evening dress that bares her talented belly from naval to breastbone." The sophomores are entranced as they try to keep up with her on the dance floor, never standing a chance as the trumpets in Wilson Pickett's "In the Midnight Hour" rock the place into a frenzy.

Meanwhile, thirty-seven-year-old Rip Torn, already a bit inebriated and looking like a "Sicilian gangster in a rumpled white-lapeled chalk-striped blue suit, wrinkled white shirt, and sloppily knotted red tie," brings a few of the previously white-blazered St. Mary's usherettes out onto the floor and dances like a "sputtering fuse, taut and intense" as his gyrations and chestward-wandering eyes cause the young women to "blush and back and sidle nervously away as he moves ever closer to them."[30]

Roma's closes to the public at 1:00 AM, making the party a private event. John Mroz and other underage sophomore committee members sneak a few drinks and enjoy the music. Mroz watches Rip Torn, now spent from his frenetic dancing, "arm-wrestling with a state trooper at three in the morning. . . . I think we stayed up all night."[31]

As the music and dancing goes on, Norman Mailer hugs the bar, his bourbon on the rocks nearby. He's momentarily greeted and praised by everyone attending, many of the students asking him to sign copies of *The Naked and the Dead*. (One people-watching film critic prods that Mailer's *Deer Park* is not even in sight.) Tonight, Mailer is on his best behavior, basking in the satisfaction of a somewhat well-received premiere. When a woman comes up to him and sincerely asks, "Are you Irish?" Mailer is too flush with praise to come up with a clever comeback. He simply shakes his head.[32]

In 1995, reflecting on his time at Notre Dame—which had "passed in a glow"—Mailer would describe Mroz as a "terrific kid. He had the kind of spirit that made it work." As for himself, "It was one of the better times of my life."[33]

4

WEDNESDAY, APRIL 3, 1968

A Hawk and a Dove Soar
Below a Mountaintop

Dr. Martin Luther King Jr. follows Ralph Abernathy into room 307 of the Lorraine Motel on April 3, 1968. Rev. James Lawson is behind King. *Courtesy of Barney Sellers, Commercial Appeal.*

LBJ Makes Plans for "Hanalua"

> *"For over 10 years now, the US imperialists have been blatantly violating the 1954 Geneva agreements on Vietnam, strenuously carrying out a policy of intervention and aggression, and waging war against the Vietnamese people. Their design is to prolong the partition of Vietnam and to turn South Vietnam into a neo-colony and a military base for the United States."*
>
> —North Vietnam,
> in reply to President Johnson,
> April 3, 1968[1]

On Wednesday morning, President Johnson's team receives a lengthy statement from Hanoi. Broadcast through the Vietnam News Agency, the text shows a still-fiery opposition stating, that the United States has committed "extremely barbarous crimes of aggression," and yet "nothing can save the US aggressors from total defeat."

The statement also displays Hanoi's political savvy, especially in the final paragraph. Knowing full well the lack of support the United States has received from many parts of the world (and within America), Hanoi "earnestly calls on the governments and peoples of the fraternal Socialist countries, the peace-loving countries in the world, and the progressive American people to extend still stronger support to the just struggle and correct stand of the Vietnamese people and the government of the Democratic Republic of Vietnam." The sentence is a knowing nod to Russia and China, the continued hands-off policies of developed "peace-loving countries" who have not, for example, sent troops in support of the United States, and, perhaps carrying the strongest sting, the anti-war demonstrators ("progressive American people") who have started to make national news.[2]

By the afternoon, it's already been a day of meetings and analysis for the president. First, he has a one-hour confidential talk with his VP, Hubert Humphrey, who would soon announce his presidential candidacy. The Humphrey meeting is trumpeted by the American Federation of Labor and Congress of Industrial Organizations (AFL-CIO), which has decided to publicly endorse Humphrey before his official announcement.

Next the president meets with Robert Kennedy, his first face-to-face with the New York senator since his Sunday announcement. The two men have never been comfortable in the same room, and during these fragile times, neither expects a bed of roses. Kennedy, perhaps in an attempt to push away the awkwardness, asks the president if the agenda can remain strictly on "international developments such as Hanoi's latest peace overture."[3]

After scrutinizing the Hanoi statement with the rest of his staff, Johnson chooses to extract the most hopeful sections of the text to the national press. At around 5:00 PM, wearing glasses and a striped tie, his hair slicked back, Johnson addresses the press just outside the White House. Reading directly from Hanoi's statement, Johnson tells the press that "the government of the Democratic Republic of Vietnam declares its readiness to appoint its representatives to contact the United States representative with a view to determining with the American side the unconditional cessation of the United States bombing raids and all other acts of war against the Democratic Republic of Vietnam so that talks may start." Despite the strong wording in the statement, Johnson seems somewhat hopeful that a dialogue can begin.[4]

Before ending the press conference, Johnson, in his trademark Texas drawl, tells the press he'll be flying to "Hanalua" (Honolulu) tomorrow night to meet with American representatives "for a series of meetings" about how to best address the current situation in South Vietnam.[5] He heads back into the White House.

Eugene McCarthy Earns His Wings

On February 18, 1965, Minnesota senator Eugene McCarthy sat with thirty other senators in a White House meeting around 9:00 PM. At the front and leading the discussion was Secretary of State Dean Rusk. A part of the briefing included an update on Vietnam. Rusk, a steadfast supporter of the war, tried to reassure the senators in the room that the South Vietnamese government currently run by General Nguyen Khanh was "stable" and "supported."

The next morning, Senator McCarthy found out the exact opposite after opening a newspaper: Khanh had been momentarily overthrown by a coup.[6]

McCarthy had been carrying doubts regarding "the accuracy of the Administration's reports about conditions in Vietnam almost from the beginning of our involvement in that country," but this was starting to get out of hand. When McCarthy factored in time zones, he realized that, at about the same time Dean Rusk was telling everyone that Khanh's government was secure, the coup was taking place.[7]

Months passed, but McCarthy kept a sharp eye on Vietnam. He, like everyone else, read the body counts and computed kill ratios in newspapers, statistics supervised by Secretary of Defense Robert McNamara, but they didn't seem to ring true as a way of judging progress. A moral, human element was missing.

McCarthy, as he had in the past, turned to poetry and literature for perspective. He read the 1960 French war novel *The Centurions* by journalist Jean Lartéguy, and the senator absorbed the hopelessness of the French cause in Vietnam, and the empathy it depicted between a French and a Vietnamese soldier. As the novel stated, "The age of heroics is over." Gone were the clear-cut days of opposing Nazi aggression. War, it seemed, could now only be fought without a sense of right and wrong, and, to McCarthy, "all the calculators and all the computers could not in any way measure the power and the strength and the willingness to die in a cause."[8]

For the next year and a half, McCarthy watched his country continue to send more resources and troops to Vietnam and did what he could as a member of the Senate Foreign Relations Committee to make sense of it. In late January 1966, one week after urging a probe of the CIA's "influence over foreign policy,"[9] McCarthy joined fourteen other senators in calling to extend the bombing pause over North Vietnam. As he told the press, there still needed to be a "burden of proof" showing if dropping bombs on the north had "any significant effect—political or military—or would in the future."[10]

As the year developed, McCarthy endured reasons to continue to have a military presence in South Vietnam. He humored Dean Rusk's worries about China becoming a growing menace. On May 15, 1966, the *Los Angeles Times* ran a furious editorial from 1964 Republican presidential candidate Barry Goldwater, who denounced McCarthy's comment to Rusk that the 1954 Southeast Asia Treaty Organization (meant to contain Communist China) was now "close to irrelevant." Goldwater saw McCarthy as disloyal, and one of several individuals in Congress who had "gone a long way toward pronouncing a new, irresponsible and altogether dangerous principle of government."[11]

During this time, McCarthy wrote a book, *The Limits of Power: America's Role in the World*, further articulating his doubts about the war. Published in October 1967, the book "one by one knocks down the justifications for the Vietnam war—defense of the U.S., containment of China, credibility of our commitments."[12]

As early as September 1967, the press began to report a "Dump Johnson" movement, led largely by "newly elected national vice-chairman of the Americans for Democratic Action (ADA) named Allard K. Lowenstein."[13] The main idea was to search and support candidates willing to send a direct message to Lyndon Johnson that his policy in Vietnam ran counter to core Democratic principles.

Lowenstein, an energetic New York lawyer highly active in civil rights, and other ADA staff began to consider candidates willing to risk their reputation and take on Johnson. First, as McCarthy would have suggested as well, they tried New York senator Robert Kennedy. He declined, even though October 1967 Gallup polls had him defeating Johnson 51 to 39 percent in a head-to-head situation, with 10 percent undecided. McCarthy, it turns out, was not listed as a choice.[14] For Bobby, the risk at that point was simply too high.

Never one to give up, Lowenstein next bent the ear of George McGovern, but the South Dakota senator was up for reelection soon, and his loyal supporters, Lowenstein realized, didn't really have the Vietnam war high on their priority list. Running two races, one possibly costing the other, didn't seem logical.[15] Another option was James M. Gavin, but the former World War II general told Lowenstein that if he ran, he'd rather it be as an antiwar Republican similar to Michigan governor George Romney. Continuing down the list, Lowenstein checked in on the qualifications of author and economist John Kenneth Galbraith, who had already helped Lowenstein's ADA promote a peace movement called "Negotiations Now." All was set up for Galbraith to run, but for one fundamental problem: he was Canadian born.[16]

It's unclear how many others passed before McCarthy, but it wasn't until Senator McGovern, as well as Lowenstein's colleague Curtis Gans, nudged the chairman in the direction of the Minnesota senator that a potential match was discussed—political passion and academic rebellion.[17]

There was a reason the senator hadn't made his interest known. Besides a few spikes of public attention reprimanding Vietnam policy as a member of the Senate Foreign Relations Committee, McCarthy was at heart a loner. He was far more comfortable with a pen than a microphone. In the 1960s alone, McCarthy had published four books while working as a senator. In this way he had remained distant from social circles at the White House, but because of his bookish tendencies had remained razor sharp on foreign policy issues. With the mind of an economist, the heart of a Catholic poet, and the bank account of a middle-class citizen, McCarthy, Lowenstein believed, was well-positioned to act as a lightning rod for the frustrated youth of the country. He was trustworthy—the kind of politician who could credibly say, "There comes a time when an honorable man simply has to raise a flag."[18]

Still, it took a bit of coaxing. Finally, on October 17, 1967, McCarthy headed over to McGovern and thanked him for pointing Lowenstein in his direction.[19] He also revealed his first four state primary targets: Massachusetts (soon to switch to New Hampshire), Wisconsin, Oregon, and California.

On the night of October 17, a somewhat regretful Robert Kennedy called Senator McGovern. He spoke with "great mental anguish" over his choice to hold off his run against Johnson, and he was surprised that "somebody else might jump in" and risk his political career. Kennedy wondered if McCarthy would be so popular as to eliminate a need for Bobby to even enter. McGovern replied, "I can tell you right now, he'll run very strong in New Hampshire."[20]

For the rest of October and into November, McCarthy began assembling a low-budget campaign, choosing general staff and campaign headquarter locations in each of the four states. By mid-November, any secrecy he wished to keep about his plans appeared to have vanished.

On November 19, conservative author and political commentator William F. Buckley opened his nationally syndicated column with this line: "It looks as though Senator Eugene McCarthy of Minnesota is the chosen instrument through which left-leaning Democrats will commit damage on President Johnson." Buckley, tongue-in-cheek, called McCarthy "splendidly qualified" to take on the president. Since he was closer to the Nixon camp, Buckley was thrilled to sit back and watch the Democrats set themselves on fire. In this column, he attempted to add lighter fluid to the infighting by documenting the decade-long animosity between Robert Kennedy and McCarthy. First, there was McCarthy's 1960 support of Adlai Stevenson, a pie in the face to the Kennedy family. Then, after John F. Kennedy was assassinated, Johnson rejected McCarthy for VP, choosing Hubert Humphrey.

Regardless of how much the two candidates actually still cared about those events, Buckley wanted the nation to gossip about them and hope for splinters. He ended his column with a prognostication: "Eugene McCarthy may well (a) sink Johnson in '68 and (b) elect Kennedy in '72." Even in November 1967 Buckley could see McCarthy, the "dreamy Stevensonian," as a man with a machete slashing his way through a political jungle, taking out the king, as Kennedy and his legions of fans stalked McCarthy from behind, enjoying the clear path.[21]

McCarthy Visits the Doves in South Bend

> "I like [Senator Eugene McCarthy's] scale of living. As against rich lawyers like Richard Nixon, and millionaires like Lyndon Johnson, and mega-millionaires like Nelson Rockefeller and Robert Kennedy, I like McCarthy for having something like $30 to $30,000 to his name."
>
> —Max Lerner[22]

At 11:00 AM on April 3, 1968, Senator Eugene McCarthy stands on a platform before five hundred of his supporters at the St. Joseph County

Airport. It appears on the surface that, as of today, he is the frontrunner for the Democratic presidential nomination. It has been a whirlwind five months for the Minnesota senator, starting with his near-miracle victory in the March 12 New Hampshire primary, where he came within 230 votes of defeating President Johnson. That 42 percent result had little to do with McCarthy's charisma. Rather, his surge of support coincided with the Tet Offensive, a "malaise with Johnson," and thousands of high school and college students knocking on over sixty thousand doors, terrified of dying in a war they did not believe in. McCarthy national student coordinator Sam Brown, a "dropout from Harvard Divinity School," divided the young New Hampshire doves into "straights" and "non-straights." The young "non-straight" men who refused to cut their long hair, shave their beards, and wear shirts and ties were placed in the back rooms of campaign headquarters, licking stamps and stuffing envelopes for sometimes sixteen hours a day, as Beatles music "boil[ed] deafeningly out of the record player." The young men and women who chose to shave and dress appropriately (think 1950s conservative attire) were sent out to canvass neighborhoods and talk to the older generation. Thus the slogan "Get clean for Gene" was born, and after the positive New Hampshire result, McCarthy's "children's crusade" moved on to Wisconsin.[23]

On March 15, Martin Luther King Jr. made his feelings toward McCarthy known to the California Democratic Council—a political organization that endorsed the Minnesota senator for president. King commended them "for endorsing one of the truly outstanding, capable, brilliant, dedicated Americans, Sen. Eugene McCarthy." But there was no chance for that endorsement to gain traction. On March 16, Robert Kennedy officially entered the race, and soon King was quoted nationally as saying both candidates are "very able and competent and dedicated men" and hoped to "see a rally to one of these candidates so that we will have an alternative to the policies that we currently have."[24]

But Kennedy opted out of campaigning in Wisconsin, leaving the state Democratic primary to McCarthy and Johnson. When the president bowed out on March 31, the media declared Wisconsin a "shadow bout," a contest offering nothing more than empty calories.* Still, McCarthy's young army of door-knockers made sure to deliver a victory: 57 percent of the Wisconsin primary vote went with McCarthy, while 35 percent remained loyal to Johnson.[25]

And so, here we are, on a gusty April morning in South Bend, Indiana, firmly in the eye of the McCarthy campaign's political hurricane. Around a thousand college-age supporters have skipped their scheduled classes to come to the airport. Some young McCarthy volunteers save money by reusing signs and posters from South Bend mayor Lloyd Allen's recent campaign. The message ALLEN FOR MAYOR is taped over and replaced with MCCARTHY FOR PRESIDENT. As has been the McCarthy campaign's style since New Hampshire, volunteers are "making use of everything they can in an uphill fight against professional campaigners," such as Kennedy, whose cash-flush, media-driven campaign juggernaut will appear in full force tomorrow.

McCarthy, meanwhile, already seems wistful while addressing his die-hard supporters. "A few years from now in 1972, or, say, 1984, you will think back on the 1968 campaign. You will say to yourself, 'I helped restore the spirit of America. I helped lay to rest the fictional 1984.'"[26]

Notre Dame student Joel Connelly stands in the audience listening to this "quiet . . . witty and intellectual" man. It's his first time seeing him in the flesh, and the Minnesota senator's character is refreshing, since to Connelly it "is all too often he who has compromised his principles [who] has survived the jungle warfare of the nominating process." As Connelly will later write in the *Notre Dame Observer*, there seems "less room these days for the quiet man, the man without much money, the man without a tightly organized professional machine."[27]

Yes, McCarthy and his campaign are quiet and dangerously underfunded, but he doesn't intend to step aside and let Kennedy take over his turf. Still at the airport, McCarthy tells the audience that his presence in the primaries still has meaning. "The people of this country want a chance to pass judgment on a complicated set of issues." He isn't

---

* Instead of choosing a Democratic nominee from the list, 10,336 Wisconsin voters (1 percent) instead chose "none of those named above." On the Republican side, "nobody" received 5,608 votes (AP report, published in the *Palladium-Item*, April 3, 1968).

attacking anyone directly, but the word "complicated" is a passive slight at Kennedy, who has yet to put forth a specific, reasonable plan for the military to withdraw from South Vietnam.[28]

But McCarthy knows that he will not receive any extra support regarding Vietnam, an issue he has maxed out. No, to win new support and have any chance of cutting into Kennedy's swath of loyalists, McCarthy plans to separate from his competition in terms of his extensive political experience and his knowledge of the economy. "I believe I have better knowledge of economics than any of the other candidates," he tells the airport crowd.[29]

He does make one subtle jab at his opponent to the crowd, many of whom hope McCarthy can become more aggressive. Did you know, he tells the audience, that Kennedy has set up "twenty-six varieties of committees to deal with twenty-six varieties of Americans." He smiles and says that there is even a committee for Irish Americans such as himself. McCarthy can't help but shake his head. "I thought we had made it."[30]

McCarthy's motorcade heads over to the LaSalle Hotel for a brief press conference. Quickly, he comments on President Johnson's plans today to discuss peace in Hawaii. "We all hope for negotiations and settlement. It is my sincere wish that the president's proposals will lead to talks in the very near future." Next, McCarthy, followed by a gaggle of a hundred-plus students, visits his campaign's South Bend headquarters located on Michigan Street, previously occupied by Mayor Allen. Nearly 150 students, including Joel Connelly, cram into the storefront. For McCarthy, eager to find some time to write a poem, it's once again a moment to reflect on how far his campaign has come. During the weekdays, "it got kind of lonely tromping the snows of New Hampshire," he says to his crowd of followers, "but we certainly don't seem to be alone anymore."[31]

As appreciative as he is of his young supporters, the antiwar McCarthy is attempting to pivot away from his already-cemented college campus attention. He could have chosen the Stepan Center to deliver a speech to a large young audience, but instead he heads over to the local Rotary Club and speaks to 350 Rotarians. It's an attempt to woo a voting-age crowd and dazzle them with his mastery of American economics. Connelly squeezes in at the back and listens to McCarthy's twenty-four-minute issues-rich speech. The young journalist is impressed with McCarthy's "total command of his subject matter. Even those who stand in opposition sit and listen." As an example, McCarthy ties the problems of "gold outflow" and the "inflation threat" to the economic toll brought upon by fighting in Vietnam, then tells the Rotarians that "the economy is so well directed and controlled that the transition could be easily made."[32]

Connelly listens and observes the crowd's reaction. They seem spellbound. "McCarthy is the only man I have ever seen to be able to hold a luncheon audience of Rotarians with a detailed discussion of economic policy."

Still, Connelly only gives McCarthy a fair chance of nomination. He foresees a Kennedy and Nixon showdown, but hopes "that the two contenders learn a lesson from the quiet man. Nixon will not be able to run simply against Communism any more. Kennedy will not win simply by having high school girls claw him. Problems must be reasonably examined and solutions offered."[33]

McCarthy's quiet persona has its issues too. After his Rotary Club speech he flies to Hartford, Connecticut, and heads over to his campaign office located "in Hartford's predominantly Negro North End." It's one of several subtle ways McCarthy is trying to combat his White middle-class identity. But the moment he arrives, several young Black men await with a megaphone. They shout, "He's not for us people! He's for the white man."[34]

And later, at the New Haven Arena, several members of the William Buckley–founded organization Young Americans for Freedom hold up signs during a speech in front of thousands. The signs read: "Don't stab our boys in the back," and also "McCarthy, Kennedy, Surrender in Vietnam." Such is life for Eugene McCarthy's campaign—detached from the minority, and traitorous to the majority.[35]

Notre Dame Students Protest
Dow Chemical

Just after McCarthy finishes his talk at the Rotary Club, a group of around fifty Notre Dame students march on campus toward the Center for Continuing Education building. Led by senior Brian McTigue, the group of demonstrators have been planning for some time to show their disapproval of "the scheduled speaking appearance of Dow Chemical president [Herbert] Doan due to his connection to the production of napalm" and the use of it for military purposes in the Vietnam War.[36]

Dow has been a common punching bag for antiwar protesters ever since the company made national news in April 1966, when local citizens petitioned against a six-month contract in Redwood City, California, after many had learned that the deal was struck between the air force and the United Technology Center, who would use Dow Chemical sites to produce it.[37]

McTigue's plan is simple: take the group to the Cities in Context conference at the Center for Continuing Education building and ask to be admitted. If they're allowed (the conference has been advertised as "open to the public"), they will listen patiently to Mr. Doan's remarks and ask questions after he's finished.

The group reaches the front entrance doors at a quarter to three. It's raining, and many have an umbrella in one hand and a sign in the other. McTigue sees that a message has been posted on the door: "Regular conferees only." McTigue has already secured permission from his architecture professor, Patrick Horsburgh, who is inside the building with a prepared statement condemning the use of napalm for military purposes.

Campus police guard the door, and McTigue grabs the attention of one of them. He wants to know why they are being denied their public right to listen to Mr. Doan's talk. The guard tells the demonstrators that he's been told not to let in anyone other than "registered architecture students." One demonstrator comes forward. *I'm an architecture student. I'd like to register.* The guards says no. Registration has ended.

McTigue decides to have everyone wait in front of the doors. They start chanting, "We shall not move!" Pretty soon several more groups of students decide to stand at the side entrances. If they can't enter, no one else should be able to, either.

Meanwhile, inside the building, Professor Horsburgh reads his statement to the conference audience members. Mr. Doan has yet to speak, and the professor hopes other conference participants will sign the statement containing the following message: "Whereas war is destructive of these essential conditions (being considered by the conference) as well as life itself: Be it resolved that as an ethical context of action the delegates of this international conference favor the immediate cessation of all willful destruction of human life and the environment of earth."[38]

As of January 1967, the current napalm formula being mixed by Dow Chemical is "50 percent polystyrene and 25 percent each of benzene and gasoline" and is "purported to be more effective than the napalm used in the Korean War."[39] It's a "jelly-like, fiery explosive that sticks to and burns its target." If a human being is near a napalm bomb when it explodes, the fire will first scorch the skin and the now-microscopic jellylike substance will remain. If you try to rub it off your skin, it will burn even more. If you pour water on your skin, the burning sensation will feel as if it is entering your bones. Full recovery is nearly impossible, and survivors must learn to cope for the rest of their lives with scar tissue that throbs in pain during even the most ordinary moments, such as a change in weather.[40]

Around 3:00 PM a late-registered attendee is let in by campus police. McTigue and others manage to enter the lobby but are held back. One protester has brought a small burned doll to represent the pain of napalm victims, while another holds a lit candle. With Mr. Doan speaking in a nearby auditorium, the group do their best to be heard by chanting and singing.

At the end of Mr. Doan's speech, he is asked by the late attendee in the question-and-answer session to explain the presence of the protesters. For the Dow president, it's not a new situation. In February 1967, student protesters at the University of Wisconsin demanded that Dow Chemical job recruiters be denied a presence on campus, staging a sit-in until a total of seventeen demonstrators were arrested. The scene had momentarily gained national attention, with several

students sacrificing their bodies by rolling under police cars and grabbing the bumpers of vehicles holding the arrested protesters.[41] Eight
months later, on October 18, 1967, the University of Wisconsin students again obstructed Dow Chemical from recruiting on campus, but
this time three thousand students demonstrated, only to be driven out
by teargas and nightsticks.[42]

Mr. Doan's answer sounds polished. He reminds the audience that
"students have demonstrated, sometimes on the verge of violence, against
Dow representatives recruiting seniors for employment in the firm."
He's "quite aware" of the moral question they are attempting to pose,
but "the individual must say whether or not he thinks his government
is trying to do the right thing—whether it has a moral policy, tactical
errors aside." Bottom line, Doan's company believes in supporting the
government, and because of this it is "moral for the firm to produce a
product asked for by the government."[43]

The protesters aren't around to dispute. The Q and A ends, and
when audience members try to leave the building, they're pushed back
at all entrances by demonstrators. Shouting and pushing occur, but no
one is hurt. To his credit, Mr. Doan offers an olive branch to several
of the head protesters. He invites three of the young men to dinner.

As they eat, they learn a bit more about Dow Chemical. It turns out
that only 0.5 percent "of Dow's profits come from napalm, and they
employ ten people to produce [it]." But since Dow Chemical has been
fulfilling war orders for the government since World War II, they stand
by the government's best interests.[44]

It's a difficult dinner for the young men, an awkward moment
of two patriotic generations colliding. Later, one of the students who
attended the dinner, Jack Lavelle, will reflect on the encounter, writing in the student newspaper that "the president of Dow Chemical is
just like your father."[45] Doan also grants a brief interview to the Notre
Dame campus magazine the *Scholastic*. He echoes what he's already
said to the protesters, but adds that he "could go on for hours telling
you of the letters we receive every day from soldiers who claim to
have been saved by napalm. The fact is, that napalm is a very effective weapon, it does a job that has to be done and prevents the death

of many American soldiers." The *Scholastic* interviewers move on to the next question, but the young journalists may have been thinking, *Does the job have to be done?*[46]

The New England Resistance

On the afternoon of April 3, forty-five-year-old activist and Boston University professor Howard Zinn sits near a podium at the Boston Common, a crowd of at least five thousand demonstrators surrounds him and the stage. The public park has enough space that thousands lie on the grass as they listen to speeches decrying the war, and 235 students come forward and turn their draft cards in to a group of "14 adults . . . college professors, ministers, and Roman Catholic priests." It is required for citizens to have their draft cards on hand at all times, so in effect, the moment students hand over their cards, they are breaking the law.[47]

This act of defiance is part of a nationally organized resistance happening on over sixty campuses across the country, including Philadelphia, where one young organizer believes the act of turning in a draft card to a respectable adult is simply how "the democratic process is supposed to be, when it is working at all."[48]

Today, Boston lays claim to the biggest crowd in the country, and when Howard Zinn is introduced, he receives a standing ovation. It's very likely that he is the only person in the entire crowd who has actually eaten dinner in 1968 Hanoi, and without question the only man who, along with poet Dan Berrigan, has acted as an intermediary in the release of three American pilots who'd been held as prisoners of war in North Vietnam. During his time in war-weary Hanoi, Zinn and Berrigan walked the capital's streets, several guards always nearby, seeing "one-person shelters, cylindrical holes dug into the streets for pedestrians to duck into," and trying to understand people who've been "responding to air raid sirens, every day for three years . . . a city without children," who've long been "evacuated to the countryside to escape the bombs."[49]

At first, the pilots didn't trust Zinn and Berrigan, since they were from the dreaded peace movement, but civility prevailed (it may have helped that Zinn served in the air force during World War II), and pretty soon one of the pilots told Zinn about his experiences in captivity. At least from what he told Zinn on the flight out of North Vietnam, the pilot said that, in his case, there was "no maltreatment, no indoctrination, just a few books on Vietnamese history, sufficient food, [and] medical care." The biggest danger, the pilot understood, was when aggrieved villagers who've lost family members to bombings would attempt to beat him to death, only to be "saved by the guards." With this surreal conversation on his mind when they went their separate ways, Zinn was surprised when the same pilot, perhaps urged on by a government looking to shore up support, began publicly discussing details of immense torture while imprisoned.[50]

As for Zinn, the professor now finds himself in a difficult position. As he stands in front of thousands at the Boston Common, he will need to keep in mind that he alone has seen the war from the other side of the conflict. He has now *seen* Communism, whereas many in the crowd have formed their perspectives from books, music, or documentaries. Also in the audience are fifty high school students. Can Zinn fairly deliver his nuanced perspective to kids and young adults whose main concern is to avoid fighting in a war they don't believe in?

He tries. "We have made something called Communism something to be destroyed," he says to the crowd, "although Communism may just mean people struggling just like people everywhere to feed and clothe themselves and run their own lives . . . this obsession with a thing called Communism is what keeps America in Vietnam and keeps all those military bases around China." When Zinn finishes, the crowd gives him another standing ovation. He's been well received, but has he been well understood?

Later, the collected draft cards and induction notices are taken to the Arlington Street Church. The leaders of the New England Resistance antiwar group are not sure yet what they want to do with the draft cards. They want to make a statement somehow. One suggestion is made in front of a crowd. Make copies and send them to Ho Chi Minh "as a gesture of sympathy and solidarity." Zinn isn't on record as commenting, but the crowd gives the idea "a loud cheer."[51]

"Mr. Conservative" Gives the
Hawks a Voice of Eloquence

It's good for his blood pressure that author and conservative critic William F. Buckley Jr. isn't in Boston to hear that loud cheer for Ho Chi Minh. If he had, he may have chosen a phrase such as "traitorously vituperative."

No, at 8:00 PM Buckley is standing near a podium inside the Stepan Center before nearly four thousand people. Above one Stepan Center entranceway is a banner reading BUCKLEY FOR PRESIDENT, while a number of attendees, Patricia Koval notices, sport buttons on their shirt with the same message. After an introduction, tonight's cosponsored literary festival speaker is given a standing ovation, and many of the two-hundred-member ROTC are in attendance, happy to finally be given a voice they can hang their uniforms on. The Dow Chemical protests and Democratic primary competition have been receiving most of the press, but the Notre Dame campus has its fair share of Republican supporters, whom Nixon would dub a year and a half later the "Great Silent Majority."[52]

William F. Buckley speaking at the University of Notre Dame's Stepan Center on April 3, 1968. *Photo courtesy of Marty Kress.*

Buckley is far from silent. As he prepares to speak to the audience, Buckley's current place in the national spotlight includes juggling three media projects at once.* The first is his magazine, the conservative *National Review*, founded by Buckley and over a hundred other investors in November 1955. In the *NR*'s mission statement, Buckley labels Communism as "satanic utopianism" and concludes by writing that "it would make greater sense to grant independence to each of our 50 states than to surrender U.S. sovereignty to a world organization." Second, but perhaps most influential to 1968 Republican voters, is his nationally syndicated column "On the Right." A common presence in nearly two hundred local small-town newspapers across the country, Buckley's weekly ruminations targeting liberal misrule stand as one of the only printed outlets of conservative intellectual pushback in the country. Take today's column, appearing in papers based in New Castle, Pennsylvania, and Waterloo, Iowa, to name a few. Buckley judges liberals for hating LBJ so much that they now "justify their hatred intellectually." This column, written before LBJ's withdrawal, ends with a line that very well can be applied to the draft-card-turn-in rally at the Boston Common: "I do not like Mr. Johnson, but I do not believe him capable of any intellectual cruelty in Vietnam. But the spirit of some of his critics is the spirit of the VC [Vietcong]. And, come to think of it, they too have their justifiers."[53]

Through his books, newspaper columns, and magazine, Buckley's written voice can be found just about anywhere, but after an attempt to become mayor of New York City in 1965 (he earned 13 percent of the vote), Buckley used his household name to launch *Firing Line*, a television program devoted to Buckley interviewing guests on a variety of controversial topics. Local television stations have picked up the one-hour program and sometimes run repeats on Wednesday night, then again on Sunday. After Buckley's Notre Dame talk, western Pennsylvania television stations will be running his interview about "Black Power" with historian and *Village Voice* columnist Nat Hentoff.[54]

---

* One other notable organization founded in Buckley's home in September 1960 is the Young Americans for Freedom, a conservative group that "promotes to youth the principles of limited government, individual freedom, free enterprise, a strong national defense, and traditional values." Young America's Foundation, "Our Mission," accessed February 21, 2020, http://www.yaf.org/about.

Buckley's flickering idiolect is fascinating to many tuned in to *Firing Line*. With his accent in a state of flux between London and the American South, his molasses-coated voice and eyes dripping with melancholic moonshine, Buckley enamors his listeners even as he tests their patience, dragging them across a carpet of silk to the end of each sentence. Paired with a volatile and contrarian interlocutor like Norman Mailer, Buckley's discussions with his guests can be likened to an electric storm of intellectualism. But tonight Buckley doesn't have a voice to bounce his own off of.

On the president's recent announcement, Buckley is clear and direct: "People, like Lyndon Johnson, do not voluntarily give up power—they are pushed out." Yes, to Buckley, "Johnson was pushed out, and [Kennedy] was the approximate pusher." Still, the sheer act of LBJ throwing in the white towel is "haunting" to Buckley. He doesn't buy that North Vietnam will now come running to the peace table. On the contrary, Buckley feels that the Vietcong's potential interest in starting peace talks is "reassuring only to stockbrokers," and makes light of what they will seek. "What will they demand in return," he asks the crowd. "The Philippines?" And then, shrugging sarcastically, "Perhaps the government may be prepared to give them New Hampshire."

There is pre-Kennedy visit buzz surrounding Buckley's visit. The political rock star is coming tomorrow, and there are four RFK advance men who have come to Notre Dame to scope out the Stepan Center and figure out logistics. One of them, Charles Nau, is onstage. During the middle of a sentence, Buckley pauses as the sound of a jet plane roars overhead. He smiles and then turns to Nau, "More Kennedy advance men?"[55]

But for as much as Buckley loves to comment off-the-cuff to breaking national news, he is here for a reason and with a prepared text; he wishes to address college students directly. His general message has edge, given the proliferation of protests across the country: practice more responsible behavior while receiving an education. Rhetorically, Buckley asks his mostly student audience, "How can you return what you find on a single shelf in your library?" He also asks the students to consider listening to their professors. "You owe [your teachers] your

respect, combined with a courteous skepticism concerning their ideo-
logical pretensions."[56]

Buckley also has a few things to say about the draft. Bottom line,
"I'm against any form of the draft," and he favors a "paid professional
army." Since the unpopularity of the war may soon make fulfillment
requests difficult, Buckley goes ahead and says that Kennedy's idea of
a "draft lottery" is a "pretty good idea." But the conservative is careful lest anyone think he is soft on war policy. Actually, to Buckley,
America's Vietnam War "policy was not bellicose enough." The war
will take time, and Buckley is sensitive enough to know how the
students may feel about it. "I recognize the inconvenience of war,"
Buckley says in response to a question delivered emotionally by an
attendee. He offers his own past experience serving in the armed forces
for two years stateside during World War II. "I was inconvenienced
by mine."[57]

Near the end, perhaps picking up a sense of dread coming from the
student crowd, Buckley attempts to place himself in their shoes. "I don't
envy you," Buckley tells them, "There are so many confusing people like
me to hack at you along the way."

When he finishes, he's given a standing ovation, but one undergraduate can't get past what he calls Buckley's "pomposity," and sophomore
committee member George Ovitt is turned off by his "trademark smug-
ness." Still, reports show that Buckley's jam-packed crowd is a Stepan
Center attendance record, breaking last night's Norman Mailer film
premiere. The two abrasive rivals will soon have a chance to verbally
spar on a May 28 episode of *Firing Line*.[58]

Dr. King's Roar from the Mountaintop

Martin Luther King Jr. wakes up early on April 3, as does Coretta. With
the children still fast asleep in their bedroom, they move quietly. King's
right-hand man, Rev. Ralph Abernathy, will soon be arriving, and Coretta
figures the two men will want breakfast before their morning flight to
Memphis. But once Abernathy arrives and says hello at the front door,
both men choose not to eat and decide against the coffee and juice in
the kitchen.

With the flight scheduled to leave at 9:00 AM, the two ministers start to head out. Coretta gives Martin a kiss at the front door, and he says he'll call from Memphis.

To Coretta, it's "an ordinary goodbye, like thousands of other times before." As King and Abernathy walk to the car, she doesn't know it will be the last time she sees him alive.[59]

On the drive to the airport, Abernathy notices his dear friend has bounced back somewhat from a deep depression. Perhaps it's the two days of rest at home and spending time with family, or simply getting a good night's sleep, but King is "in good spirits."[60]

The two ministers join three other members of the SCLC, and together they board the plane. King is seated next to longtime SCLC member and nonviolence instructor Dorothy Cotton. Over the PA system, the pilot makes an announcement: "I have to ask everyone to leave the plane because Dr. King and some of his staff are on the plane, and there has been a bomb threat."[61]

Almost all the forty-three passengers hurry off the plane. Not King, however. Cotton begins to leave the plane, and she steps on King's foot. She says to her good friend, "Don't you think we should move it? There's been a bomb scare." King still doesn't move and instead gives Cotton a melancholic glare.[62] Ever since the front porch of King's home in Montgomery, Alabama, had been bombed on January 30, 1956, he has received phone calls, angry letters, packages, and face-to-face threats. This very well may have been his hundredth bomb threat, and he has become numb to the fear.

Andrew Young, the executive director of the SCLC, watches too as King allows everyone else on the plane to go by, even his protection, unarmed bodyguard Bernard Lee. The bomb threat announcement had prompted Lee to jolt out of his seat; and Young notes that Lee is "the first one off the plane." Young glances back at King and sees a smile form on the minister's face. *There goes my protection.*[63]

Eventually, King does come off the Eastern Air Lines plane, allowing trained dogs to roam up and down the aisles in search of anything suspicious. Nearly an hour passes, and the dogs don't find anything. Abernathy and King head back onto the plane. "Well, it looks like they won't kill me this flight," King says to his friend.[64]

A little past 10:30 AM, King and company arrive at gate seventeen of the Memphis airport. A crowd of onlookers surrounds the gate, and four police officers approach King immediately for protection. Supporter and Memphis civil rights activist Tarlese Matthews is the group's transportation. Matthews had earned the respect of the local Black community, and also King, by orchestrating the desegregation of the Memphis Zoo. Before Matthews's lawsuit, Black residents could only attend the zoo on Thursdays. The court ruled in her favor, Matthews won, and perhaps in order to avoid further public embarrassment, the city moved "to desegregate not just the zoo but also the nearby municipal park and golf course."[65]

Before leaving with Matthews, King decides to stop along the terminal and indulge the flock of reporters following the group as they walk.

Will you obey the mayor's injunction forbidding you to march?

King's public answer? "I have my legal advisers with me, and conscience also has to be consulted." King's private answer? *Absolutely not.* He has every intention of helping the sanitation workers' strike, now deep into its second month.

King also tells the press that the injunction is a "basic denial" of the first amendment.

What can you do to make sure the group of people who acted violently at a prior march (on March 28) *won't do the same thing?*

"We have been meeting with them. . . . These groups have committed themselves to cooperation with us." This is only half-true. The group the reporters are referring to are the Invaders, a local eighty-member organization founded on the principles of Black Power. King's colleagues have been talking to the Invaders, but they have yet to secure their total cooperation with a future nonviolent march. King hopes to change that today.

Would complications here in Memphis affect your plans for the Poor People's March in DC?

"Our plan in Washington is going on. Memphis will not in any way curtail or deter it."

After a quick dismissal of NAACP president Roy Wilkins's fears of the Poor People's March turning into a riot (King: "That's not new.")

and a brief comment on president Johnson's recent actions toward Vietnam (King: "I hope the president orders an immediate cessation of all bombing, even around the demilitarized zone. It would be the kind of good faith that would make talks fruitful."), they head out of the airport and into Matthews's Buick.[66]

It's sunny today in Memphis, but the forecast shows a storm coming in soon. On the surface, the city seems to be going about business as usual. The mayor of Memphis, Henry Loeb, has managed to see his city come back to normal after nearly four thousand national guard troops roamed the curfewed city back on March 28, after King's first attempt at a peaceful march in support of the sanitation workers turned hostile. Now, the curfew has ended, most of the troops are gone, and the newly elected mayor—in office for three months after receiving less than 2 percent of the Black vote—hopes to take back control of the city and show his supporters that they haven't made a mistake voting for his law-and-order message.

King checks into room 306 of the Lorraine Motel around noon. The hotel structure was bought by African American businessman Walter Bailey in 1945, deciding to rename it "Lorraine" after his wife, "Loree," as well as Nat King Cole's 1940 version of the jazz staple "Sweet Lorraine." Bailey later added the second floor, but no elevator.

Staying long enough only to put his stuff down, King, along with Abernathy and Jesse Jackson, heads over to the nearby Centenary Church to talk with a group of local Black clergymen. King is quick to ask for unity, despite March 28's march turning violent on account of a group of youths who should "actually be pitied" for their actions, "for all they have ever known is poverty."[67]

King hands the spotlight over to Jackson, who believes the best way to get the sanitation workers a better deal is to begin an economic boycott of large corporations, temporarily crippling the local economy and squeezing Memphis officials into giving in.

Starving, King heads back to the Lorraine around 2:30 PM and digs into a late lunch. At this point, a federal injunction is delivered to King forbidding him to organize a march for ten days. King has been expecting it to come and has assembled a group of pro bono lawyers to scrutinize the injunction to see if there is any wiggle room to avoid being jailed. Even if they can't, King has no plans to back down. Though not ideal, a nonviolent march that ends in mass arrest but no violence would be an improvement to the March 28 media debacle.

With a good meal in him and head lawyer Lucius Burch looking into the injunction, King's top priority now becomes securing a march completely devoid of looting, rioting, and destruction of property. This means heading over to talk with the Invaders, the group mainly responsible for the March 28 failure.

The Invaders' name comes from the 1967 TV show about an architect attempting to convince officials that aliens have landed on earth. The first episode begins with an ominous question, "How does a nightmare begin?" The show concluded its two-season run on March 26, 1968. As for the group, the FBI estimated its total membership at around seventy-five, consisting of high school, college, and graduate students eager to infuse the Black Memphis community with confidence and pride. At 3:30 PM, seventeen Invaders, led by Charles Cabbage and John Burl Smith, are waiting to talk with Dr. King in the dining room of the Lorraine.

King knows why they are there, and it's not just to have a chat. The Invaders want money, and in exchange for $2 million dollars to help start a local school geared toward assisting inner-city Black children, they would pledge their compliance to a nonviolent march.

Wow. King knows that two million is an astronomical number, far larger than the Southern Christian Leadership Conference can offer. But King, knowing his audience, takes the group seriously. He doesn't laugh but instead mentions how in the past an assortment of Black churches has helped organizations like the Invaders launch projects such as schools geared toward aiding inner-city struggles. King even calls a connection in New York. With the group of Invaders looking on, King discusses over the phone the possibility of funding with his contact. He then hangs up, turns to Cabbage, and says, "OK . . . We have a commitment to partially fund your program."[68]

Now it's King's turn to request something. He asks for "twenty-five of their members to serve as parade marshals" and asks for a pledge of nonviolence. Cabbage, perhaps still gobsmacked about the immediate funding success, tells King the Invaders "will try to do our best."

It's almost 5:00 PM, and King needs to rest. After a bomb scare, a press conference and two crucial meetings, he heads back to room 306 nursing a sore throat that's not getting any better from smoking a pack a day of Salems. He tries to grab a few winks back in his room that has "double beds, a rabbit-eared TV perched on a simple wooden dresser, two small table lamps, and a chair with striped upholstery."[69] After a few minutes, Abernathy comes in to check on him. King is exhausted and tells his best friend, "I really don't feel like speaking." The men also notice the moody weather and storm clouds. Tornado warnings have already been reported, which means a small crowd at the Mason Temple.

Low turnout, sore throat, exhaustion . . .

Abernathy agrees to go in King's place and takes Jesse Jackson with him.

Several hours later, King's phone rings. It's Abernathy, calling from a lobby at the Mason Temple. "Martin, all the television networks are lined up waiting for you. This speech will be broadcast nationwide. You need to deliver it. Besides, the people who are here want you. Not me."[70]

King knows his friend, and he knows his honesty. They've been side by side ever since the Montgomery Bus Boycott back in 1955. Into the phone King says, "I'll do whatever you say. If you say come, I'll be there."

"Come."

So King suits up. Before leaving, he calls Coretta and, perhaps making sure he has the latest news before his speech, asks if she has heard of any progress made by President Johnson regarding peace talks. Coretta tells him that she missed the six o'clock news.

King tells her it's OK. "I'll watch the eleven o'clock news. I have to go and speak at the mass meeting, but I'll be back in time to watch the news. Don't worry about it."

Just before hanging up, King speaks to his wife for the last time. "I'll call you tomorrow night."

The weather in Memphis that night borders on apocalyptic—horrible for a resident, but perfect for a Baptist preacher's rhetoric. At around 9:00 PM King, "in a very dark brown suit; white shirt; and copper-tinged, dark brown tie," takes a seat behind Abernathy.[71]

Perhaps it's the Four Horsemen–like weather, or the spirit of the crowd knowing they're about to hear the man they came for, but even Abernathy is feeling loquacious. He begins a grand, slow-cooked Southern drawl introduction, "Brothers and sisters, ladies and gentlemen. Too often we take our leaders for granted. We think we know them, but they are really strangers to us. So tonight, I would like to take a little time to introduce you to our leader, Dr. Martin Luther King Jr."

By "little time" Abernathy means twenty-five minutes. Near the end, Abernathy can't help but tie King to LBJ. "He is the man who tells the president what to do."[72]

King can't help but grin at the overwhelming buildup. In fact, King feels the need to crack wise as he finally stands at the pulpit around half past nine. "Thank you very kindly my friends. As I listened to Ralph Abernathy and his eloquent and generous introduction . . . I wondered who he was talking about." Still, Abernathy has been with him on the civil rights battlefield since the beginning, and King, with great sincerity, tells the audience that "it's always good to have your closest friend and associate to say something good about you, and Ralph Abernathy is the best friend that I have in the world."

King thanks them all for coming despite the weather and then takes everyone on a tour through history. Starting in Egypt, he comes to Greece, with "Plato, Aristotle, Socrates, Euripides, and Aristophanes assembled around the Parthenon." Reeling off the names of philosophers is something King has been doing since his seminary days, and the crowd releases a mix of impressed laughter and cheers.

For the next forty minutes, King's voice sounds as powerful and authoritative as it's ever been. Gone is the sore throat and exhaustion:

> Something is happening in our world. The masses of people are rising up. And wherever they are assembled today, whether they are in Johannesburg, South Africa; Nairobi, Kenya; Accra, Ghana; New York City; Atlanta, Georgia; Jackson, Mississippi;

or Memphis, Tennessee—the cry is always the same: "We want to be free."[73]

The crowd is close to King, literally. Because of the architecture of the Mason Temple, no one sits more than sixty yards away from him, and amid intermittent thunder and showers of rain, King encourages everyone to stay together and use nonviolent methods to help the sanitation workers. He implores the crowd to take their money out of downtown Memphis banks and start accounts at African American owned Tri-State Bank, to avoid corporations with biased hiring practices such as Coca-Cola and Wonder Bread. As long as they stay together, demonstrate, and economically withdraw from the Memphis economy, they will help deliver a victory to the sanitation workers.

But it is moments from near the end of the speech that television decides to capture. After telling the audience about his early-morning bomb scare flying from Atlanta to Memphis and the threats he's heard from his "sick white brothers," he tells his responsive audience how little he now fears death:

> Well, I don't know what will happen now. We've got some difficult days ahead. [Audience: *Yes!*] But it really doesn't matter with me now [*Yes!*] because I've been to the mountaintop. [*Yeah! Cheers . . .*]
> And I don't mind.
> Like anybody, I would like to live a long life. Longevity has its place. But I'm not concerned about that now. I just want to do God's will. [*Yes.*] And He's allowed me to go up to the mountain. [*Yes! Go ahead.*] And I've looked over. [*Ah yes.*] And I've seeeeeen the Promised Land [*YES! All right.*] I may not get there with you. But I want you to know tonight [*Yeah! Yes!*] that we, as a people, will get to the promised land! [*All right. Cheers . . . Go ahead, go ahead.*]
> And so I'm happy, tonight.
> I'm not worried about anything.
> I'm not fearing any man!
> Mine eyes have seen the glory of the coming of the Lord!! [*Cheers*][74]

King moves away from the pulpit, emotionally drained, and into the arms of Ralph Abernathy. Just before embracing his best friend, well past 10:00 PM, King tries to finish his last line, "Mine eyes have seen the glory of the coming of the Lord . . . *his truth is marching on.*"[75] But he is too overwhelmed, and tears are in his eyes.

5

THURSDAY, APRIL 4, 1968

The Death of a King and
the Life of a Millionaire

Robert Kennedy and his wife, Ethel, waiting to be introduced at the Stepan Center. April 4, 1968. *Photo courtesy of the University of Notre Dame Archives.*

"The victims of the violence are black and white, rich and poor, young and old, famous and unknown. They are, most important of all, human beings whom other human beings loved and needed. No one—no matter where he lives or what he does—can be certain who will suffer from some senseless act of bloodshed. And yet it goes on and on and on in this country of ours."

—Robert F. Kennedy[1]

"He and His Followers Should Be Hobbled"

Despite his incredible speech the night before, public support for King, especially his Poor People's March, has started to dwindle. In several newspapers across the country, editorials appear in the morning edition on April 4.

The *Orlando Sentinel* publishes an opinion piece meant to stand for the entire newspaper. Under the headline KING MUST BE DISSUADED, the paper warns, "If Memphis was a sample of what 'nonviolence' can lead to, the worst riot in history is likely to develop from his assault on the District of Columbia." The paper calls on Lyndon Johnson to do more to keep King from bringing "three thousand demonstrators" to the Capitol. "Whether the power of the office of president is sufficient in itself to deter the Reverend King is uncertain, but Lyndon Johnson should try. If he can prevent the widespread bloodshed and looting which will surely be a part of the march on Washington, he will have made a great contribution to his nation."[2]

In the *McKinney Weekly Democrat-Gazette* over in Texas, an editorial written by Norman Scott starts with the headline IT'S TIME TO ACT. In the last paragraph, Scott doesn't hold back. "The United States gets involved in trying to stop Communism in other parts of the World . . . but, it's time to put a halt to it in our own country!"[3]

But in Jefferson City, Missouri's *Post Tribune*, one editorial reaches a new level of anger. Written by frequent contributor Major General Thomas A. Lane, the military veteran criticizes the media for letting King off the hook about the Memphis march that turned violent. "How long will editors go on pretending that Dr. King is an apostle of non-violence? How long will a credulous public go on believing these transparent pretensions? Dr. King is no Gandhi . . . Martin Luther King is an apostle of Marx, and Marx was an apostle of violence." Like the *Sentinel*, he calls on Johnson once again. "Does President Johnson have the political courage to tell Dr. King there will be no march against the Congress of the United States? Perhaps he will do that only when our editors of big city dailies stop promoting anarchy."

The same publisher also distributes a morning edition newspaper under the title *Daily Capital News*. Their words, written in the "we"

This sketch was printed in a variety of newspapers on the morning of April 4, 1968. Several of the newspapers, such as the *Palladium-Item* (Richmond, Indiana) would later issue an apology. The acceptance of the sketch does, however, show how King was perceived as a troublemaker by a large portion of the public just before his assassination. *Don Hesse,* St. Louis Globe Democrat.

voice, are far stronger than Lane's: "Dr. King, we believe, should be exposed for what he is. A dangerous man . . ." And then, a direct threat: "Since it apparently does no good to point out to Dr. King that his 'marches' often lead to violence and hence that he should discard them, he and his followers should be hobbled before new marches lead to further violence."[4]

What may be one of the most glaring examples of how public opinion was beginning to shift away from Dr. King comes from a political cartoon sketch published in several newspapers across the country on the morning of April 4. The sketch shows Dr. King holding a pistol with two hands, a self-made halo above his head. At the top is the caption 'I'm Not Firing It—I'm Only Pulling the Trigger.' It is a reflection of the popular criticism at the time—that King's peaceful marches are only creating a greater chance for violence.

Dr. King's Final Hour

In Memphis around 5:00 PM, SCLC executive director Andrew Young is driving back to the Lorraine Motel. He has good news to share with Dr. King, and King needs it. After a day of recovery and unsuccessful meetings attempting to further persuade the Invaders to be cooperative in the next nonviolent march (King's power phone call on April 3 wasn't enough), Young is eager to let him know that, after a day sitting in a Memphis courtroom and on the witness stand, he and the SCLC's team were able to get the injunction lifted. Bottom line, they'll be able to march and not be sent immediately to jail.

Young finds King in his brother A. D.'s hotel room on the first floor. When he enters, he sees that King and others have been "eating . . . talking and clowning," waiting for a report from Young. Before he can tell him about the day, King grabs him and pushes him down on the bed. King grabs a pillow and starts swatting at Young. Standing over Young "like a big kid," King keeps swinging as Young ducks. "You have [swings] to let me know [swings] what's going on [swings]." Young grabs and a pillow and soon "everybody piles on everybody."

At 5:50 PM, Dr. King notices the time and says to the group, "We're due at dinner."[5] King heads back up to room 306 to put on a suit and tie.

After he finishes, King steps out onto the balcony and spots Rev. Jesse Jackson and musician Ben Branch standing in the parking lot below. King invites Jackson to dinner at Billy Kyles's wife's home but teases that Jackson doesn't "even have a tie on." Jackson smiles then defends himself. "The prerequisite to eating is an appetite, not a tie."

King lets out a laugh and then says, "You're crazy."[6]

Jackson introduces Branch to King. King says, "Oh yes, he's my man. How are you, Ben?"

"Hello," Ben yells back.

King requests a gospel song to the skilled trumpeter. "I want you to play 'Precious Lord' for me tonight."[7]

As King lingers on the balcony in front of room 306, he wonders if he should grab a coat before heading out to eat. As he thinks, a sniper who had checked into a rooming house seventy-five yards away has propped open a bathroom window above a tub. He said his name was John Willard (perhaps a nod toward Lincoln assassin John Wilkes Booth). "Willard" has a direct line to the motel, and he sticks his rifle out the window and looks out across the lawn. With the rifle and "the magnification of a 7x [Redfield] scope," King appears through the lens as if a mere ten yards away.[8]

Robert Kennedy Roars Through Indiana

"It is difficult for me to see a single qualification that the man has for the presidency. I think he is shallow, vain, and untrustworthy—on top of which he is indecisive."

—Dwight D. Eisenhower, March 1968[9]

Back in Indiana around noon, hope is in the air as a crowd of a thousand watches a politician's Convair 550 airplane roll to a stop at South Bend's St. Joseph County Airport.[10] Many of them are high schoolers and received permission from their parents and principal to be excused from class. Young women hold up signs as the anticipation builds. When the airplane door opens, the crowd erupts. You'd think the Fighting Irish football team had just returned with the national championship. But no, this burst of youthful glee is for a forty-two-year-old married father of ten (and one more on the way). His name, Kennedy, is synonymous with hope and idealism, and he's well aware that part of his appeal lies in the glorified memory of his slain brother. To his throng of supporters, it's a Kennedy, not a McCarthy, who can win the election and solve the Vietnam quagmire. It's Bobby, not LBJ, who can fix the draft, end domestic poverty, and calm the racial tension that persists throughout the South and urban slums.[11]

Robert Kennedy tells the crowd, his brown hair messy from a stiff, cold wind, that he's "delighted to be here," and the word "delighted," delivered in his Bostonian style, causes dozens of high school girls to squeal and swoon.[12] Thanks in large part to a swath of under-eighteen attendees, the size of the crowd is double that of McCarthy's the day before. It's flattering, but Kennedy knows he needs to deliver his vision with actual registered voters and community leaders if he wants to build a sustainable campaign. But at this point, only several weeks after officially declaring his candidacy, he'll take all the support he can get. "I need your help," he says. "If we can win here in Indiana, I could go on to win the Democratic presidential nomination and turn this country around."

Kennedy thanks the cheering crowd and makes his way toward his idling motorcade. Bobby, in a dark gray suit and tie and black jacket, climbs into the backseat of an open convertible. He waves back at the "we-love-you-Bobby" throng and the caravan moves away from the plane. Everything is going according to plan. After visiting fifteen states in the previous two and a half weeks since his official March 16 announcement, Kennedy knows his core voting base: under-twenty-nine youth and minorities.

The caravan passes through predominantly Black West South Bend. Many residents line the sides of streets and whistle for "Jack's brother." The route has been planned to maximize crowd support and show that Bobby is trying to reach out to everyone, especially those who feel forgotten. However, only minutes after driving away from the airport, the motorcade is blocked by swarms of people who flood the street and surround RFK's car. Bobby has been standing on the backseat of the convertible, and as the car carefully pushes through the crowd, a few overenthusiastic teens yank Kennedy from his spot. Bobby falls out and slams against the street pavement. Four members of his security team vault out of their own cars and help the presidential candidate up. He's OK, but several aides choose to sit in the backseat and hold tight to his lower body. One aide wraps his arm around Bobby's midsection to keep him from being dragged out again.[13]

Driving along Angela Boulevard, the caravan passes supportive signs taped and stapled to telephone poles, slowing to a crawl as it passes Central High School. Hundreds of students and young adults jam into each other as they lunge for Bobby's outstretched hands. Where there aren't people, there are cars lined along the street, many of which were parked hours earlier so the drivers could catch a glance of the man who is "trying to turn this country around." A fifty-five-year-old woman named Pearl lunges toward Kennedy in the hopes of shaking his hand. Before she can, however, she's shoved to the ground by others and fractures her right shoulder. As children run into the street, Janet, a local schoolteacher, injures her foot attempting to keep them safe. After hundreds of manic handshakes and much grasping, the motorcade powers through the mob and glides toward the Notre Dame campus.[14]

At the Stepan Center, there are around 1,200 people crowded around the front entrance. Some have even climbed onto the roof in the hopes of snagging a better view of the event. These devoted fans would gladly wait inside, but each and every one of the 3,800 wooden chairs is filled, and the aisles overflowing with local high school and university students who've been waiting for hours to hear Kennedy's speech. Forty-five members of the marching band stand ready to triumphantly announce Senator Kennedy. In the back of the Stepan Center, a local rock 'n' roll band plays head-bobbing tunes. Signs premade by the Kennedy for President campus organization ("We spent 150 bucks") have been passed out to the crowd. Some of them are standard (KENNEDY IS THE ONE!) while others are larks (ARA [Parseghian, ND football coach] AND BOBBY FOR AMERICA!). A film crew is there to record every moment.

Thanks to the Student Union Athletic Committee, the Kennedy for President group, and volunteers from the sophomore literary festival, all of this has been put together in around three days. The local newspaper interviews Notre Dame's student body president, J. Richard Rossie, just before the motorcade arrives for the event. After mentioning that there will be voter registration support in North and South Dining Halls from 5:30 to 6:30 PM, Rossie attempts to deliver a well-crafted comment amid the madness: "We who first organized for McCarthy did so for two reasons: because he was a peace candidate and because we wanted to bring Kennedy into the campaign. As soon as Kennedy declared his candidacy, like that, we switched over. If Kennedy hadn't, we would have stayed with McCarthy as the peace candidate."[15]

These are the feelings of many, but not all. Sophomore literary festival committee member George Ovitt doesn't trust Kennedy and equates most of the current excitement to Bobby's youthfulness and his ability to "talk a good game." To many of the new generation, Kennedy has a kind and sensitive glow. He wants peace and an end to domestic poverty—two pillars anyone can stand behind. Ovitt, and many in more established political circles, are looking for pithier statements. As the motorcade reaches the Stepan Center, Kennedy is, to Ovitt and many Indiana politicians, nothing more than a name-brand contender flinging promises he's not sure he can keep. As of April 4, Kennedy is behind both "favorite-son candidate" Indiana governor Roger Branigin and McCarthy. Governor Branigin has chosen to stay in the race to keep the sixty-six Indiana delegates up for grabs at the Democratic National Convention. Embracing his exalted Hoosier status, Branigin calls McCarthy and Kennedy "strangers" and "tourists" of Indiana. Until Kennedy can deliver a complex message to a broad audience, he'll never make inroads with Indiana's county commissioners.[16]

Kennedy weaves his way through the packed audience and reaches the stage. For forty-five seconds, the crowd roars their support, the sound deafening, in part because of the aluminum-lined ceiling of the Stepan Center. The cheers sound like a buzzing speaker. Literary critic Granville Hicks, one of thousands crammed into the geodesic dome (and perhaps the oldest), can barely take the audible high-pitched growl. "If a Notre Dame football rally is more excited or noisier, I don't want to attend one," he comments. Ovitt, lingering around the edges of the "show," deems it more appropriate for a rock star than a politician.[17]

Bobby knows the audience in front of him is young, hopeful, and exuberant about helping him. After the explosion of applause, Kennedy first tries on a bit of modesty as he gives the crowd one of his "Aw, shucks" smiles: "This must be the warmest reception anyone has had in this auditorium since William Buckley spoke here last evening."[18]

With his wife, Ethel, sitting behind him, Kennedy delivers a few zingers he knows will land well with his young college-age audience. "Number one, I'm really here not as a presidential candidate but to see if Notre Dame will ever have the courage to play [football against] my college, Harvard." The crowd produces a smiling groan, and Kennedy, while grinning, shrugs, "It's all right! [Harvard] is willing to do it."[19]

But soon Kennedy heads back into more of a serious and urgent tone, keeping as much focus as he can on the younger generation. "I think this world belongs to you," he tells them. "You are obligated to take an interest in our political processes. I and those associated with me must bear a share of the blame for the policies we have made, but if we are to form a policy of progress at home and a policy of peace abroad, you must help."[20]

Robert Kennedy at the Stepan Center on April 4, 1968. *Photo courtesy of Marty Kress, taken by John Mroz.*

Robert F. Kennedy's April 4 Schedule
All estimated times are Central Standard Time

- **11:30 AM** Left Washington, DC
- **1:00 PM** Arrived at the St. Joseph County Airport
- **1:00–1:45 PM** Motorcade through South Bend
- **2:00 PM** Spoke at Notre Dame's Stepan Center
- **3:00 PM** Visited St. Joseph County Nursing Home
- **4:00 PM** Left South Bend
- **5:40 PM** Arrived at Muncie Airport
- **5:45–6:15 PM** Motorcade through downtown Muncie to Ball State University
- **6:20 PM** Spoke at Ball State University's Irving Gymnasium
- **7:15 PM** Left Muncie Airport (first heard about MLK being *shot* around 7:00 PM)
- **8:00 PM** Arrived at Indianapolis's Weir Cook Airport (heard news that King had been *killed*)
- **9:15 PM** Delivered remarks on the death of MLK to a crowd at an outdoor basketball court near Broadway Christian Church.
- **10:00 PM** Back at Indianapolis's Marriott Hotel, arranged a plane for Coretta Scott King and met with "black militant organization" as scheduled by John Lewis.[21]

As he has since the beginning of his campaign, Kennedy does his best to impress upon his young audience the issue of poverty. "Here in America, there are children so underfed and undernourished that they are crippled for life. Families in our ghettos huddle ten to a room fighting off the cold and the ravages of rats and disease. . . . The life expectancy of the American Indian is twenty-five years less than that of the white man. . . . This is indecent."[22]

For Kennedy, the issue of poverty *is* his reason for campaigning. Ever since being stunned into silence during his visit to the Mississippi Delta and seeing malnourished children with distended stomachs and little to no chance of escape, Bobby has made the issue central to all other problems in America. "There are children in the United States who eat so little that they fall asleep in school and do not learn. We must act, and we must act now. . . . If we cannot . . . we must ask ourselves what we really stand for."[23]

The audience roars. They are with him. Kennedy has a sensitive, thoughtful delivery. The students seem to trust every fact he utters. One reporter, awestruck by the blind support, quips that Kennedy could have started swearing at the crowd, and they "still would have applauded."[24]

In regard to Vietnam, Kennedy makes sure to communicate his position that the draft is "inequitable and unfair." But when he tells the crowd that one of the first actions he'll make as president is to end college deferments, many in the audience lose a bit of joy. Kennedy, perceiving the change in atmosphere, smiles, "Did I just lose you to Hubert Humphrey?" The youthful crowd rumbles back to life. The senator has charm to spare, justifying his position by stating that "at least until the Tet Offensive, the burden of war has been carried by the poor." In addition, "Twenty percent of Vietnam casualties are black." To Bobby, a dedicated refocus on civil rights, domestic poverty, and an end to Vietnam stand as the only way to bring about a long-lasting peace in the United States.[25]

Kennedy is able to articulate these viewpoints even more at his next stop in South Bend, the St. Joseph County Nursing Home. As positive as the response has been from the younger generation, Kennedy doesn't want to be pegged as a politician for the youth only. He decides to leave behind the motorcade and asks most of the traveling media for some space. Besides his wife and a few campaign officials operating film equipment, Kennedy only allows a *South Bend Tribune* reporter to attend. The visit is so the campaign can have film footage of Kennedy talking to the oldest generation, rather than always fending off the loving screams of the youngest.[26]

Approximately a hundred elderly residents of the County Home await Kennedy, and they are ready with questions. Kennedy takes a seat on a sofa in the dining room lounge, happy and relieved somewhat to be temporarily out of the circus of people awaiting him all around the fence of the nursing home. "First, I want to say how nice it is to be here." He pauses, gathering his thoughts. "I think that it's important that elderly people be able to live lives of dignity and honor. It's terribly, terribly important." He wants his words to sound authentic . . . trustworthy, even though cameras are rolling nearby. "If this country amounts to anything now, it's because of what you've done."

He has one more thought to share with them. The national media has painted him as a political figure for the youth of the country, but in this moment he hopes to reform that image. "The younger generation has a special responsibility to the elderly." Then a rhetorical question: "Why should older people have to worry about being ill and losing their life savings? It couldn't be wronger."[27]

His introductory remarks finished, he fields questions. According to Thomas Jewell, the *South Bend Tribune* reporter, many of the elderly live only off Social Security. Their fears are real and immediate. *Will Social Security run out in a few years? Can benefits be increased?*

Kennedy answers *no* and *yes* to the questions, but for benefits to increase there needs to be an adjustment to the way it's funded, from "general revenues rather than a payroll tax." Other questions allow Kennedy to dig into his feelings on medical care and the war in Vietnam, saying the two are financially connected. In short, as the war continues, less funding can be budgeted for health care. One elderly man tells Kennedy he's had sons fight in World War II and Vietnam and wants to know Kennedy's thoughts on the current war. It's a difficult question for Bobby to answer. At this moment in time there is a partial halt to bombing in Vietnam, and President Johnson has sacrificed his own position as president in order to advance peace talks. "I hope peace will come," Bobby tells the man. "I would like to see negotiations start now so that no more American boys are sent there."

In the middle of the Q and A, the topic turns to racial violence and the sporadic rioting occurring around the country. Kennedy is quick to respond to the fears his predominantly White listeners have, saying that the problems with racism are "not a problem for any one group. It is an American problem. We must treat people equally and make it clear we will not tolerate violence." An elderly Black woman takes command of the conversation. With a heavy heart, she tells the senator that most Black people "are ashamed of the rioting and looting. . . . We just want a job and a chance to make an honest living."[28]

It's a smooth forty-five-minute visit. Before leaving, Bobby and Ethel meet in a room for ten minutes with St. Joseph County Democratic chairman Ideal Baldoni. He is honest with Ethel and Bobby; they have a lot of work to do in Indiana because they "came into the picture late." McCarthy and Branigin already have significant political networks throughout the state. Because of this, county organizations have already pledged their support for the other candidates. "And we keep our commitments," Baldoni says.

Bobby and Ethel leave the nursing home. Before reaching the backseat of his convertible, Kennedy walks toward the fence border and attempts to shake the hands of everyone who'd waited for him. After a few dozen smiles and thank-yous, the motorcade makes its way back to the St. Joseph County Airport.[29]

The chartered plane flies 140 miles south to the Muncie Airport, landing at 5:40 PM. He's quickly greeted by hundreds of supporters and a high school marching band blaring "Born Free." Unfortunately for them, Kennedy's running thirty minutes late, and the Notre Dame scenario begins all over again as the motorcade, now with a fire-engine red convertible, drives toward the Ball State University campus. They park near the Irving Gymnasium, and Kennedy, as he's done many times before, requests a common entrance into the gym so that he can wade his way through the crowd. "He likes it this way," one campaign manager tells local reporter Floyd Creech. "Don't make the students clear a path for him—he likes to step over them."

Kennedy may like it, but his staff thinks differently. Three days earlier, while standing outside a restaurant in Philadelphia, eggs were thrown at Bobby and Ethel. The couple weren't hit, but several staff members had their coats ruined.[30]

The demographics and atmosphere of the crowd are roughly the same as Notre Dame—under the age of thirty and crazed to a Beatlesesque level. Around eight thousand supporters, packed tight enough to starve the room of oxygen, jump to their feet as Bobby and Ethel navigate their way to the stage. Students who've been waiting for several hours wave signs that read ALL THE WAY WITH RFK and THINK YOUNG—RFK. To Creech, it's Kennedy's "appearance and manner" that fires up the students. Young women who are close to the senator and Ethel comment to each other about their looks. "He has some grey hair," and "Look how tanned Ethel is."

Eugene McCarthy's presence is felt somewhat. A gigantic sign reading McCARTHY FOR PRESIDENT hangs over the edge of the gymnasium balcony, and, either through forgetfulness or genuine admiration for the candidate, remains visible throughout the event. However, when a student attempts to advertise the candidacy of Richard Nixon by displaying a snapshot of his face, he's greeted with "a mixture of hisses, boos" but also a few scattered cheers. The audience is here to see Kennedy, but who they will trust as president is undecided.[31]

After a quick introduction, Kennedy addresses the crowd at 6:20 PM. The content of Kennedy's speech echoes his safe and generalized remarks at Notre Dame. As the senator rehashes his familiar statements regarding Vietnam and poverty, a few young men grab the attention of Mrs. Kennedy. They hand her a copy of the April 8 edition of *Newsweek*. Bobby's face graces the cover, but Ethel scoffs. "Gracious! Isn't that a terrible picture?" she shouts at the young men. She scribbles a message on the magazine: "*He's really better looking than this* —Ethel Kennedy."[32]

Thirty-four minutes later, Kennedy concludes his speech and opens himself up to a Q and A. One bold student stands up and verbalizes his disgust with the shallowness of Kennedy's speech. "You've given us ten minutes of jokes, another twenty minutes of double-talk. Do you have any solution to the grandiose problems you have outlined?" Kennedy nods, then delivers a few policy-rich statements such as private industry earning "tax credits by building low-cost housing and by hiring workers now on welfare rolls." But his more detailed solutions are drowned out by thousands of people booing the questioner "into submission."[33]

This isn't the case when a Black student stands up and asks Kennedy to talk more about "uplifting children in Black ghettos who are now starving." "You're placing a great deal of faith in white America. . . . Is this faith justified?" the student asks.

No boos this time, and Kennedy responds with hesitation. "Yes, it is, but we must also place our faith in black America."

Perhaps learning a lesson from his hiccup at Notre Dame, Kennedy asks the crowd to raise their hands if they are in favor of student deferments regarding the Vietnam draft. It's a nearly unanimous yes, but Bobby, hinting at his own opinion, reminds the young crowd to take responsibility for the "nation's major issues." Near the end of his time onstage, Kennedy tells the students that "we need to decide what we can do during our lives to help. What is our purpose in life? . . . Like Plato, we need to examine everything."[34]

After a closing thank-you, a mob of students rush to the front of the stage. Media tables collapse, and a young woman gets trapped by the stampede. Security helps her escape, but this crowd chaos is a continued part of the Kennedy campaign's request to allow students total access to their candidate. Bobby doesn't mind being swarmed, and this sense of closeness continues as he and Ethel head back to the red convertible and leave in the motorcade to the airport.

It's dark when Kennedy reaches his chartered plane. Before boarding, he runs over to a five-foot-high metal Johnson Field terminal fence to shake hands with people waiting for him. He hadn't had enough time to reach them in the morning, but he makes sure to do so now. As he moves down the line, a young supporter approaches.

"Did you hear about Martin Luther King?"

Bobby stops walking for a moment. "Was he shot?" Kennedy asks.

"Yes."

"Was he killed?"

"No, he's in critical condition."[35]

The local Muncie reporter sees Bobby shake his head as he finishes greeting supporters along the fence line. He boards the plane with his wife, Ethel. His flight to Weir Cook Airport in Indianapolis will take less than an hour. With Dr. King heavily on his mind, he knows a crowd of hundreds of African American supporters are awaiting his arrival.

The Family's Special Bulletin

Back in Atlanta, around half past six, Dexter King and his older brother Martin are relaxed and sitting on the floor. The television is on. Usually the boys are watching game shows or *American Bandstand*, but whatever they're watching now is soon interrupted by a "Special Bulletin."[36] Dexter's older sister Yoki is in another room when "an unforgettable voice" tells the two sons what has happened to their father. "Dr. Martin Luther King Jr. has been shot in Memphis, at 6:01 PM."

Speechless, the boys give each other a look before bouncing up off the floor and running to their parents' bedroom. Dexter quickly takes note of his mother's state. Her ankles are crossed, and her hands are holding the beige phone tightly to her face. "Mother? Mommy? Mama? You hear that?" Dexter asks. "What do they mean?"

Coretta puts her index finger to her lips, and the boys stand still and wait for her to put the phone down. Dexter hears her repeat a phrase, "I understand . . . I understand." Dexter wants her "to get off the phone and make me understand."

She does, and the sadness in her eyes is enough to cause the children to fear the worst. Yoki enters the room, and immediately she puts her hands over her ears. She can't. It's too much. "Don't tell me! Don't tell me!"

Dexter and Martin move toward their mother—desperate for a hug. Dexter can feel her take "a deep breath, as if about to dive underwater."[37]

Maya Angelou's Tragic Celebration

It's 6:00 PM in New York City, and Maya Angelou is in her kitchen cooking for a group of friends, mainly from the Harlem Writers Guild. It's her fortieth birthday, and she's decided to celebrate with a feast before heading out for a monthlong sojourn across America in support of Dr. Martin Luther King Jr.'s Poor People's March. Dr. King had asked for her support. "I need someone to travel this country and talk to black preachers. I'd like each church to donate one Sunday's collection to the Poor People's March." No doubt with a smile, she adds "Not too many black preachers can resist a good-looking woman with a good idea."[38]

Angelou has prepared a feast in her apartment: "Texas chili without the beans, baked ham and candied yams, rice and peas for the West Indian palate, macaroni and cheese and a pineapple upside-down cake." But before anyone has a chance to come over, Angelou answers her phone. Her friend Dolly has an urgent tone to her voice. She tells

Angelou to promise not to turn on the television or the radio. "Give me your word."

Angelou complies. "I give you my word."[39]

As she sits overlooking her beautifully arranged dinner, with ice buckets filled and daffodils "as perky as their name," Angelou can only sit and wait for her friend to come deliver news that, to her, seems unimaginable.

Angelou has had a deep connection with the civil rights movement ever since being pulled into the fire by Malcolm X, whom she'd met during her four years in Ghana. Malcolm X had inspired her to help (pro bono) strengthen his organization, called the Organization of Afro-American Unity. Tragically, however, one month before she was due to start, he was killed while speaking in Harlem.

Dolly arrives and tells Angelou the news now making its way through society like a ferocious tremor. Dr. King was shot and killed while standing on the balcony just outside room 306 at the Lorraine Motel in Memphis. When Dolly reports the news, Angelou's senses shut down. It's simply too much.

With nothing more than a glance back at what now appears to be a showy birthday celebration, Angelou is desperate to leave her home immediately. She needs to be surrounded by suffering, by sufferers trapped in despair.

She makes her way on foot through the streets of Harlem and down 125th Street. Accompanied by a neighbor, Angelou's pain sits within. "I turned my thoughts over as one turns pages in a book. In the silence I spoke to myself, using the time to comprehend the emptiness."

Around her she hears "raw screams," the breaking of glass, yet she can still remember Dr. King's voice, "which sang out of radios and televisions and over altars and pulpits, which intoned from picket lines and marches and through prison bars." Now, that voice has been "stilled. Forever stilled."

She watches complete strangers hug each other as tears flow. She passes televisions showing footage of Dr. King preaching. A crowd gathers, unified by misery.

Eventually, Angelou finds herself at a diner. She's the only customer. The owner sits at the end with "his head on the counter."

When she pleads for some service, the owner tells her despondently, "Get it yourself."

It takes a moment, but the owner composes himself and talks with Angelou. He explains to her the anger, anguish, and desperation in the streets, "You know this is all about Malcolm. . . . See, they killed him not far from here, and we didn't do anything. Lot of people loved Malcolm, but we didn't show it, and now even people who didn't agree with Reverend King, they out here, just to show we do know how to care for somebody. Half of this is for Malcolm X, a half for Martin King, and a half for a whole lot of others."[40]

James Baldwin's California Rage

Across the country in Palm Springs, California, Angelou's friend James Baldwin sits by the pool of a luxurious home. He calls the neighborhood a "millionaire's graveyard" and has been sent to this house by a producer to continue work on a film script of Malcolm X's *Autobiography*. Billy Dee Williams, perfect in Baldwin's mind for the role of Malcolm, sits nearby. The locale is meant to relax his artistic spirit, but the "sunshine as bland as milk and honey, the eerie streets paved with gold," and "the thunderous silence of wealth" make it very difficult to tackle Malcolm's gritty, darkened soul.[41]

A reporter comes to the home and chats with Baldwin and Billy Dee about the film version of Malcolm. In this climate, talking feels much better than writing, so Baldwin charms the reporter and feels in command of the film's future vision. Baldwin acts "in charge of the film," despite what the studio actually wants him to do, which is not to speak publicly about it. Still, Baldwin divulges a few of the film's details as they drink by the swimming pool. After Billy Dee and Baldwin guide the reporter back to her car, they return feeling as if the film is theirs. Billy Dee jumps into the pool and begins singing "African improvisations to the sound of Aretha Franklin" as a nearby record player blares her music. Someone, a butler perhaps, has brought a phone out to the pool. At around 3:30 PM Pacific time, it rings. Baldwin picks up and hears the voice of actor and friend David Moses on the other line.

Moses exclaims, "Jimmy? Martin's just been shot." The gravity of the sentence stuns Baldwin. "He's not dead yet . . . but it's a head wound—so . . ."

For the next several hours, Baldwin feels lost. He weeps, but more "in helpless rage than in sorrow." Two days later, Baldwin leaves behind the divisive helplessness that exists between Palm Springs and Watts and flies to Atlanta to attend King's funeral.[42]

The Public's Apathy

Rev. Samuel McKinney, a former Morehouse classmate and longtime friend of Dr. King, takes a red-eye from Seattle to Philadelphia. After he collects his luggage from the baggage claim, a friend meets with him and tells him that they've got to go the radio station as soon as possible: *King was killed.*

McKinney is speechless. He walks past a restaurant and sees two servicemen being served breakfast by a young White woman behind the counter. They're talking about Dr. King, and the young lady shakes her head—"I could care less."[43]

The servicemen don't see anything wrong with that.

Joseph Heller's *Catch-22*

Heller on April 4. Sophomore committee member Marty Kress is to his right. *Courtesy of Martin P. Kress.*

Back at the South Bend airport, the Kennedy crowds have long gone. It's the early afternoon, and sophomore literary festival committee members Marty Kress and John Mroz watch a plane roll in. Mobile stairs are attached to the exit door. Along with other passengers, Joseph Heller walks down the steps and sees his "audience" of four Notre Dame students in suits and light-brown jackets.

The author of *Catch-22* is dressed as if he's just come from a board meeting—dark blue collared jacket, business suit, and a leather portfolio envelope under his arm. His hair is slicked back, with a streak of white that extends to the back of his head. With no Kennedy supporters around, Heller shows off his McCARTHY FOR PRESIDENT button to *South Bend Tribune* journalist Patricia Koval, who has been assigned to cover the literary festival. "If you're going to write anything," Heller tells her as they walk to the car waiting for him, "will you please tell them I wore a McCarthy button?" As if on cue, the four students show their solidarity for their author by opening their coats, revealing their own McCarthy buttons.[44]

Before his 8:00 PM lecture, Heller drops in on an eighteenth-century English poetry class that Mroz and Kress have scheduled, the goal being, according to Kress, to "get [the authors] to engage in lectures" on campus.[45]

Heller stands at the head of the room and responds to any questions students might have about his novel. Phil Kukielski, a Notre Dame sophomore, sits in the back and enjoys the banter between Heller and the class's "stuffy" professor. Kukielski can already tell that Heller is an "adman" and a "New Yorker who doesn't suffer fools kindly." When the professor of the class wonders aloud about the origin of his Snowden character in *Catch-22*, instead of asking Heller directly, the professor takes this as an opportunity to pontificate on the possibilities he's thought of: "Did the name come from Wordsworth? Oh, it must have been Wordsworth. Also, there is a mountain in Wales called Snowden. Yes, yes, that must be it! Surely that is where you found it. Please, tell us, Mr. Heller? Was it from Wordsworth and this mountain in Wales that you chose the name Snowden?"[46]

Heller, already tired of listening, turns to the self-amused professor, looks him square in the eye, and says, "Nope. Next question." For

Kukielski, who's been listening to his windbag of a professor all semester, it's an absolute pleasure. "Heller cut off his balls in front of the class." Immediately, Heller becomes one of Kukielski's heroes.[47]

Still on the Notre Dame campus around six o'clock, Heller visits Professor John Matthias's home for cocktails and a meal. A few dozen students have found a way to be invited to this private dinner event. One of them, James R., in his final year at Notre Dame, earns an invite thanks in part to taking a modern novel class. Upon entering, he notices that Heller is "dressed like a New York banker in a dark suit." To James, Heller looks good and tanned as he fields "questions and comments from a circle of about a dozen admirers."

James eventually wanders into Matthias's kitchen, waiting on an opportunity to talk to Heller about *Catch-22*, a novel he's devoured. As he waits, he notices a man in his forties, sitting "in the corner on a stool slouched over the counter—as far away from the living room . . . as one could possibly get without leaving the house." The kitchen is too crowded for the student to introduce himself to this man, who seems "crazy, imaginative, and gentle . . . but always with a touch of depression." This man, Kurt Vonnegut, has set himself up in the kitchen, away from his new author friend's zone of popularity. He'll soon leave quietly and head back to his room at the Morris Inn.[48]

Around seven, the group starts to negotiate rides back to the Notre Dame campus. A student rushes into the living room and cuts into the discussion by saying, "This doesn't have anything to do with the festival, but we've just heard that Martin Luther King has been shot." The television is turned on, and when the news appears, all becomes subdued. *Martin Luther King Jr. has been killed in Memphis.* As a pall of mute sadness descends on the home, Heller doesn't know what to think. Five-hundred people are waiting for him at Washington Hall. Such devastating news causes him to second-guess his appearance.

After a bout of confusion, Heller chooses to go on with his talk. There is a very good chance that many have been sitting in the crowd, unaware of the breaking news. In April of 1968, one either hears immediate news over a radio, the television, a phone call at home from a friend, or face-to-face. Because of this, a large percentage of the literary festival audience would now have to hear this news from the author of *Catch-22*.

At Washington Hall, a near-breathless Joseph Heller stands offstage a little before 8:00 PM. If he doesn't tell the audience the news, there is the risk that people will find out that he knew but didn't mention it, which might be construed as insensitive to Dr. King. If he does tell the audience, he risks losing their attention, the news eclipsing anything he can say or read. As he clears his throat, Heller knows he's about to enter a dramatic moment.

While Heller paces, just outside, sophomore committee member Tito Trevino walks with Kurt Vonnegut toward Washington Hall. Neither Trevino nor Vonnegut have heard the news about King, and they're enjoying the cool night. They are about to go into a door that leads backstage when they see Norman Mailer in a suit leaning against a tree trunk, smoking a cigar. Vonnegut finishes his cigarette, and Mailer walks over to Vonnegut and Trevino. "I'll never forget it," Trevino later said. After an exhale of resignation, Mailer looks at Vonnegut and says, "Did you hear the news?" Vonnegut shakes his head, and Mailer tells him blankly, "Martin Luther King's been shot and is dead."

Trevino is quiet. He then glances at Vonnegut, who appears as if someone has "punched him in the gut." Vonnegut has been stunned into silence. Nearly a minute passes, and he utters to Mailer, "Well, what are we going to do? Does Joe know?"[49]

Mailer says "Yes," and the three of them go backstage. Soon they find Heller in the dressing room, who at this point is a standing tower of nerves. Granville Hicks is nearby, and the group devises a plan. Mailer volunteers to tell the crowd before introducing Heller. But by the time they've figured out what to say, they hear a sophomore committee member speaking to the crowd. Mailer, Vonnegut, Trevino, and Hicks all quickly file into their reserved front-row seats.

Once the sophomore has everyone's attention, he says, "I think everyone should know that Martin Luther King Jr. has just been shot."[50]

A sudden collective gasp yields way to a wave of panicked murmurs. *South Bend Tribune* journalist Patricia Koval records how the "breezy, intellectual casualness disappear[s]" from the event. Just before the sophomore leaves the stage, he introduces "our featured speaker" this evening, Joseph Heller.[51]

What can Heller say? Besides their shared desire in ending the war in Vietnam, Heller has no personal connection to Dr. King. Heller shares his anxiety with the crowd: "Oh, my God. I wish I were with [my wife] Shirley now. She's crying her eyes out." He may be worried that the section of *Catch-22* he's chosen to read will come across as inappropriate. He stands there, borderline speechless. "I don't know what to say. I'm stunned."[52]

Not everyone in the audience is sad about King's death. Notre Dame graduate student James McKenzie is with his pregnant fiancée, Elaine, during Heller's talk, "sitting in an upper balcony in the rear." Behind the couple are two undergraduates, and they begin to do a bit of "stage whispering." As the topic of King's death is addressed onstage, the undergraduates say "About time" loud enough for others around them to hear. McKenzie is infuriated by their insensitivity, but the news is too devastating for him to confront them directly, so he lets it go. For the graduate student and soon-to-be father, "It's a silence I regret."[53]

Around the same time as the Heller talk, another sophomore committee member, Tom Schatz, sits in the Dylan Hall dormitory lounge. The television is on, and a group has gathered around, sitting on couches, stricken with a sense of despair as they listen to the news. One college student, however, stands up and pronounces, "God bless the man who shot Martin Luther King." Schatz can only shake his head, calling the moment "sad" and recalling how everyone in the room despised the statement.[54]

Heller plows through the gloom by keeping the discussion on *Catch-22*, a book that took him eight years to complete. In what must have been a hold-your-breath connection between King's decades-long fight for civil rights and the world of literature, Heller lets out a high-wire attempt at a one-liner: "If it were up to me to write *Uncle Tom's Cabin*, we might still have slavery." Heller then shrugs his shoulders.

Still visibly upset, he proceeds to tell the audience that while writing *Catch-22*, the novel "became an intensely moral book in spite of myself." The moral center involves the main character, Yossarian, and his struggle to survive World War II, "or die in the attempt."[55]

As he'd planned after hearing the news of King's assassination, Heller chooses to read "the Snowden death scene," perhaps the most powerfully dramatic section of the novel.

In chapter 41 of *Catch-22*, Yossarian has been stabbed under his arm and is put in a drug-induced haze by several untrained doctors. Soon, Yossarian enters a mind-set of "a prisoner in one of those sleepless, bedridden nights that would take an eternity to dissolve into dawn." Left with nothing to do but think, Yossarian reminds himself of Snowden, a young man who'd been viciously wounded by flak. It is arguably the most serious scene in the book, and also one of the hardest to take, thanks to Heller's visceral description of Snowden's two wounds: "The raw muscles inside twitched like live hamburger meat." When Yossarian opens Snowden's flak suit, he discovers underneath "God's plenty . . . liver, lungs, kidneys, ribs, stomach." As Yossarian tries to save his life, Snowden can only mutter, "I'm cold," over and over again. The only thing Yossarian can say in return is "There, there."[56]

The literary festival audience does not know the details of King's assassination, but they know he's been wounded—and many may have heard of his death. Heller's decision to read such a gut-wrenching and visual scene is bold, given the situation.

After his reading, there is a short Q and A. One college-aged student asks the author about Yossarian: *Could you put his existentialist nature into perspective?*

Heller, "good-naturedly," doesn't try to put on airs. "I'm almost ashamed to admit it, but I don't know what existentialism means." Heller's naked modesty wins over the uneasy crowd, and a local reporter writes that the "answer brought relieved applause and laughter from the audience."[57]

For McKenzie, the Heller event is a moment that will remain with him for a long time. He remembers Heller "mentioning that Snowden's refrain about cold came to him from Lear on the heath [Act III, Scene II]." It's "an unforgettable, powerful reading on a solemn, horrible night; I can never separate thoughts of King's assassination from the absurdities of *Catch-22*."

Later, when their son is born, Elaine and James McKenzie would give him the middle name King.[58]

Bobby's Moment

During the flight from Muncie to Indianapolis, Bobby Kennedy has only a little time to jot some thoughts down regarding King's death. It has already been a long day, and as he sits and broods, Kennedy's thoughts go back to the Black Ball State student he replied to. "You know," Kennedy says to *Newsweek*'s John J. Lindsay, "it grieves me . . . that I just told that kid [to have faith in white America] and then walk out and find that some white man has just shot their spiritual leader."[59]

When their Convair 550 lands at Weir Cook Airport in Indianapolis, Kennedy still thinks that King is in critical condition, as he'd heard in Muncie before boarding. He sends his campaign manager, Fred Dutton, to find out the latest news. Dutton comes back quickly and confirms that King is dead.[60]

Though he's had a plane ride to absorb the potential for bad news, Kennedy breaks down. Journalist David Murray, standing nearby, finds it unbearable to watch Bobby's reaction. "Oh God," Kennedy says. "When is this violence going to stop?" The manner in which King was killed multiplies the sense of devastation Kennedy must feel. The agony of November 22, 1963, opens up all over again, and Murray believes the news causes Bobby to relive "his brother getting it in the same way."[61]

A few short moments later, a reporter asks for a statement. Kennedy, perhaps using some of the language he'd prepared on the plane, dispenses a few sentences, appearing "tired and strained." "[King] dedicated himself to justice and love between his fellow human beings. He gave his life for that principle, and I think it's up to those of us who are here—fellow citizens, government—to carry out that dream, to try to end the divisions that exist so deeply within our country, to remove the stain of bloodshed from our land."

It's roughly a twenty-five-minute ride from Weir Cook to the Broadway Christian Center's outdoor basketball court, the site the Kennedy campaign had requested. They are already an hour late, so Bobby decides against visiting his campaign headquarters. He wants to reach the site as soon as possible. Telling Ethel to go to the hotel, Bobby sits alone in the backseat of the car.

With not much more than darkness to look out at, he wonders aloud, "What should I say?" Dutton is in the front seat, but his campaign manager doesn't have much to offer. At the moment, most of Kennedy's staff fears rioting and violence. Indianapolis mayor Richard Lugar asks the campaign staff to cancel the speech. He can't guarantee adequate protection if things get out of hand. But Kennedy refuses. A campaign staff member tells Lugar over the phone, "You're not going to get [Bobby] to do anything he doesn't want to do."[62]

They reach Broadway Christian Center. They're now running ninety minutes late, but a crowd of several thousand local residents, predominantly Black, wait around a flatbed truck parked on the basketball court. Two floodlights on either side illuminate the area.

Briefly, Bobby and his staff huddle together to discuss what to say. John Lewis, a member of the Student Nonviolent Coordinating Committee who'd already heard the news about his close friend and mentor Dr. King and who had helped the Kennedy campaign set up the event in Indianapolis, urges Bobby's staff to deliver the news. "You can't have a crowd like this come, and something like this happen, and then send them home without anything at all. Kennedy has to speak, for his own sake and for the sake of these people."

Kennedy, with a folded piece of paper in his hands, climbs onto the flatbed truck "stage" and gets the attention of the audience. The fringes of the crowd have already heard the news, but when Kennedy tells them that "Martin Luther King was shot and was killed in Memphis," there are gasps and screams for several seconds. Many in the middle of the audience hadn't yet heard.

Without looking at the paper in his hands, Kennedy takes his time with his words. In his mind are sentences he's put together on the plane from Muncie to Indianapolis, and also the work of Aeschylus's Oresteia. In the years after his brother was killed in Dallas, Bobby rediscovered his love of the Greek poets and plunged himself into their worlds in hopes of finding any semblance of reason to the universe: "Even in our sleep," Kennedy recites to the crowd, "pain which cannot forget/falls drop by drop upon the heart/until, in our own despair, against our will/comes wisdom/through the awful grace of God."[63]

As he speaks, the listener can sense Bobby reaching into himself, drawing out the words that help alleviate his own anguish:

> In this difficult day, in this difficult time for the United States, it is perhaps well to ask what kind of a nation we are and what direction we want to move in. For those of you who are black—considering the evidence there evidently is that there were white people who were responsible—you can be filled with bitterness, with hatred, and a desire for revenge. We can move in that direction as a country, in great polarization—black people amongst black, white people amongst white, filled with hatred toward one another. Or we can make an effort, as Martin Luther King did, to understand and to comprehend, and to replace that violence, that stain of bloodshed that has spread across our land, with an effort to understand with compassion and love.[64]

Without question, *this* is the Bobby Kennedy many Indiana county commissioners are hoping to see more of—a man full of depth and substance. In the future it will go down as one of the greatest speeches of the century, but since he delivers his remarks well past 9:00 PM, many national newspapers and television stations do not have the allotted space or time available to inform the public. Still, local newspapers find room for it on their back pages. Back near the Notre Dame campus, the *South Bend Tribune* manages to hear about the speech just in time to place a few of his remarks on the bottom left corner of page forty of their morning edition.[65]

As for the end of his April 4, Kennedy heads back to his hotel, where Ethel is waiting. He calls Coretta Scott King and tells her he wants to "help in any way I can." Coretta is grateful and mentions that she's "planning to go to Memphis in the morning to bring back Martin's body."

Bobby doesn't hesitate. "Let me fly you there. I'll get a plane down." Kennedy also hears from Coretta that dozens of well-wishers are calling her one phone line hoping to get through. He sees the need for more phone lines, and he calls on a few of his employees to bring to Coretta's house three extra telephones.

Exhausted, Bobby has one last planned engagement: a meeting with a local Black militant organization that John Lewis scheduled. They've been waiting a long while for Bobby to meet with them, and when he finally shows up, they're not happy: "Our leader is dead tonight, and when we need you we can't find you." They call him "the Establishment" and say he doesn't really care.

Kennedy replies with exasperation, "Yes, you lost a friend, I lost a brother, I know how you feel. . . . You talk about the Establishment. I have to laugh. Big business is trying to defeat me because they think I am a friend of the Negro." Kennedy's willingness to be honest and open impresses the organization. As the meeting concludes, the group pledges its support.[66]

Kennedy is finally able to head to bed. As he sleeps, over a hundred cities across the United States report fires, riots, and looting. Many later credit his calming, empathetic speech for helping Indianapolis avoid a similar fate.

LBJ Gets the News

President Johnson's April 4 starts around eleven o'clock in the morning, with Luci and her nine-month-old son Patrick Lyndon. They take a helicopter from the White House lawn to the air base, then a plane to New York, where they enter St. Patrick's Cathedral. Three-thousand Roman Catholics are seated and waiting to witness the installation service of Archbishop Terrence J. Cooke as "spiritual leader of the archdiocese of New York."[67]

Johnson is still riding high on a general wave of positivity. After his surrender of the office, a Lou Harris Poll will soon report his approval rating at 57 percent. A "complete reversal," according to an aide, since on March 30, one day before his announcement, 57 percent were against him.

As he, Luci, and his grandchild walk down the main aisle of the cathedral, the tightly packed congregation turns and gives him a standing ovation. Johnson tries to take it all in as the family makes their way to their seats in the first pew. Before today, only Pope Paul VI has "received a standing ovation in the cathedral."[68]

The service is two hours, and afterward President Johnson greets Jacqueline Kennedy for a moment and later promptly congratulates the archbishop at his home. Before heading out he meets up with New York governor Nelson Rockefeller and his wife, Happy, handing her a framed photo of them at the White House.

Perhaps still riding high from the applause and socializing, the president asks the helicopter pilot waiting for him in Central Park to head over to the United Nations for a quick chat with UN Ambassador Arthur J. Goldberg and UN Secretary-General U Thant in the hopes of applying more international pressure on peace negotiations in North Vietnam.

At 6:01 PM, Memphis time, the exact moment King is shot through the jaw, President Johnson is most likely in a helicopter flying from the DC air base to the White House. He hears nothing about King as he heads back into the White House. It's only while conversing with the president of Coca-Cola, Robert Woodruff, that someone informs him of the news around 6:30 PM.

Let's talk later, Bob.

A gauntlet of fears begins to enter the president's mind. *How bad is the wound? How will the public respond? How should I respond?* Johnson cruises through an abbreviated meeting with US ambassador to the USSR, Llewellyn Thompson, hoping to prep him for the time when North Vietnam finally does come up with an offer for peace. But all rational planning in this area is extinguished at around 8:20 PM EST. It's announced that Dr. Martin Luther King Jr. has been killed.

Just like that, the standing ovation at St. Patrick's fades from memory. . . .

Johnson immediately cancels his appearance at a $250-a-plate Democratic fundraising dinner with Vice President Hubert Humphrey, an event he wants no real part of anyway. He also cancels his plans to fly to Honolulu at midnight. With his schedule now open, the president starts crafting a message to be spoken on national television. Before any television appearance, a barber is necessary, so as Johnson gets his sides touched up, he and Joseph Califano thread together sentences meant to calm the general public: "I ask every citizen to reject the blind violence that has struck Dr. King, who lived by nonviolence."[69]

The statement ready and his appearance suitable for television, Johnson manages to get Coretta Scott King on the line and has flowers sent to her home. At 9:07 PM Johnson records his 175-word statement on the assassination: "I know that every American of good will joins me in mourning the death of this outstanding leader and in praying for peace and understanding throughout this land. . . . It is only by joining together and only by working together that we can continue to move toward equality and fulfillment for all of our people. I hope that all Americans tonight will search their hearts as they ponder this most tragic incident."[70]

He has a late dinner with Lady Bird, who calls it a "strange, quiet meal." She feels as if she and her husband have been "pummeled by such an avalanche of emotions the past four days" that they can't "feel anymore . . . poised on the edge of another abyss, the bottom of which we could in no way see."[71]

Later, as the president watches the three television sets in the Oval Office, he begins to hear reports coming in from across the nation— Americans staring into their own kind of abyss.

A Dark Minnesota Night

In Minneapolis a twenty-seven-year-old Black barber named Clarence Underwood sits in his home with his wife, six-year-old daughter, and newborn son. It's a little past ten at night, and he is deeply anguished by the news on the television—Dr. King has been assassinated, and Underwood is furious. "My King is dead," he says to his wife, who tries to calm him down.[72]

Tonight, however, is different, and with reports of rioting beginning to come across the television, Underwood is filled with a helpless torment. He is tired of being considered a second-class citizen, of being pushed down and bullied by the White power structure. He wants a revolution. From Underwood's perspective, the oppression is endless, and while he respects King's approach of turning the other cheek, what is there to do when the "enemy" turns for no one?

His wife pleads for him to come to his senses. They fight enough for their daughter to remember it for the rest of her life. Underwood grabs a .45-caliber pistol and says flatly, "My King is dead. I'm going out to get me a honky."

At 10:09 PM, John Francis Murray, a White twenty-five-year-old management trainee at F. W. Woolworth Company, sits on the bus. Recently married, Murray and his wife, against his father's wishes, have decided to live in north Minneapolis as proof that "whites could live in black neighborhoods." Ever since taking guff for hanging out with Black students in his university days, Murray has felt comfortable talking to the Black community.[73]

At 10:10 PM, the bus stops and the doors open. Murray walks down the bus aisle, and as he steps off, he sees Clarence Underwood moving along the sidewalk with his .45 aimed at him. A second or so passes and Underwood shoots Murray in the knee. He marches up to Murray, who is now on the ground as other witnesses surround the scene. Murray pleads to Underwood to stop, but the gunman is past the point of reason. He shoots Murray in the head three times.

Underwood doesn't try to escape. Local officers patrolling the area soon find Underwood, who now points his gun at the officers. "Shoot me," Underwood says. "They killed my King."

They don't, and after police fire a warning shot, Underwood puts his gun down and is taken away, his revolution incomplete.[74]

The Stoking of Carmichael

The phone rings around 8:00 PM in the DC apartment of twenty-six-year-old Stokely Carmichael, coauthor of *Black Power* and a core member of the Student Nonviolent Coordinating Committee (SNCC). It's his wife, Miriam ("Zenzi") calling just before appearing onstage at the Coconut Grove in Hollywood. "Are you all right, Stokely? I'm coming home. No way can I go onstage tonight. We have to be together at a time like this. Be on the first plane flying east."[75]

Carmichael is not all right. Like Underwood, he's seething with anger, but with his wife sobbing over the phone, he knows she is only partially crying because of Dr. King. She's also terrified that Stokely is next in line to be killed. After talking to his wife, who insists on returning home, Carmichael heads over to the DC office of the SCLC. He wants to know *who* exactly shot Dr. King.

The radio is on, and Carmichael tries to relax in a chair, but he can't. He calls a friend, and his comments drip with an end-of-the-world, do-or-die tone. "Well, if we must die, we better die fighting back," he says into the phone. It's as if his core is vacillating between violence and nonviolence, heart versus mind. "Now that they've taken Dr. King off . . . it's time to end this nonviolence bullshit."[76]

Carmichael can't continue to wait on the radio. "I'm going to get my guys," he tells a few of the SCLC staff members. They're worried. Is he about to join the rioting? What "guys" is he talking about?

For Carmichael, his "guys" means SNCC, and once outside he's able to get a few of the members in one place. Together they go "store to store, asking all businesses to close as a sign of mourning and respect."

But very soon after the stores close, Carmichael begins to "see and feel grief and loss turning to anger . . . rage . . . no one could have stopped it—you kidding?—no one." Nor does he "particularly want to."[77]

Carmichael's wife has reason to fear he'll be killed. In today's *Star-Gazette*, a newspaper out of Elmira, New York, Carmichael is called "a folk hero of his people," a firebrand with words that echo the separatist philosophy of Marcus Garvey but contain the urgency Malcolm X used to inspire crowds toward a new brand of confidence: "Never apologize for hate," Carmichael writes in a November 1967 letter to Black youths, quoted by the *Star-Gazette*. "If we hate white people, we hate them because we love our people so much."[78] With Malcolm X and now King assassinated, it appears to the general public that Carmichael better watch his back.

Hours after their call, Miriam comes through the door, and they embrace. Outside, smoke from riots fills the air; armed military has been deployed across DC's downtown, and a curfew has been established. It's enough for Miriam to recall her days growing up in apartheid South Africa, and she's relieved her husband is not "lying dead somewhere in the streets."[79]

Carmichael knows that the spotlight will be on him, and that the media will be awaiting his words. But tonight he grieves over the senseless death of a good friend and mentor. In his late teens, Carmichael burned with anger when he saw on the television Black students being "knocked off lunch counter stools, sugar in their eyes, ketchup in their hair." Working his way up through the ranks of the more nationalist-minded SNCC, Carmichael started seeing White terrorists shoot bullets into the homes of nonviolent supporters in Mississippi and Alabama, and as early as 1963, SNCC organizers started arming themselves with guns, pulling away somewhat from King's absolute belief in nonviolence. "If nonviolence could work, great. If it can't work, we'll try something else."

That something else turned out to be a phrase he uttered in June 1966 during a 220-mile march from Memphis, Tennessee, to Jackson, Mississippi, called the March Against Fear, or the Meredith March. Carmichael and others in SNCC had prepared to speak of Black Power in front of a loud crowd in Greenwood, Mississippi. Dr. King had left to do a media appearance that night, and the moment Carmichael shouted "BLACK POWER!" to the audience, the jubilant reaction surprised him, and he knew a philosophical repositioning toward individual authority, empowerment, and pride had started, and there was nothing the SCLC could do now to stop it from catching on. That same year, Carmichael helped form and launch the Black Panther Party of Lowndes County, Alabama.[80]

As he waits for the morning, blocks of downtown DC in flames, his thoughts remain with King, a man who Carmichael believes was one of the greatest mobilizers of the twentieth century. Carmichael reflects on the last time he spoke face-to-face with King. Although he can't remember the context, he does remember the last sentence King spoke before parting.

"Stokely, promise me you'll be more careful," King said.[81]

At the New School of Afro-American Thought tomorrow, there is a press conference planned. Originally scheduled to deal with SNCC member H. Rap Brown's controversial imprisonment for inciting a riot in Cambridge, Maryland, SNCC knows they will need to address Dr. King's death directly. They could simply cancel and send out a written statement, but Carmichael knows that the press will be looking to record his words and publish them nationally. It is a unique chance for his voice to be heard by the nation. He'll be careful, but not in the way Dr. King would have liked.

A Boy's Hope

In a house near Atlanta, a White nine-year-old boy named Billy Rankin sits on a couch in front of the television. His parents are in the living room down the hall, and hundreds of baseball cards are scattered around him. A special report flashes on the screen, and Billy sits frozen for a moment. He's heard about this man, usually good things, and he's now confused.

He vaults off the couch and thunders down the hall. "Daddy . . . Mommy . . . Dr. Martin Luther King has been shot! It said so, right on TV!"

Mr. and Mrs. Rankin miss the TV bulletin but flick on the radio and hear the news. A grim air fills the room, and for the next half hour the family sits together. He hears from television about marches Dr. King has done in the past.

As they wait for a new report, Billy asks his parents what seems like a simple question: "Was Martin Luther King a great man?"

His father answers him with quickness and certainty. "Yes, he was a great man."

Billy becomes even more confused. "Well, why would anybody want to shoot him?"

For Mr. Rankin, it's a simple question . . . "so pure." And yet he can't seem to come up with a satisfying answer. Perhaps it's Billy's innocence, or perhaps he himself is too saddened to come up with something that makes sense. But he tries. He tells Billy the truth, and the boy "becomes unusually quiet." Without any kind of a fuss, Billy takes a bath as his father heads over to the *Atlanta Constitution* newsroom to "help put out a newspaper."[82]

After his bath, Billy, still unusually quiet, remains close to the television. Inevitably, he hears the news that this great man he's heard of has now died. Mrs. Rankin encourages Billy to find a book to read to help calm his thoughts. Billy does, but the book remains closed as he sits in the same room as his mother.

It's at this point Billy decides to take out his 1967 Christmas present—a miniature squonk organ he'd neglected for many weeks. With his mother nearby, Billy decides on a marching song. In the middle of the living room, Billy plays "Onward Christian Soldiers," the smooth and mellow electric tone filling the room. Perhaps Dr. King would have liked the choice.[83]

It's a hectic night at the newspaper for Mr. Rankin. Atlanta is King's home, and the paper wants to do right by him and his family. After all the hard decisions have been made—*Which editorials do we run? How will people feel about the front-page headline?*—the paper heads to the printer.

When Mr. Rankin finally reaches home after midnight he checks on Billy and sees that his son is sound asleep in his bed. Mr. Rankin heads to bed himself, but not before hearing from Mrs. Rankin how his son played a marching song for a great man.

6

FRIDAY, APRIL 5, 1968

The Fallout of a Nation

Westside Chicago after the MLK riots, near Madison Street and Albany, April 1968. *Chicago Sun-Times.*

In the Mountains of Vietnam

On a rainy and windy night near Tam Ky, South Vietnam, on November 30, 1967, flight surgeon Capt. Floyd Harold "Hal" Kushner was "hanging upside down in a burning helicopter." His chopper had just crashed against a mountain and his left forearm and collarbone were fractured. During the collision he lost seven teeth and was eventually shot in the shoulder and neck by the random firings of a damaged M-60. He was lucky.

His pilot died immediately. When the crew chief headed for help away from the crash site, he was shot and killed after being spotted by North Vietnamese—a fact the twenty-six-year-old Kushner wouldn't learn until six years later.

Hal Kushner managed to crawl out of his crushed seat and wait near the helicopter with his badly wounded and immobilized copilot. That's what they were supposed to do—"wait with the aircraft until you get rescued." But after nearly three days of waiting without food or water, Kushner watched his copilot succumb to the darkened hands of death. Alone, he had a choice to make: Should he endure as long as he could at the crash site and hope for rescue or climb down the mountain with what strength he had left and search for help?

He chose to move.

Soon, Kushner found a rice farmer after reaching flat land. His uniform stood out, and he hoped that the medical insignia on his shirt would be spotted before he was shot. The rice farmer didn't shoot him. But that night, after Kushner guzzled a can of condensed milk, he was shot in the shoulder by a Vietcong member, his arms were tied, and he was forced to march for thirty days and hundreds of miles up into the mountains. The bottoms of his feet lacerated and torn, Kushner knew he had become a prisoner of war, or in the eyes of the North Vietnamese, a "criminal."[1]

In early January 1968, Kushner ended up in a jungle camp "in the Truong Son Mountain range of western Quang Nam Province, South Vietnam."[2] It was "triple-canopied," meaning next to impossible to be spotted by airplanes. As Kushner spent his days eating three coffee cups of "old, red mountain rice" laced with rat feces and sleeping on a bamboo palate with other POWs, he wondered if he'd ever see his then-pregnant wife and their three-year-old daughter again. Before the crash he was 5'8" and 165 pounds, but he had dropped about sixty pounds since. His maggot-infested wounds had been cleaned out by a fiery hot rod.[3]

He was joined a month later by a small group of POWs. They wore black pajamas and were asked to record antiwar messages in exchange for their potential release. Kushner refused, saying he would rather die, but two Puerto Rican soldiers who spoke Spanish decided to take the offer. Kushner, who also spoke Spanish, slid a handwritten message with ID information to one of the soldiers before their release, asking in Spanish for them to deliver it to someone in command. They did, and in March 1968, Kushner's family identified Hal's handwriting.[4]

Around this time, the Vietcong attempted to separate Kushner and other POWs by race. They placed five Black soldiers in one hut, or "hooch," and the Caucasian soldiers in a separate hut. The North Vietnamese had been following reports of racial discrimination in the United States and believed they would be able to indoctrinate the Black Americans against their country. But their plan failed, and the prisoners "let them know that" they preferred to remain together as Americans. And so they did, battling malaria and dysentery as they were put to work carrying wood and elephant grass and building shelters. Through it all, they took care of each other, cleaning and nursing the men who had become too weak to work.[5]

On April 4, after Dr. King was assassinated, the news reached a North Vietnamese newspaper. They published a report with the headline A BLACK LEADER IS MURDERED BY SUBVERSIVES.[6] The news reached Kushner's jungle camp, and soon the Vietcong were attempting to leverage King's death to convince Americans to speak out against their country, claiming the death and the resulting riots were "part of the struggle of the American people against their government."

Then Kushner witnessed firsthand the will of the North Vietnamese to win the war outright. "You can kill ten of us to one of yours," a Vietcong told Kushner and the others, "but your people will turn against this, and we will be here, for ten years, or twenty years, or thirty. Unless you can kill every one of us, we're going to win this war."[7]

Hate Mail in Atlanta

On the morning of April 5, cities across the United States put on peaceful but fractious marches in honor of Dr. King. In Atlanta, a thousand Black students and the six local college presidents gather at the nearby Morehouse gymnasium and decide to march through the west side of Atlanta. When White Atlanta mayor Ivan Allen—one night removed from breaking the news to Coretta Scott King at the airport about Dr. King's death—asks to participate, the main student organizer rejects him: "This is a black people's march."[8]

Meanwhile, the *Atlanta Constitution*'s seventy-year-old White publisher, Ralph McGill, has written a provocative editorial about the assassination titled "A Free Man Killed by White Slaves." McGill, no stranger to controversy, writes that "at the moment the triggerman fired, Martin Luther King was the free man. The White killer, (or killers) was a slave to fear, a slave to his own sense of inferiority, a slave of hatred, a slave to all the bloody instincts that surge in a brain when a human being decides to become a beast."[9]

McGill is well known for fighting against segregation and helping Dr. King's cause over the years with supportive editorials that have gone against the Deep South's status quo. King respected him enough to even name him an ally in his 1963 "Letter from Birmingham Jail."

Like King, McGill has received his share of death threats over the years, and now, since major newspapers such as the *Boston Globe* have also decided to run McGill's April 5 editorial, angry phone calls, telegrams, and letters come in throughout the day.[10] Most of the messages are kind, McGill will later write, but intermingled with these are spikes of hate.

"I just want to say that the death of old King is the greatest news since the Second World War ended," says one caller to a secretary working at the *Constitution*.

An unsigned letter comes in that day as well: "Many of us peace-loving, God-loving humans today unite in thanks to our God for delivering us and ridding humanity of one who has caused so much violence, bloodshed, and discord . . . we thank God that King is dead."

And one handwritten grenade, lobbed from Massachusetts:

Mr. Ralph McGill,
I read your article about how the white beast and slave who shot down Martin L King is an animal. Well Mr. McGill a son of a bitch like you don't come out and say in print anything in your paper about the poor cab driver that the niger [*sic*] students killed and burned his cab in South Carolina, at the Negro Colledge ten days ago. You Godamn Bum your just a poor excuse for a white man you son of a Bitch I hope some <u>goddamn</u> niger does the same to you you Bastard. Long live a Real American Mr. George Wallace[11] a real whiteman not a <u>shit</u> <u>Bum</u> like you you should drop dead you half ass white no good son of a Bitch.

I hope your daughter, if you have one, gets raped by some godamn Niger.[12]

Perhaps most disconcerting to McGill is when one writer attempts a twisted logic to validate the assassin's actions: "It is sad that Dr. Martin Luther King Jr. was shot in cold blood in America, but he also reaped what he sowed. He taught people to disobey laws, and his assassin simply disobeyed the law against murder."[13]

From one extreme to another, however, a White poet named Sara Schulman contributes a poem titled "April 4, 1968" and sends it to the *Atlanta Constitution*. The shame Schulman feels, the desperation and desire to connect with Black people flows over:

Today I'd like to black my face
and walk among the human race

I'd like to stand somewhere and shout
Look—I know what you're all about

But I'm afraid that they would say
Bullshit—your conscience hurts today

My conscience hurts—today I feel
that part of me just isn't real

That someone made a bad mistake
and gave me something—something fake

That I must destroy and throw away
Or else I can't survive today

and so before it is too late
I'll decide which part to amputate

If I could cut away my skin
no one would know just who I've been . . .[14]

Aloha Nonviolence

Nearly 4,500 miles away, at the University of Hawai'i at Mānoa's Hemenway Hall, six Black students sit behind a podium, poised to speak their mind to an interracial crowd of five hundred about how Dr. King's death has affected them. Organized to be a memorial service, there is no solemnity to be found here. Not today. The young men onstage are angry, and the first student, Bob Cole, lets the audience know it. "The death of Martin Luther King, my black brother, killed any hope I had that there is any decency in this country. . . . I don't want to be accepted any longer. I don't want to be assimilated any longer. I want blood!"

Wally Fukunaga, a local coffeehouse owner, has sponsored the event after listening to Cole and other Black students mention a need to communicate their feelings to a large audience. Initially, the Black students had asked other students, White and Asian, to talk, but just before the meeting starts, they change their mind. At least today, only Black people get the podium.

Cole continues, speaking directly to White students, "It's time to take up arms and live or die for a cause. Honky, you blew your game when you thought we were harmless, ignorant, oversexed people, and if you still believe that today, I want you first!"[15]

Cole sits down, and another student onstage takes his spot. Quieter than Cole, he mentions his heartbreak, saying to the crowd that "what happened last night was that the white man killed the black man who loved him most, and if you think all the people up here hate you, you're right, because the man that loved you most is dead and there's nothing but hate left."

One of the Black students then leads the audience through a version of "He's Got the Whole World in His Hands" (changing "He" and "His" to "We" and "Our"). The crowd goes with it, but once it's over, a Black student sitting with the rest of the crowd requests the speaker's platform. He has "things I want to say from my heart to the people here in this room."

The young man collects himself before he tells the crowd, "It's very easy to come to a memorial service and shed tears and feel bad and get angry and then go home and forget it—this is what's been happening in this country for three hundred years."

At first he sounds reasonable, near defeat, but he can't remain civil. He lets it out. "There's nothing but hate left! You'd better get that straight, baby—the summer has begun!" He looks over the quiet crowd and sees that a few avoid making eye contact. "I am Ralph Ellison's Invisible Man—Goddamn it, look at me! Don't sit there—I'm trying not to be invisible!"

He takes a moment to regain his composure. He's lost and frustrated, but today he has company and a chance to speak from the heart. "Hate isn't an easy thing to say, and neither is love, but I think before I can love my white brother, my white brother is going to have to love me—and before the barriers can be brought down, we're all going to have to live together like decent human beings."[16]

Hope and Apathy in La Jolla

On the University of California, San Diego, campus, college administrators organize a morning meditation event in the hopes of providing a safe space for students to grieve and ponder the death of Dr. King. For many enrolled students, this is not nearly satisfying enough, and several hundred young men and women have already decided to organize and march into downtown La Jolla, an area they choose because of its "wealthy and conservative . . . whiteness." Along the way to the downtown area, local La Jolla residents see the swell of interracial student demonstrators and decide to join the crowd. Soon the number of marchers reaches six hundred.

Now in the center of La Jolla, several of the main organizers ask store owners who have an American flag on display to fly them at half-staff. This doesn't go smoothly. *No, thanks . . . his death hasn't impacted me that much,* several owners say. A back-and-forth takes place, but no violence. Instead, organizers hand-deliver a flyer to anyone in the community who will take one. On the flyer is a three-hundred-word message:

> For the past few years, the oppression of the black people has become inescapably real to virtually every American. It has been brought into every living room on the television screen; its reality has been affirmed by politicians and expert panels after expensive and lengthy investigations. But the oppression of the black people in America has been a hard and clear fact for the past two hundred years. White America stands guilty of the crime of silence—of evasion, cruelty and injustice for that whole period. But at this point these evasions and injuries cannot be avoided. White America must face up to its past and its present.
>
> The murder of Martin Luther King by a white man means, unfortunately, the virtual end of efforts by the black community to try to talk reason, peace, and love to the white majority and the white politicians who run this country. Peaceful attempts to demonstrate the reality of the oppression of the black community have been answered for years by political platitudes which come to nothing. Now these attempts have been answered by violence. The murder of Martin Luther King is, for a very great number of blacks, the last straw of tolerance. There will be riots this summer and the summer is starting early. Can white America face up to the real cause of the problem— that the real cause is the white community itself? Is it too late for white people to respond with a humility that springs from an awareness of what they have been doing for the past two hundred years? Or is this country going to be torn in two?[17]

In a UC San Diego classroom the same morning, a distraught biology professor named Michael Soulé, talking to his nearly empty Biology 113 class, derails his lesson plan to talk about the tragic interconnectedness of the '60s assassinations. He implores his "apathetic" students to take more initiative and resist the urge to remain passive. Several of the students don't share their professor's sense of urgency, however. One smart aleck who believes in his own inactive passivity, says that if the King assassin "had been apathetic," instead of angry and proactive, King would still be alive.

Professor Soulé gives up. *Best to stick with biology.*[18]

Missoula, Montana, Locks Arms

On the University of Montana campus in Missoula, three hundred students, faculty, and administration attend a silent ceremony in honor of Dr. King, similar to the one in UC San Diego. After the event, several hundred decide to march into downtown Missoula, but forty marchers have other ideas.

This group, led by UM professors, decides to go into a downtown realty office and demand an end to racial discrimination to off-campus housing. One of the professors indicts the fair-housing injustices of the realty office on a portable loudspeaker. Police are called in, and when the group of students and professors are asked to leave, they refuse, choosing instead to lock arms and legs. Eventually, seventeen are arrested, but not before bringing local media attention to a longtime issue of Dr. King's—better fair-housing laws, a political issue currently on the mind of President Johnson.[19]

A President Is "Hobbled"

In Jefferson City, Missouri, the *News-Tribune* responsible for publishing two excessively angry editorials about Dr. King on the day of April 4, finds itself surrounded Friday morning by two hundred students from historically Black Lincoln University. They carry signs that read, "Your newspaper killed nonviolence—let's see you kill racial hatred." Another sign grabs the attention of company staff. "You have only your newspaper to blame for his death."

Setting aside a few thrown rocks and glass bottles breaking near the building, the group, organized by Lincoln University's Student Government Association, remains nonviolent while standing in the parking lot. As local residents drive by and see the crowd, newspaper employees come out to ask what they want. The president and president-elect of Lincoln's SGA come forward and ask to enter the building.

Once inside, the young men talk directly to Robert Blosser, the president of the *News-Tribune* newspaper. "We have come here because of the discontent regarding the editorial you ran on Dr. King . . . your editorial aroused many of the students because we are Negroes. We want something run showing the good side of Dr. King."[20]

They also want a statement of apology and a retraction. Blosser agrees.

Several minutes later, Blosser steps outside the *News-Tribune* building and speaks loudly to the hundreds of demonstrators: "The *News and Tribune* deeply regrets the assassination of Dr. Martin Luther King in Memphis, Tennessee. The *News and Tribune* is definitely not opposed to the Negro and his efforts toward gaining equality in all facets of community living." As for the editorials, "We certainly had no idea at that time that violence would take the life of Dr. King—and, nor do we feel that our words encouraged the Memphis sniper to pull the trigger. We, as loyal Americans, must pull together. We are in sight of peace in Vietnam where our soldiers, Negro and white, are fighting as brothers. This was the goal of the Reverend Dr. Martin Luther King Jr."

"Boo!" shout many of the students. Blosser sounds insincere and, perhaps most offensive to the students, incorrect. Dr. King's goal was not for Americans, Black and White, to fight side by side in Vietnam. King wanted the war to end, and for Americans, Black and White, to *resist* fighting in Vietnam. Perhaps Blosser only means King's goal is for Americans to become "brothers," but his lack of accuracy is costly. As he's strongly jeered, a rock is thrown and hits him in the leg. Another rock whizzes by his head, and Blosser heads back inside, the crowd moving closer to the building.

After a brief meeting, the editor of the newspaper opens the front entrance and announces that the *News-Tribune* will "run material reflecting credit to Dr. King for his achievements."

But a fraction of the crowd is still unsatisfied. "We want a complete retraction!" Another demonstrator shouts, "Say what you said was wrong."

A group of no more than fifteen then pushes ahead and forces the front door open. The two SGA leaders shout for them to stop, but it's too late. A plate glass door is torn off its hinge and broken, and a group of young men get into the office. A telephone is thrown to the ground, but soon police come in with hard hats and nightsticks and move the demonstrators back outside. The crowd disperses, many of the marchers now angry at the newspaper and the small group who decided to use force. "They're ruining the whole thing," says a female marcher. "They said this was going to be nonviolent."[21]

Stokely Carmichael's Message to the Nation

Later on April 5, in the lobby of DC's New School for Afro-American Thought, Stokely Carmichael has the attention of the national media. He wears dark sunglasses, a white-collared shirt, and a loose-fitting jacket, and stands behind a waist-high table filled with microphones. Behind him on the wall to his left is a photo of H. Rap Brown, to his right a poster of Malcolm X. The looting, arson, and vandalism in DC, especially along Fourteenth Street, has been unrelenting since last night, but since there hasn't been a figurehead to pin the blame on, Carmichael is aware that he may just be that man.[22]

He starts in a mellow tone and asks that "Brother" H. Rap Brown be set free for crimes he has not committed. "When white America killed Dr. King last night, she declared war on us. . . . We have to retaliate for the deaths of our leaders. The execution of those debts will not be in the courtrooms, they're going to be in the streets of the United States of America. . . . There no longer needs to be intellectual discussions, black people know that they have to get guns."

The press conference lasts only twelve minutes, despite SNCC organizers only wanting it to last five. After Carmichael's initial two-minute statement, SNCC formally sends its condolences to the King family. Then the Q and A starts, and tempers flare . . .

Reporter: Mr. Carmichael, don't you believe that a vast majority of Americans feel just as badly as you do about what happened in Memphis?

Carmichael: The white press . . . from honky Lyndon Johnson to honky Bobby Kennedy will not co-opt Dr. Martin Luther King. [King] fought for his people. Was it not but four weeks ago when Johnson told King that if he came marching into the district he'd meet a force, because he should bring his trouble to him? And now tonight he's trying to make as if Dr. King was his hero. He fools no one. Bobby Kennedy pulled that trigger just as well as anybody else. 'Cause when Dr. King was down in the South and Bobby Kennedy was attorney general, every time a black person got killed, Kennedy wouldn't move because he wanted votes, so he's just as guilty. All of white America killed Dr. King. And those who feel sorry ought to feel sorry.

[. . .]

Reporter: Mr. Carmichael, what do you think will happen to the Poor People's Campaign now?

Carmichael: I understand that the Southern Christian Leadership Conference will carry it on, and as we said before we will be glad to give support. Whatever the Southern Christian Leadership Conference asks for today, we will give to them, except our tears. We will give no more tears for any black man killed in this co—

Reporter (*interrupts*): Mr. Carmichael do you see anybody replacing Dr. King as a nonviolent leader?

Carmichael: No, that's why America lost when she shot him down last night.

[. . .]

Reporter: When you say the "execution of those debts" will be not in the courtroom but the streets, can you be a little more specific about the course of action you expect?

Carmichael: I think that is quite explicit.

Reporter: Do you expect an organized rebellion?

Carmichael: I think it is quite explicit.

Reporter: Mr. Carmichael you talked a lot about how black people have to die in what you're proposing . . .

Carmichael: That they take as many white people with them as they can.

Reporter: Yes, but what about the black people who have to die.

Carmichael: Uh, we die every day. We die in Vietnam for the honkies, why don't we come home and die in the streets for our people? We die every day, we die cutting and fighting each other inside our own communities. Why cut and fight and kill each other off? Let's kill off the real enemy. Black people are not afraid to die. We die all the time. We die in your jails, we die in your ghettos, we die in your rat-infested homes. We die a thousand deaths every day.

[. . .]

Reporter: Mr. Carmichael what's the alternatives for the kind of retribution in the streets that you're talking about. Is there any way to stop it?

Carmichael: I don't think so. I do not think so. I think White America is incapable of dealing with a problem.

Reporter: How will Dr. King's death affect your leadership as you see it, Mr. Carmichael?

Carmichael: Well, Dr. King's death will not affect my leadership. It will affect me as a black man, because he was my brother, flesh of my flesh, and blood of my blood. See the mistake they made when they shot Dr. King was, even though Dr. King talked about nonviolence, he was always in the streets, ready to lead a demonstration. All of the other so-called leaders who talk about nonviolence are not on the streets with their people. So, many people respected Dr. King even though they didn't agree with his philosophy 'cause at least he was in the streets. So now there is really no one else to respect who talks about nonviolence, because the people who talk about nonviolence are not in the streets.

Reporter: Mr. Carmichael, are you declaring war on white America?

Carmichael: No, white America has declared war on black people. She did so when she stole the first black man from Africa. The black man has been sufficient, has been patient, has been resisting, and today the final showdown is coming. That is clear. That is crystal clear. And that black people are going to have to find ways to survive. The only way to survive is to get some guns, 'cause that's the only way white America keeps us in check, because she's got the guns.

Reporter: What do, uh, what do you see this ultimately leading to? A bloodbath of which nobody wins?

Carmichael: First, my name is Mr. Carmichael, and secondly, black people will survive America.

SNCC Organizer: Last question!

Reporter: What accomplishments or objectives do you visualize from the retaliation of what you sp—what do you think to hope to acc—

Carmichael (*interrupts*): A black man can't do nothing in this country that we're gonna stand up on our feet and die like men, and if that's our only act of manhood, then goddamnit, we gonna die . . . [*Organizer shouts one last question.*] . . . We're tired of living on our stomachs!

White Reporter: Do you fear for your life?

Carmichael: The hell with my life, you should fear for yours. I know I'm gonna die. I know I'm gonna die. [*Scattered applause.*][23]

Hours later, at the end of the half hour of *CBS Evening News with Walter Cronkite*, fifty-five-year-old journalist Eric Sevareid delivers his ritual two-minute segment, lauding King as "the most important American of his time, white or black. He more than any other man wielded a cutting edge to history for this time and place. He preached love so hate of course destroyed him, as it destroyed two thousand years ago the man whose gospel he followed, as it destroyed twenty years ago in India the man whose strategies he adopted."

As for Carmichael, Sevareid, after hearing the New School press conference, can't help but compare the young revolutionary to the most heinous villain of the twentieth century: "To blame everyone [for Dr. King's death] is to blame no one. Only the Hitlers of this world, and their spiritual kin like young Mr. Carmichael believe in mass guilt and genocide as justice."[24]

LBJ Searches for a Middle Ground

The White House's American flag has been lowered to half-staff, and all day thick plumes of smoke from the nearby DC riots waft by, blocking out the sun. In the morning and on little sleep, a beleaguered Johnson leads a meeting with twenty-one civil rights leaders. He has heard Carmichael's threatening words, and as the group sits around the long table of the Cabinet Room, Johnson starts the meeting by quoting Carmichael's volatile words challenging "black people to strike back at white America."[25]

Supreme Court justice Thurgood Marshall is then called on by Johnson to give his thoughts. Marshall, being a man of law, has always had mixed feelings about Dr. King's methods, believing that people "have a right to disobey the law," but also have "the right to go to jail for it." But with entire blocks of DC on fire, he doesn't see the patient tactical strategies King often employed throughout his life. He sees anger reaching a boiling point. Bottom line, he tells Johnson, the demonstrations need to stop. "The important thing is to keep people out of the streets and change the mood of the country."[26]

It's a reasonable statement, but not something Johnson needs right now. He needs potential solutions, not measurement.

It's not exactly a civil meeting. Several attendees allow their frustration to show. One man, thirty-four-year-old Gary, Indiana, mayor Richard Hatcher, carries the unsettled air of the Carmichael generation. He declares America a fundamentally racist country.

Rev. Leon Sullivan, a pastor at Philadelphia's Zion Baptist Church, understands that Johnson has not called this meeting simply to grab reasonable statements and understandable anger. Reverend Sullivan hits the pulse point of everyone sitting around the table. "The large majority of Negroes are not in favor of violence, but we need something to fight back with. Otherwise we will be caught with nothing."[27]

Yes, that *something*. To Johnson, that means passing unprecedented legislation in support of civil rights. Ever since 1966, Johnson has been attempting to pass through Congress a national fair-housing bill. On the surface, the bill sounds harmless enough, but as White House aide Joseph Califano witnessed in the last two years, the fair-housing issue "prompted some of the most vicious mail LBJ received on any subject," even death threats toward Califano. Dr. King also saw firsthand in Chicago this anger when placing the issue on the lap of Mayor Richard Daley. King "had never seen such hate—not in Mississippi or Alabama—as I see here in Chicago." Back in August 1966, King had even devised a strategy of going into random Chicago real estate agencies to see how direct the discrimination had become. "Every time Negroes went in, the real estate agent said, 'Oh, I'm sorry, we don't have anything listed.' And then, we sent some of our fine white staff members in to those same real estate offices, and the minute the white person got in they opened their book, 'Oh yes, we have several things, now. What exactly do you want?'"

At the midway point of the meeting, the group heads over to the Washington National Cathedral to attend a memorial service for Dr. King, where the minister had preached five days ago about "remaining awake through a great revolution." It seems everyone is awake now. The crowd at the cathedral is in the thousands, larger than the ceremony after the assassination of John F. Kennedy in 1963. With ongoing violence and turbulence throughout the country, the government now stands at his attention. All it took to get it was his life.

When the meeting starts back up again, Johnson tells the group his plan to push through his fair-housing bill and lets them know its current status. As of April 5, 1968, the bill has been approved by the Senate, but would have met its death in the House. Johnson hopes, and he isn't shy in saying this, to use King's death as a way of getting the bill through the House, where stubborn politicians must balance the interests of their local constituents with their own opinions.

The bill will not come close to achieving King's dream of a beloved and integrated community, but it can, Johnson thinks, be a start.

In the afternoon, the mayor of Washington, DC, Walter Washington, has had it. The looting and rioting have overwhelmed the downtown area, and he puts in a request for Johnson to send in federal troops to restore the peace. He does, but without ammunition. "I don't want Americans killing Americans. I may not be doing the popular thing, or even the right thing, but no soldier in Washington has killed a citizen yet."

Now with federal troops, the mayor sets down a 5:30 PM to 6:30 AM curfew and forbids retailers to sell liquor or guns. In the White House,

Califano's room becomes a "command center" as he continues to receive reports of rioting in major cities, such as Chicago, where police do have ammunition.[28]

Four Dead in Chicago

> *"I say to the power structure in Chicago that the same problems that existed and still exist in Watts, exist in Chicago today, and if something isn't done in a hurry, we can see a darkened night of social disruption."*
>
> —Martin Luther King Jr., 1966[29]

At 2:00 PM, police superintendent James B. Conlisk places a call in his office to Chicago mayor Richard Daley. For the last several hours, Conlisk has witnessed a large gathering of young Black teenagers, many high schoolers, breaking windows and stealing from various businesses. Conlisk has already dispatched most of his 11,500-officer police force to break up the crowds, but there are simply too many, and they aren't listening. "The problems are so widespread, Mr. Mayor," Conlisk says on a private line, "that I feel the national guard should be sent in to assist us in maintaining law and order."[30]

Mayor Daley has been hearing reports as well. Quickly he calls the Illinois governor and puts in a request. At 2:30 PM, on the West Side of Chicago near the intersection of Oakley Boulevard and Madison Street, the first fire alarm goes off at a furniture store.[31] Hundreds more will soon be set off.

A firefighter witnesses the arsonists and reports that "they're walking west and burning as they go."[32] Two miles south in North Lawndale is the building where King had decided to live in January 1966 and to push for fairer housing practices. This will also soon be on fire.

In the next forty-eight hours, 162 buildings on the West Side will be destroyed by fire and 268 broken into.[33]

By 4:00 PM, businesses and factories begin seeing the fires and smoke in the distance. Sensing trouble, managers begin sending their employees home early, and eighty elementary and middle schools close to protect their teachers and students. It appears everyone in the city has the same idea: *Get home, quick.* While this seems like a sound idea, it turns into a disaster. Soon highways are clogged with traffic. Police cars have trouble reaching problem spots because of the congestion, as do firetrucks.[34] People who are injured and trying to call the hospital or police department must contend with jammed phone lines.

As the sun begins to set, businesses find themselves with no protection from looters, so they make rash decisions like asking "gang members" to help protect their inventory, but, perhaps predictably, as the riots become more intense, the gang members help themselves to a bit of the merchandise. Even more dire, some small business owners strapped for cash recognize a chance to collect insurance and secretly ask a trusted acquaintance or two "to help torch" their own places.[35]

The first rioter killed is a teenager. At sixteen years old, Ponowel Holloway is more privileged than some of his Chicago friends. He has a mother and father at home, three brothers, a sister, and a grandmother to look after him. He's a sophomore at John Marshall High School and "crazy about science." He hopes to one day work in the electronics field. To help pay bills and for a bit of pocket change he's taken a job at a nearby restaurant as a busboy. Around seven at night on April 5 Holloway is making his way home from his part-time job through Chicago's West Side.[36]

There is smoke and fire around him from the riots, groups of Black Chicago residents, most under thirty years old, going in and out of stores stealing. There is the sound of gunfire in the distance. Finding himself in the middle of the frenzy at 4135 Madison Street, he sees the Maybrook's department store with a large amount of its merchandise already stolen. On an impulse, Holloway makes his way to the rear of the store to grab what he can. As he does, several eyewitnesses see multiple police officers with automatic rifles right outside the store. The officers "shoot the lock off the front door and enter the store." Holloway is shot in the "upper right chest" and found dead at 7:15 PM. He is unarmed.[37]

At thirty-four, Cyrus Hartfield has been grinding it out for nine years as a packer for the Central Soya Company, carving out enough time to sing for a local church choir. With a wife and four sons living nine hundred miles south in Beaumont, Mississippi, Hartfield has been sending as much money as he can home. Tonight, at around 7:30 PM, he's made his way over to Madison Street and plans to send a fifty-dollar money order overnight using a currency exchange. He has made plans to leave Chicago for Beaumont to spend Easter with his family. Hartfield has written to his wife stating that he'll "bring the children clothes."

At 7:35, twenty minutes after Holloway's death, Hartfield decides to enter a women's clothing store very near Maybrook's. Perhaps he sees the dozens of looters around him, the fire, and thinks he can grab a gift for his wife . . . but instead he is shot and killed inside the store. Hartfield's brother, who lives nearby, hears the news and sits in "horrible shock." Hartfield "just worked hard all the time, trying to pay his way. . . . All he could talk about was putting his kids through high school and college."[38]

It's 8:00 PM, and thirty-one-year-old Robert Dorsey and his wife are having dinner with his sister. For the last several hours they've been keeping their eye on the fires two blocks south along Madison. They've heard gunfire as well, and Dorsey grows concerned that it will soon spread into his sister's neighborhood.

Dorsey is no newcomer to Chicago. For the last six years he's worked as a truck driver for a local equipment company. His boss calls him "a hard worker, a real good man" and "very reliable." As for Dr. King's death, Dorsey feels it is a "terrible shame" but simply believes "the law should take care of the murderer." For Dorsey there are other priorities to consider, such as one day fulfilling a dream and buying a home on the South Side and adopting some children.

They finish dinner around 8:30 PM, and Mr. and Mrs. Dorsey debate whether to walk home. They're expecting a long-distance call from Mrs. Dorsey's mother, who lives in St. Louis. This, combined with worries about their own apartment, is enough to give the walk a try. Before they leave, Robert tells his sister to "keep the kids in the house . . . stay back from the windows, and don't have no lights burning."

Their apartment is a mile away, and they choose to avoid the darkness and volatility of Garfield Park and walk west along Madison Street, but everything they see is on fire.

They make it to Keeler Avenue, their turn-off, but down the street police officers are firing their rifles in the air. They choose to walk one more block down Madison and take a left on Kildare Avenue.

As they do, they reach an alleyway, a shortcut to their home. At 9:15 PM, a half block away from their apartment, the couple hears shots fired, "like a machine gun." Dorsey shields his wife and pushes her to the ground, falling on top of her back. Dorsey asks his wife, "Are you all right?" She is, but blood gushes from Dorsey's stomach as he sits up—a bullet has hit him in the back and come out the other side.

Minutes later nine policemen, four with rifles, run to the couple. Mr. Dorsey is bleeding out. "Who shot him?" the policemen ask Mrs. Dorsey, but she doesn't know. Nearby, young children shout at the police officers. "Stop shooting! Stop shooting! You've already killed one man!" At 9:30 PM, before an ambulance can arrive, Mrs. Dorsey feels her husband "give a little jerk" and pass away. It's not until 9:45 PM that police carry Mr. Dorsey into their squad car and take him to the local hospital.

His wife is clear on one thing: "I didn't see anyone shooting but the police."[39]

————————

At twenty-four, Paul Evans is trying to turn his life around. People who know him call him "quiet," a people-watcher. He has struggled for awhile to find work, but an employment agency called the Urban Progress Center lands him a job washing dishes. It's not a dream job, but it'll do. On Friday morning, he asks his sister for carfare and meal money. She helps him out but warns him, "There is going to be trouble tonight. Don't stand around and be watching, you come on home and be careful."

But at 5:30 PM, after his shift has ended, he's "watching boys and girls breaking up all the windows."

Hours pass as Evans looks at the looting occurring around Maybrook's department store. At 10:45 PM he is only one block away from where Robert Dorsey was killed, and behind the store where Holloway was killed. One of his sisters sees him, but Evans isn't rioting. He's not armed. He's simply watching the fires. There's a shout: *Here comes the police!* In the same alleyway, police come running both ways. His sister runs in one direction, but Evans, running west, is shot in the neck, chest, and abdomen. Taken to the hospital, Evans hangs on long enough for his mother to see him. Just before his mother is able to call on a pastor to enter the room, he passes away at six in the afternoon of the following day.[40]

Within a three-and-a-half-hour span on April 5, four young Black men have been mortally injured by gunshots "within a two-square-block area" along Madison Street.[41]

Despite eyewitness testimony from people literally across the street, police float the idea that "sniper fire was coming from a city parking lot south of the buildings during most of the evening."[42] But since Holloway and Hartfield are killed *inside* a building, a sniper *outside* seems geographically impossible.[43]

Not until midnight do six thousand national guardsmen finally reach the West Side, but by this point a two-mile stretch of roaring fires blazes as thousands of firefighters fight to extinguish the flames. Over a thousand West Side sanitation workers help clear rubble and assist the firefighters.[44]

The night sky is red, and it appears chaos has momentarily taken over the city of Chicago. But a pattern emerges from the arson. Setting aside a few Black businesses committing insurance suicide, just about all the businesses burned down or looted are "white institutions" or "white-owned stores." Many witnesses to the burning say that looters feel "joy" as they steal, a "dance of death."[45]

But as buildings unsupported by city funds crumble, as an underfunded infrastructure is burned to the ground, residents say that Friday, April 5, is not about Dr. King's death but instead "the first step in the political independence of the [Chicago] black community." For those traumatized and physically wounded, however, local residents only see "senseless violence" that doesn't "prove a thing. [It] just hurt so many innocent people."[46]

South Bend Grieves

At ten in the morning, ninety miles east from Chicago, the city of South Bend grieves over the death of Dr. King. An interracial crowd of four thousand local residents—construction workers, students, teachers, businessmen, politicians, and police officers—marches to the St. Joseph County Courthouse for a one-hour ceremony. Many in the crowd are led there by Black students from John Adams High School as the Catholic church bell tolls. All the surrounding Catholic schools have closed out of respect for Dr. King. Public schools, however, go on as usual, although administrators do excuse any student who wishes to attend the ceremony, as long as they get parental approval.[47]

Mayor Lloyd Allen, hoping to avoid the anger rippling throughout the country, addresses the thousands while standing at the top of the courthouse steps: "[Today we mourn] the senseless hatred (that) has taken an authentic apostle of nonviolence. The cowardly act of a sick personality has created new tensions in a nation that is striving to build an atmosphere of freedom and opportunity for all its people. These tensions must not be allowed to penetrate our city. Instead, we must use this sorrowful occasion to rededicate ourselves to the cause of human rights." The mayor brings the county courthouse American flag to half-mast and tells the crowd it will stay there until after Dr. King's funeral.

Conrad Kellenberg, a White professor of law at Notre Dame who had helped the city rewrite South Bend's fair-housing laws in the early '60s, uses words more direct than the mayor: "There is a virus of white racism in our land, and there is racial injustice and inequality in our nation and in our community. There is also poverty [and an] inactivity of those whites who know better and can provide the leadership to do better."[48]

The service ends with the crowd singing "We Shall Overcome," but the civil rights anthem, at least for today, has lost its resiliency. Over the course of the day there are no riots, only a lingering sadness.

Back on the Notre Dame campus, the literary festival crowd is demoralized. A fatigued John Mroz doesn't attend the downtown ceremony, and Granville Hicks senses a "terrible sadness" hanging over the day. Meanwhile, Wright Morris, devastated by the tragedy of Dr. King's death, is battling doubts about participating in tomorrow's symposium.

With satirist Kurt Vonnegut set to speak at 4:00 PM, no one knows what to expect, but, at least to Hicks, laughing at anything feels like an "embarrassment" and disrespectful to people in mourning.[49]

The Tragedies Within Kurt Vonnegut

On Sunday morning, May 14, 1944, Mother's Day, Kurt Vonnegut's sister Alice woke him up early. *It's Mom*, she whispered, her eyes concerned.

Vonnegut slid out of bed. He was twenty-one, and on a three-day furlough from the army. Together they walked to their mother's bedroom; their father was asleep in another room.

Normally, their mother would be writing a romance. A writer for years, she had yet to have one published, but continued to try. Ever since the start of the war and her youngest son's efforts to go over to Europe to fight, her depression had deepened. Before marrying a Vonnegut, Edith had been raised in a high-class lifestyle, but over the years Kurt's father's modest salary had constricted her dreams of travel and adventure.

Kurt walked in that Sunday morning and bent over her bed to see that she appeared more than asleep. She was dead. Sleeping pills. Not even a note.

It affected Kurt on a fundamental level. He had always been closer to his mother and sister than his conservative father and older brother, Bernard. In fact, it was around the dinner table as a child that young Kurt developed his wit. With Bernard and his father discussing science and architecture, and his sister and mother enjoying a bit of daily gossip, the only way the youngest son could attract any attention was to tell a few jokes. After all, he had already been called "an accident." To Kurt, "the only way the youngest kid . . . can hold attention is by being surprising."

At times, Alice, five years older, joined him as they perfected comic timing via the radio, memorizing bits from "Abbott and Costello, Burns and Allen, or Laurel and Hardy." Unifying his serious-minded family through humor was the glue to Vonnegut's childhood. He continued to think of himself as a humorist for a while at Cornell, writing pieces for the college newspaper, but soon World War II yanked his mind toward an obligation to his country, and away from a mother who had left him behind.[50]

Seven months after his mother's devastating suicide had wreaked havoc on his thoughts (*Why Mother's Day? Did she ever love me?*), on December 16, 1944, Vonnegut found himself on the front lines fighting Hitler's troops in western Germany. It was Hitler's last stand, the beginning of the Nazi leader's last gasp—the Battle of the Bulge—and Vonnegut's 423rd Division was being used as bait, one of its purposes being to "step on mines or draw fire." The German forces overwhelmed his division's position, and after three days of fighting he was captured.

He was one of thousands of prisoners of war, marching along a river for two days until they reached a freight train. When Vonnegut sardined himself into one of the boxcars, he smelled a powerful dose of "fresh cow dung." As Vonnegut will later write, the boxcar became "a single organism which ate and drank and excreted through its ventilators. It talked or sometimes yelled through its ventilators, too. In went water, loaves of black bread and sausage and cheese, and out came shit and piss and language."

On December 23 British planes spotted the train and, thinking it was full of German cargo, proceeded to drop bombs and open fire. One boxcar filled with sixty-three soldiers exploded, their bodies spattered across the snowfield. Vonnegut could see them through narrow slats. One wounded man, on the verge of death, shouted, *Will someone please shoot me?*[51]

After a weary Christmas, Vonnegut, along with tens of thousands, finally arrived at a prison camp, but had to wait overnight to be processed. The Germans ordered them to sleep in the snow. Weakened already, some around Vonnegut froze to death. He battled frostbite, but lived.

For two weeks, Vonnegut recovered. He'd been given his Geneva Convention–required postcard and wrote home, but the correspondence didn't reach his family for months. They'd only been told he was missing in action. "That's that," said his uncle.

Through random selection, he was one of 150 chosen for prison labor in the city of Dresden.

In Dresden he was bossed around by a man with a black eye patch who yelled at the prisoners and called them "gangsters." Vonnegut cleared rubble off streets and would forage for mouthfuls of expired food within the piles. Others risked being shot by hiding some for later.

Around 10:00 PM on February 13, 1945, a squadron of hundreds of Royal Air Force bombers flew over Dresden. Throughout the night, and on and off for the next two days, bombs were dropped on roads, munitions factories, railroad storage facilities, and historic buildings filled with centuries-old artwork. An estimated twenty-five thousand people were killed in the firebombing, and Vonnegut waited it out in an underground structure filled with large slabs of raw beef on hooks attached to rafters that shook from the concussive blasts.

Vonnegut emerged from the bowels of *Schlachthof-fünf* (Slaughterhouse-Five) and saw that Dresden was but a skeleton of its former self. He was ordered to dig into basements of buildings and bring out the corpses of those who had suffocated. Working with a line of prisoners, Vonnegut opened basements that resembled "a streetcar full of people who'd simultaneously had heart failure. Just people sitting there in their chairs, all dead."

When the piles of bodies were burned and soldiers and prisoners exhausted, the Germans realized there were simply too many bodies to pull out. Plan B: Vonnegut and others were to "recover items of identification and valuables only." The corpses were then set ablaze by a flamethrower.[52]

In late March 1945, one POW working in the basements, Michael Palaia, took a "jar of pickled string beans" and hid it under a coat he'd randomly taken from a pile. The coat had the letters CCCP, written on the back—once worn by a Russian. Many Germans had a deep hatred for anything reminding them of the Russians, and demanded he take it off. He did, and out came his jar of string beans. That night, Palaia, Vonnegut, and four others were ordered to take shovels and march to the top of a nearby hill. They dug two holes. To show the other prisoners not to steal, the Germans executed Palaia and a Polish soldier. They ordered Vonnegut and others to bury them.

After the war ended and Vonnegut was reunited with Alice and the rest of the family, it was Palaia's merciless death that caused him to cry out in anger. "The sons of bitches!" he shouted to his uncle Alex. "The sons of bitches!"[53]

September 15, 1958. Vonnegut was now a married father of three juggling the short story magazine market, sending works of fiction to the *Saturday Evening Post*. His brother-in-law, James Adams, was visiting Alice in the hospital. She was in the last stages of breast cancer and didn't have long to live. Adams stayed with her as long as he could before heading to work on the 9:14 AM New Jersey Central commuter train. He needed to continue providing for their four children.

It turned into tragedy. The engineer controlling the train's speed suffered a massive heart attack and lost control. With not enough time to stop, the first two passenger cars careened off a drawbridge and into Newark Bay. Adams, in the second car, died, as did forty-six others.[54]

With Alice near death at the hospital, Kurt and Bernard believed it would be too devastating to deliver the news. But Alice called home and found out anyway. She asked Kurt, her childhood comedic partner in crime, to take the kids. He said yes, and just before she passed away, thirty-six hours after her husband, she muttered her final words to Kurt and her four boys: "Don't look back."[55]

Kurt had lost his authorial end point, his muse. Alice was "the person I had always written for. She was the secret of whatever artistic unity I had ever achieved. She was the secret of my technique." With her passing, Vonnegut's own life train had derailed. He would need to live as if floating—disconnected from certainty.[56]

A Comic Waltz Through Tragedy

> *"Sons of suicides seldom do well. Characteristically, they find life lacking a certain zing. They tend to feel more rootless than most, even in a notoriously rootless nation."*

> —Kurt Vonnegut, *God Bless You, Mr. Rosewater* (1965)

Novels of satirical madness followed—*The Sirens of Titan* (1959) had a "chrono-synclastic infundibulum," a place "where all the different kinds of truths fit together," and *Mother Night* (1961) included one of the only morals Vonnegut has ever believed in: "We are who we pretend to be, so we must be careful about what we pretend to be."

But it is *Cat's Cradle* (1963) that gave him a strong presence on college campuses and struck a positive chord with writers such as Theodore Sturgeon, who jokingly warned readers that they "better take [the novel] lightly, because if you don't you'll go off weeping and shoot yourself."[57]

In the novel, Vonnegut invented a religion, Bokononism. A Bokononist believes "that humanity is organized into teams, teams that do God's Will without ever discovering what they are doing." It is a religion of lies, but lies meant to make the world a better place. On page five, he offered a warning to the reader: "Anyone unable to understand how a useful religion can be founded on lies will not understand this book either."[58]

For devout Christians and many over the age of thirty, the novel was tossed to the side as fluff, but as ripples of revolution began to overtake the '60s, *Cat's Cradle* struck a chord with a counterculture seeking to upset the absolutism of the government and its military. At Notre Dame in 1968, sophomore committee members passed the novel around, but two English majors took their Vonnegut obsession to another level. Since Notre Dame required all undergraduates who declared themselves Catholic to take eight theology courses, and all non-Catholic students four, these two students decided to take *Cat's Cradle* to the head of the theology department. *We are no longer Catholics*, they told the professor. *We are Bokononists now. Please halve our theology requirement.* Since the religion was in a published book, and Vonnegut had defined its principles specifically in his novel, the students' request was granted.[59]

On April 4, a few hours before Dr. King's death and before heading over to where Heller is staying, Vonnegut has an early dinner with Notre Dame professor Dr. Richard Bizot—his wife's prized burgundy beef. Bizot has also invited one of his students—one of the two Bokononists. "Mr. Vonnegut," says Bizot. "I'd like you to meet John Grima, who subscribes to a religion you invented."

Vonnegut is thrilled. He and Grima head into the living room and take off their shoes and socks. They sit on the floor and push the bottoms of their feet together. It's called *boko-maru*, or a meeting of the *soles*. It's meant to help lighten the pain people carry within.

Yet it is his "Dresden book" that drives him mad during his stay at Notre Dame, a book that has haunted him for over twenty years, ever since surviving World War II. In a January 1966 letter to his editor, Vonnegut wrote that the novel, eventually to be called *Slaughterhouse-Five*, was "going slowly, because I am busting my ass sentence by sentence, but you should have it all handily by June." He headed back to Dresden for a bit of on-the-ground research, but found it now resembled "Cedar Rapids in 1936."[60] Tweaks on top of tweaks, then, in a March 18, 1968, letter to a former student named Charlotte, he wrote that "I guess my book will be done in a month." He called it a "teeny-weeny thing," a "series of telegrams. It takes a long time to accumulate a book of really good telegrams."

He ended the letter by telling Charlotte, a participant in McCarthy's "children's crusade," that she had Vonnegut's "permission to go to bed with Eugene McCarthy. Give him anything he wants."[61]

On April 5, in the early afternoon, Kurt Vonnegut and Joseph Heller have set up a peculiar press conference in the lobby of a building on the Notre Dame campus. They want to make an announcement: *We are actively raising money for Eugene McCarthy.* They will be the "special guests in the home of Dr. and Mrs. Harry A. Ludwick." Between 4:00 and 7:00 PM, they will mingle with others and coax them into donating to the one politician who actually needs it.[62]

Kurt Vonnegut circa 1968. *Photo Courtesy of Indiana University Lilly Library.*

Vonnegut tells reporters, such as the *South Bend Tribune*'s Patricia Koval, that he'll "do all he can for McCarthy's presidential ambitions by campaigning in the Indianapolis area [his birthplace] when he leaves South Bend."

Vonnegut allows Heller to do most of the talking. In one of his comments, Heller, perhaps unaware, lifts the Minnesota senator into the ether of a Bokononist. "McCarthy is a candidate about whom it is not necessary to tell any lies. He profits from every comparison with all other candidates." Vonnegut also mentions McCarthy's popularity among "authors, artists, and entertainment people," such as Paul Newman and Dustin Hoffman.

But who will you support if he doesn't get the nomination?

Vonnegut is mum. Koval offers Kennedy as an answer, and Heller shrugs, but he's not happy about it. Without explaining why, Heller says, "I would actually prefer Governor [Nelson] Rockefeller."[63]

With cameras around, Koval notices that the authors seem "uneasy" in this kind of spotlight. Vonnegut eventually does speak. "The trouble is, we don't know anything." He gives Heller a bit of a nudge. Heller then says, "It doesn't stop anybody else from talking."[64]

———————————

Hundreds of students pack into the library auditorium at 4:00 PM. The gloom of Dr. King's death still hangs over most of the crowd. Granville Hicks grabs a seat and wonders how this man known for his off-brand sense of humor can push through this doom-filled day, as does journalist Patricia Koval.

Vonnegut stands onstage with a chalkboard by his side. His talk is titled "Teaching Writers to Write," and many of the sophomore committee members sit in attendance. One of them, William Locke, sits with a copy of *Mother Night* on his lap. As he waits for the talk to start, he observes an "extremely nervous" Vonnegut waiting to be introduced. His sophomore guide, Tito Trevino, meanwhile, waits off to the side, not yet having read any of Vonnegut's novels.[65]

After being introduced, Vonnegut opens by pretending to confess a deep secret: "I don't like my profession very much. I feel like I'm sick most of the time." He's not serious, but he pretends to be, and the audience can't help but become hooked to the "witty, salty and very casual" delivery. He goes on to talk about his time teaching at the University of Iowa, but again undercuts anything he may represent. "English departments don't produce writers, because they teach taste too soon." Still, he doesn't regret his time attempting to *teach* writing. He was rewarded, and, as the former PR man for General Electric tells the audience, "[Money] definitely cheers people up."[66]

Now that he has detonated anyone's expectation to be taught the art of writing, Vonnegut attempts it anyway. He draws a vertical axis and puts a G at the top and an I at the bottom: Good Fortune and Ill Fortune. He then draws a horizontal axis in the middle and writes B on the left and E on the right: "B is for Beginning, and E is for Electricity." He means "Ending," but everyone knows that. Vonnegut does not smile too much as he draws his rudimentary graph, but the audience can't help but feel lifted into his mind for the moment.

Vonnegut goes on to draw the plot lines to *The Scarlet Letter*, and *Cinderella*, the latter being his go-to for hilarity:

> Surprisingly enough, it's depressing that people usually don't like stories about below-average people . . . but we're going to start at [low ill fortune]. Worse than that, who is so low? It's a little girl. What's happened? Her mother has died. Her father has remarried a vile tempered ugly woman with two nasty big daughters.

At this point, Vonnegut waits for the snickering to subside, then, in what Hicks describes as an "expressionless" manner, delivers the punch line. "You heard it?"[67]

Yes, they have. Vonnegut continues, perhaps briefly relating to Cinderella's situation due to his own tragic past. "Anyway, there's a party at the palace that night and she can't go. She has to help everyone else get ready. Now, does she sink lower [on this chart]? No, she's a staunch little girl and she has had the maximum whack from fate, and that is the loss of her mother. She can't go any lower than that."

Without showing vulnerability, Vonnegut dials up the laughter once again, drawing "stairs" on the board and shows how Cinderella is able to lift herself out from ill fortune. Eventually, Vonnegut reaches the end by drawing a sharp diagonal upward, telling the crowd laconically that Cinderella "finds the prince, the shoe fits, and she achieves off-scale happiness."

The audience loses it. One sophomore committee member, fifty years later, still thinks it's "one of the best stand-up comedy routines" he's ever seen. Tito Trevino remembers "spasming" with laughter, while others struggle to breathe. He goes on to talk about writer's block, writing sex scenes, and for more than a half hour the audience forgets the doom and gloom floating through the nation's streets. Granville Hicks, not exactly a natural laugher, calls Vonnegut's timing "perfect . . . he seem[s] again and again to be throwing a joke away and then suddenly, in an offhand, absentminded fashion," gives "it the unexpected twist that" brings a "burst of laughter like an explosion."[68]

Hicks also very insightfully notices that, considering the circumstances, the audience's laughter is "embarrassing to him as well as to us." But both speaker and audience understand that a healthy release is occurring. To Hicks, Vonnegut's humor is a "necessary relief" amid such dark times. Later, Hicks will help launch a new look for Vonnegut's future speaking lectures. After seeing this performance, Hicks compares his method to "that of Mark Twain—at least as interpreted by Hal Holbrook." Vonnegut does value Hicks's opinion, and from the time *Slaughterhouse-Five* is released and beyond, Vonnegut will grow a mustache and floppy hair—as if declaring himself the second-coming of Mark Twain.

Vonnegut's performance will spike his popularity around the country, but today's talk/act hasn't come easy. When Joseph Heller walks up to congratulate him at the end, he notices that Vonnegut is drenched in sweat. Later Vonnegut will undercut himself again by saying that "all I had to do [that day] was cough or clear my throat and the whole place would break up. . . . People were laughing because they were in agony, full of pain they couldn't do anything about."

Vonnegut's pain never seems to fade, however. After signing a few books he has a little bit of time to kill before hearing Ellison speak, so he asks Tito Trevino to take him to see the Grotto of Our Lady of Lourdes on campus—a replica built in honor of the famous French shrine. As he stands and stares at the hundreds of lit candles underneath a ceiling of boulders, he doesn't pray to the Virgin Mary but instead, according to Trevino, tries to wrap his mind around why the University of Notre Dame would "go to all this trouble to make a copy of this."

Vonnegut chuckles to himself and mutters, "Are you kidding me?"[69]

Like many, he is still bothered by King's death. On April 5 he is nearing the end of the completion of a draft of *Slaughterhouse-Five*. In two months, in the wake of Robert Kennedy's assassination after winning the California primary, Vonnegut will add a mention of their deaths in chapter 10 of the novel:

Robert Kennedy, whose summer home is eight miles from the home I live in all year round, was shot two nights ago. He died last night. So it goes. Martin Luther King was shot a month ago. He died, too. So it goes. And every day my Government gives me a count of corpses created by military science in Vietnam. So it goes.[70]

Vonnegut's timing is off regarding King's death (it would have been two months ago) but the sincerity remains, and it's a reflection of the times—how so much has happened in such a short window of time.

So it goes. . . .

Kurt Vonnegut Meets Ralph Ellison

In the early summer of 1966 Vonnegut was teaching graduate-level creative writing at the University of Iowa. Andre Dubus, who had been teaching undergraduate rhetoric and composition, was asked by his director to go in person to Vonnegut's home and see if the author could meet Ellison at the local airport. Ellison was scheduled to appear on the Iowa campus.

Dubus, a young aspiring novelist at the time, went ahead and invited himself along on what he foresaw as a fun road trip with two popular authors, Vonnegut being far less known than Ellison, but excellent company, especially if drinks were involved.

Vonnegut picked up Dubus and they headed off to the airport. Soon enough, Dubus confessed to Vonnegut that the University of Iowa "didn't really ask for both of us to pick up Ellison. Just you."

Vonnegut smirked. "I knew that."

Along the way, Dubus and Vonnegut soon realized that neither of them had actually seen Ellison in the flesh. Without coming out and saying it, both men assumed, being in the Midwestern cornfields of a predominantly White city, that Ellison would be easy to spot. . . .

Dubus attempted to bat away the awkwardness. "How are we going to recognize him?" he asked Vonnegut. "Do we just walk up to the only Negro who gets off the plane?"[71]

Vonnegut, his eyes previously on the road, glanced at Dubus and said one word: "Shit." Dubus was unsure if Vonnegut said *shit* because, by stating the problem out loud, Dubus had actually doubled the potential awkwardness of finding someone based solely on their skin color or if Vonnegut was simply perplexed as to whether they'll be able to find Ellison without a picture.

Dubus bet on the former. "We could just walk past him, pretend we couldn't see him."

Vonnegut gave a smiling shake-of-the-head reply. "That's so good, we ought to do it."

Eventually, the two men reached the airport terminal and watched as "one black man" came off the plane. Vonnegut went up to the man and said, "Ralph Ellison?" The man replied with a knowing smile, "Yes."

Dubus sat in the back seat, and Ellison saw a paperback copy of his novel *Invisible Man* while climbing into the front. At first, Ellison ignored it, and instead talked about hunting pheasant with Vonnegut's current colleague and friend, novelist Vance Bourjaily. Soon enough, however, Ellison picked up his first and only novel and flipped through the pages. "It's still around," he said, Vonnegut driving them all past cornfields back to campus. Vonnegut wanted to make sure Ellison knew that he hadn't simply placed the book on his seat out of some generic gesture of courtesy, so he told Ellison that he was using the novel in one of his workshops. Before going too far into their art, however, Vonnegut asked Ellison a very important question: *Do you want a drink?*

Ellison did, and pretty soon the three men were putting down vodka martinis at a bar just off campus. An enthralled Dubus and a now-relaxed Vonnegut sat on one side of the booth as Ellison riffed on jazz and books.

Ellison, who had grown very accustomed to talking about his novel since its electric debut in 1952, told Vonnegut about the massive impact André Malraux's 1933 French novel *Man's Fate* had on his own novel. Malraux's book was loaded with philosophical yet revolutionary overtones, and Ellison had blown through it "forty times" along with a heavy dose of Dostoyevsky just before and during the creation of *Invisible Man*.

Somewhat randomly, Dubus then brought up "In Another Country," a short story by Ernest Hemingway that Dubus had grown to love and recently reread. Ellison, also an admirer of Hemingway, dazzled his two travel companions by reciting from memory the first part of Hemingway's story: "In the fall the war was always there, but we did not go to it any more."[72]

The two men were impressed. After a few rounds, Vonnegut dropped a travel-weary Ellison off at his room on campus. Ellison's wife, who disliked flying, was now waiting at the train station, and Vonnegut had been told by the director to pick her up as well. Before leaving his room, Vonnegut asked Ellison a question, perhaps tongue-in-cheek, perhaps not: "How will we recognize her?"

Ellison played along. "She's wearing a gray dress and a beige raincoat." Oh, "and she's colored."[73]

Ralph Ellison and MLK—Separate Roads (1956–1968)

For just about the entirety of the Montgomery Bus Boycott, Ralph Ellison lived with his wife in Italy. He'd accepted a position as a fellow at the American Academy in Rome. As Martin Luther King Jr. was beginning to become a national figure, Ellison watched his rise from a distance, far more invested in making progress on his second novel, a manuscript that would eventually balloon to over two thousand pages and remain unpublished until his death in 1994.[74]

Ellison's first reaction to King and the bus boycott came in a private letter to close friend and novelist Albert Murray. When Ellison and Murray corresponded with one another, they were close enough to have in-jokes, such as calling *Invisible Man* the "you-know-what" during its creation and calling African Americans in general "mose"—a creative mix of a biblical Moses seeking the promised land and, according to Ellison's literary executor, John Callahan, a "sly and cunning Negro trickster whose subservience is a mask behind which he slips the racial yoke and turns the joke on the white folk."[75]

Ellison expressed genuine excitement about the news coming out of Alabama. "I feel a lot better about our struggle though, mose is still boycotting the hell out of Montgomery," Ralph wrote on March 16, 1956, three months after the bus boycott had started. When he mentioned seeing photos of old Black preachers, Ellison let his language fly: "Some of them look like the old, steady, mushy-mouthed, chicken-hawk variety; real wrinkle-headed bible pounders . . . in the pictures [they] look like they've been to a convention where they'd caught some son of a bitch not only stealing the money, but sleeping with all their own private sisters!" Still, Ellison had to admit, "They're talking sense and acting! I'm supposed to know Negroes, being one myself, but these moses are revealing just a little bit more of their complexity."[76]

At that point in time, Ellison and most of the world knew very little about King, but, judging from his opinion of old-time preachers and how they acted as if the year were "1915," his clever list of job titles shows that Ellison may have believed King would have to be a little bit of everything to galvanize such an archaic group of authorities. "Leader [possibly MLK] is a young cat who's not only a preacher but a lawyer too, probably also an undertaker, a physician, and an atomic scientist. And they're standing their ground in spite [of] threats, assassinations, economic reprisal, & destruction of property." Ellison went on to blast an idol of his, Southern author and first Notre Dame literary festival honoree William Faulkner, who'd written an editorial for *Life* magazine suggesting the movement "wait a while" and talk things through. But Ellison, as King believed too, knew that "mose isn't in the market for his advice, because he's been knowing how to 'wait-a-while' for over three hundred years, only he's never been simply waiting, he's been probing for a soft spot, looking for a hole, and now he's got the hole."[77]

After Rome, Ellison, thanks in large part to the help of friend Saul Bellow, accepted a teaching position at Bard College in New York. In 1958, Ellison was a bona fide professor, an academic who had never graduated from college. The steady income was a welcome change for him and his wife, but Ellison had never been one to enjoy too much comfort. This was the same man who had so little money to attend Tuskegee Institute that he had to hop trains as a "hobo" from Oklahoma to Alabama. Ellison was also a semi-professional trumpet player and photographer. The comforts of university life were reassuring, but he soon found himself needing to feel closer to his own artistic pulse.[78]

In a September 28, 1958, letter to Murray, Ellison revealed his insecurities. Eight days before he wrote the letter, Martin Luther King

Jr. was stabbed at a Blumstein's department store in Harlem during a book signing of *Stride Toward Freedom*. It may have been a surprising yet empathetic moment for Ellison to conjure, since he too, during the release of *Invisible Man*, had sat down in stores to sign books. Izola Curry, the woman who stabbed King near his heart with a six-inch letter opener, was Black, and after her arrest, Ellison was gobsmacked to see newspapers reporting that White Southerners had been sending her donations to help with court fees. This incident, mixed with his own precarious situation, rolled into one during his letter to Murray:

> I know how depressing it is to see Negroes getting lost in the American junk pile and being satisfied with so little after all the effort to break out of the South. It makes you want to kick their behinds and then go after Roy Wilkins [head of the NAACP] and that crowd who still don't see that Civil rights are only the beginning. Or maybe I should go after myself for not being more productive and for not having more influence upon how we think of ourselves and our relationship to what is truly valuable in the country. I'm trying in this damn book [his second] but even if I'm lucky one book can do very little. And wouldn't a damn nutty woman pick King to kill instead of some southern politician? I'm surprised that she wasn't torn to shreds right there on the spot. The New York papers are reporting the gifts of money and letters of well-wishers which the crackers are sending this bitch . . . and they think we're fighting to become integrated into that insanity![79]

The closest Ellison ever came to being publicly linked to King's cause was on February 6, 1965, when he, along with sixteen other "authorities in the field of human relations" attended a conference in New York City for a program the SCLC called "Operation Dialogue." Spearheaded by two White employees in King's SCLC, Harry F. Boyte and intercultural education expert Rachel Davis Dubois, the purpose of Operation Dialogue was to reach across racial and economic division and work out differences through "group discussion and conversation." But after several months of false starts, Operation Dialogue never really took off, and Ellison didn't stay with it long enough to help with promotion, nor did he bond in any way with King (who decided not to attend the February meeting) during its implementation.[80]

Two weeks after the conference, Malcolm X was assassinated in Harlem, and as time moved on and the idea of Black Power became popular, Ellison started to receive questions after his lectures such as *Do you think your* Invisible Man *is a precursor to Malcolm X?* and *Would you ever write about someone like Malcolm X in your fiction?* Ellison, a strong believer in using myth to communicate truth, responded as only he could, "I wouldn't dare to tell the truth about him. It would destroy the same myth. And this myth is a valuable myth." Still, Ellison had no desire to communicate his support of Malcolm's cause; his intellectual pride wouldn't allow it. "I don't want Malcolm telling me what American history is, and I don't want him to tell me what my experience has been."[81]

Ellison had never liked being nudged toward one side. He was the kind of artist who seemed more comfortable fluctuating between ideologies. He had never wanted to be a "man of the times" but rather a "man of times." Pigeonholes were for the gullible. And when there was controversy, Ellison tended to run to the middle and point out the shortsightedness of those around him.

In 1967, as Dr. King moved farther away from the Johnson administration's policies involving Vietnam, Ellison continued to move closer to the besieged president. Pretty soon, the author could be found on several committees helping to shape Johnson-pushed organizations, such as the National Endowment for the Arts. Ralph and Fanny attended luxurious White House dinners. They were complimented and wined and dined by important political figures. In an essay titled "The Myth of the Flawed Southerner," Ellison, who grew up in segregated Oklahoma, showed sympathy for Johnson's struggles to be taken seriously as an intellectual, blaming Northern liberal elites for judging how intelligence is supposed to sound. Ellison went on to compare LBJ to Lincoln and encouraged the American public to look at what the president had done domestically as opposed to "staring blindly at the fires of a distant war."[82]

By siding with an unpopular president, resisting a full nod of approval toward Dr. King's integrationist approach, and dismissing Malcolm X as nothing more than a necessary myth, Ellison inevitably provoked backlash from the younger generation, White and Black, who believed the author was simply afraid to take a stand and would rather mingle with the predominantly White power structure than connect with his own race.

One especially painful moment occurred on the weekend of October 27, 1967. Ellison and Dr. King visited Iowa's Grinnell College campus as a part of a three-day convocation. Ellison agreed to be a part of a panel discussion titled "Urban Culture and the Negro." From his Friday start, Ellison's support of Lyndon Johnson and blurry opinions of Vietnam seemed out of place among liberal arts students hoping to make an impact. As *Harper's* editor Willie Morris pointed out, the people in attendance at the panel were "especially hard on Ralph Ellison."[83]

Perhaps unafraid of the self-righteous attitudes of college students, Morris brought Ellison over to a student's apartment late Saturday night. The party was "a mold of the decade," according to Morris, with folk singers, guitars, and candles all around the room. Future California senator H. I. Hayakawa was enjoying the vibe, along with CBS News president Fred Friendly. Ellison and Friendly were bantering with students about the poison of television advertising when there was a "loud roar of a motorcycle outside." Within moments, a man dressed like a Black Panther ("black leather jacket and black beret") burst through the door. He'd ridden his motorcycle four and a half hours from Chicago. Quickly, Ellison was surrounded by this man and another Black student. The young men had read *Invisible Man* but hated the ending for what they believed it stood for: "giving in to oppression rather than fighting it."

Ellison, a bit drunk, disagreed, but the defense of his novel quickly turned into a defense of himself against this Chicago Black Panther. With a raised voice that stunned the party into silence, he delivered a verbal blow to the author: "You're an Uncle Tom, man! You're a sellout. You're a disgrace to your race."

If words could knock the wind out of someone, this was the time. As Morris observed, Ellison became so stunned with anger that his features were "transmuted, the muscles of his body tensed." Once the initial blow had been absorbed somewhat, Ellison fought back. "I resent being called an Uncle Tom," and followed it with a wave-of-the-hand dismissal. "You don't know what you're talking about. You don't know anything. What do you know about my life?" He pointed his finger at the man. "It's easy for you. You're just a straw in the wind. Get on your motorcycle and go back to Chicago and throw some Molotov cocktails. That's all you'll ever know about."

The confrontation over, Ellison felt a wave of shame overwhelm him and placed his head on the shoulder of a Black Grinnell student from Mississippi. "I resent being called a Tom," Ellison said while sobbing. "I'm not a Tom. I'm not a Tom."

It only took a moment or two for Ellison to put his shield back up. While sitting on the outside front steps, Morris apologized to Ellison for bringing him to the party. Ellison didn't need the apology. His tears, it turned out, had been building over the years. "I've heard that kind of thing for a long time. I'm used to it."[84]

The next day, Sunday morning, Dr. King expressed his moral outrage over Vietnam, sermonizing that the fight "could turn into a third world war." Wearing a black robe and preaching to a congregation of five thousand Iowa residents packed into Grinnell's gymnasium, King was in his antiwar element. Meanwhile, a rally on the same day called for LBJ's impeachment. By this point Ellison had retreated to his vacation home in predominantly White Plainfield, Massachusetts, where his unfinished manuscript awaited his attention.[85]

One week after the Grinnell debacle, on November 5, Ellison received John Mroz's invitation. Perhaps still rattled by his poor Midwestern experience, Ellison sent his swift reply to Mroz, deferring his decision to a Chicago speakers bureau.

However, three weeks later, on November 29, he and his wife were driving back to their house in Plainfield when they saw it in flames. "Faulty electrical wiring" was the unsatisfying explanation. The home had burned to the ground, and a massive portion of Ellison's manuscript was lost. They would have to wait months until their insurance company made a decision on their home. In the meantime, thanks to a frantic, divided society in need of Black authorities, his speaking skills were in high demand. So, when Mroz and company knocked on his New York home in December, Ellison gave in, his price to speak in the prime-time slot $1,500, rivaled only by the undisclosed Mailer fee.[86]

Ralph Ellison in New York City, 1968.
Photo © Bob Adelman Estate.

Ralph Ellison Doesn't Need a Standing Ovation

At around 5:30 PM on April 5, while walking back to the hotel after Vonnegut's talk, Granville Hicks and Wright Morris see Ralph Ellison arriving at the front door. Hicks is somewhat surprised. *He came, despite the circumstances.*

Hicks has known Ellison for decades, ever since their brief allegiance under a Communist banner in the 1930s while writing for *New Masses*. The moment Hicks sees Ellison, he notices that the author has been affected by King's assassination. "His face, always gentle and sad," has now become "gentler and sadder than ever."[87]

Ellison knows what awaits him. Here he is, a Black man, about to speak to an audience about "Life and Literature," and just because another Black man has been killed, he will be expected to deliver some kind of profound insight—a temporary "Moses" spouting commandments to the deaf. He may look gentle and sad, but it is probably less to do with

King's death and more to do with White society's irrational expectations toward Black intellectuals. He knows what they want, and he knows he'll try to give it to them.

At the Morris Inn, Ellison orders a New York strip steak for dinner. Eating with sophomores Tito Trevino, John Mroz, Marty Kress, and others, Ellison shows off his Oklahoma cattle roots and offers questions to the group: "Do you know where the 'strip' comes from?" Ellison describes the exact location on the cow. Trevino listens intently, in awe of Ellison and his elegance and intellect. It's a good meal, and at least from Trevino's perspective, Ellison seems relaxed, and not too worried about tonight's presentation.[88]

At 8:00 PM, the audience in Washington Hall is overflowing and, similar to the entire week, mainly young and White. Hicks and his wife, along with the Morrises, Vonnegut, and Heller, all sit together in the front row. (Mailer is . . . somewhere.) As Ellison listens to a sophomore introduce him, Hicks is impressed with the turnout, but when the speaker finally says, "And now, Ralph Ellison," there is a blast of applause. It is far and away the most emotional reaction an author has received from an audience this week. Soon the crowd is on its feet, and Hicks internalizes a wince. He hopes the students are "paying tribute to his courage as well as his literary stature" and not simply because of the color of his skin.[89]

Finally, Ellison, in suit and tie, his hands resting on the podium, begins his talk. After a few words of gratitude, he moves right into the pulse of the day. "We are in for some rough times."[90]

Indeed, times already are rough. As Ellison speaks, ninety miles west is Chicago, currently in flames as Ponowel Holloway walks home from work, soon to be killed. In Washington, DC, Fourteenth and U Streets are on fire as federal troops attempt to retake control with Stokely Carmichael nearby.

Ellison stays above the fray in his talk, delivering an academic presentation on the history of American literature and not mentioning King by name. "We have a false history—a false conception of who we are and what we are."[91]

As Hicks notes, Ellison addresses the "terrible discrepancy between America's professed ideals and the condition of the Negro, to which, through centuries, most white people [have] succeeded in blinding themselves." At least now it appears that White America has stopped willfully being blind to the effect Black people are having on the culture. Ellison reminds the audience of all the unrecorded race riots that had occurred during the turn of the century. This willful ignorance is now wreaking havoc on the country. In short, Ellison tells the crowd, the country is being punished for all "the things in life we don't want to hear about." It is a damning statement, coming from the author of *Invisible Man*, a novel dedicated to the unheard.[92]

Still, Ellison doesn't want to get too far off track. "I came here to talk about the art of fiction . . . and that is what I am going to do." It is in art, in *literature*, where Ellison believes the country can save itself from ruin. He lists his favorites—Herman Melville, Henry James, Mark Twain, Stephen Crane, Ernest Hemingway, F. Scott Fitzgerald, and William Faulkner—but the recent literary output frustrates Ellison. Yes, there have been some successful works, but "far too often in the last decade of our novels, we have not cut deeply enough, been tragic enough, and you [the audience and country] have not demanded enough of us besides entertainment."[93]

This comment may cause the front row of literary festival authors to sit up a bit more. After all, they are fighting the same battle Ellison is describing. Unanimously, each author has professed in his own way the incredible achievement of *Invisible Man*. Besides Vonnegut, Granville Hicks is on record as writing that Ellison's novel "demonstrate[s] that the American Negro is deserving of not only political and economic but cultural equality."[94] Wright Morris is far more profuse, and in a very important book review for the *New York Times*, printed two weeks after the book's release, he calls the novel "a resolutely honest, tormented, profoundly American book. . . . *Invisible Man* belongs on the shelf with the classical efforts man has made to chart the river Lethe from its mouth to its source."[95]

Not all bow down to Ellison. Leave it to Norman Mailer to stir the pot:

> When the line of his satire is pure, [Ellison] writes so perfectly that one can never forget the experience of reading him—it is like holding a live electric wire in one's hand. But Ralph's mind, fine and icy, tuned to the pitch of a major novelist's madness, is

not always adequate to mastering the forms of rage, horror, and
disgust which his eyes have presented to his experience, and so
he is forever tumbling from the heights of pure satire into the
nets of a murderously depressed clown.[96]

Mailer may have stumbled into the reason Ellison has remained
on pause about publishing book number two. Yes, *Invisible Man* is
something that cannot be repeated, but it is Ellison's "fine and icy,"
perfectionistic mind that keeps him from delivering even more work
that cuts deeply into American culture. Plus, more practically, when
you have colleges paying you $1,500 to deliver the same lecture you've
been delivering for years, financial urgency is off the table.

To many who sit in the audience, Ellison's lecture feels more like
a "potted academic lecture," so it's not until the Q and A period when
students begin to ask him his thoughts on Dr. King. Ellison, never in
a mood to suffer fools, shrugs a bit when asked about his view of the
riots currently going on in dozens of cities across the country. Reflecting
upon prior tragedies such as John F. Kennedy and Malcolm X, Ellison
is terse and neutral: "You don't have leaders of this nation assassinated
without chaos."

One other audience member asks him more directly: *Why haven't
you mentioned the assassination of Martin Luther King Jr.?*[97]

Ellison, perhaps with a dramatic pause, says three words: "Literature
goes on," then attempts to throw in a dash of optimism. "In times like
this one must have hope."[98]

At the reception after the speech, Ellison is surrounded by Notre
Dame professors. Several are satisfied with Ellison's talk, calling it "savvy
and sophisticated," but others have questions. One man, possibly from
the sociology department, asks Ellison to refine his criteria for hope:
What do you mean, exactly? But Ellison doesn't give him a clear answer.
Still, this professor pushes Ellison to answer, but a colleague stands in
the middle of the two and stops the scene from escalating. "I want you
to know," the man tells Ellison, "that you're only talking to a stupid
goddamn Milwaukee Pole."

Ellison laughs it off, then takes the slight a step further. "The next
thing someone's going to call me a nigger, and then we're really in for it."

Off to the side, two professors are overheard discussing why Ellison refused to confront Dr. King's death head-on. "Look, anyone can mourn and will, but Ellison was not going to let the [presumably] white assassins reduce him to just another black mourner. Fiction is his weapon, and that's what he used."[99]

Before the reception ends, a rather quiet Wright Morris finds John Mroz and hands him a typed letter in an envelope. He tells him privately that he can't attend the symposium tomorrow—King's death has proven too much for himself and his wife. They will take the first train out of South Bend in the morning, heartbroken but not wishing to publicly air their feelings. For anyone who knows Morris, his actions are not out of character. It is what makes his stories so intensely personal, but also what keeps him from ascending to a Mailer-level of outspoken fame.[100]

You can read the letter tomorrow to the crowd, if you'd like, he tells Mroz.

Julian Bond Debates William Buckley in Front of Thousands

> *"My men went over every square inch of this building and we didn't find a thing. And, in addition, I want you to know that I have distributed ninety-five plainclothesmen throughout the audience."*
>
> —Vanderbilt chancellor Alexander Heard to Buckley and Bond, moments before their debate[101]

At around 9:00 PM on April 5, twenty-eight-year-old civil rights activist Julian Bond, his eyes appearing troubled and weary, walks up to a podium inside Vanderbilt University's Memorial Gymnasium in Nashville, Tennessee. Taking part in Vanderbilt's IMPACT, their annual two-day weekend symposium, Bond is the main speaker tonight, paired intentionally with William F. Buckley, still going strong forty-eight hours after his talk at Notre Dame. Billed in press releases as an event similar to *Meet the Press*, Bond and Buckley have already delivered stand-alone forty-five-minute talks and will now discuss their views in front of a panel of three moderators as a predominantly White audience of six thousand looks on.

Bond and Buckley have been preparing for this event, but they've had little to no time to prepare remarks regarding Dr. King's assassination.[102]

Bond starts, not intimidated in the least by the crowd, nor by Buckley. At this point in time, Bond is mentioned in press releases as a "civil rights and anti-war leader from Georgia, who gained national recognition when he was twice denied his seat in the Georgia legislature because of his opposition to the Vietnam war." In 1965, Bond, taking advantage of a newly created 136th House District in Atlanta, won over eighty percent of the vote, thanks in large part to the district being 95 percent African American, in addition to knocking on doors and personally introducing himself to voters.[103]

But just before officially taking his seat in the House of Representatives, SNCC publicly announced its opposition to the Vietnam War. Since Bond was employed by SNCC and supported the statement, the Georgia state legislature, perhaps looking for a way to deny Bond his seat, called SNCC's declaration an act of "treason."

Enter Dr. King.

Bond had known Dr. King ever since 1960, when he joined a philosophy class of eight students at Morehouse College that King was coteaching. King, finding the Georgia state legislature's act "unconscionable," was ready to support a young man looking to make change without resorting to violence. King led a rally in support of Bond and then acted as a coplaintiff when the case was brought before the Supreme Court. They ruled unanimously in favor of Bond.

And so here he is, a member of the Georgia House of Representatives—a young politician who has now lost an important mentor.[104] As has been the case around the country, nonviolence as a method has been put into serious question, and Bond is pressed on this. "Violence as a political tool has not yet been given a test, and I'm of the opinion that it's not likely to be much of a success. Nonviolence as a political tool has been tested—with limited success. I'm hopeful that in the future nonviolence can be a useful tool, but I'm of the regrettable opinion that because of what happened in Memphis, the likelihood of effectiveness and success is very dim."[105]

Perhaps worried the audience may think he's endorsing the riots currently disrupting various neighborhoods surrounding the campus, Bond makes himself clear. "I'm not advocating violence." But—and here is where Buckley begins to perk up—Bond does see a direct connection between the war in Vietnam and the fight for racial equality at home. Bond, showing no fear, believes that violence is the official policy of the United States, and this aggressive state of mind has "seeped into police stations." As examples that help his argument and at the same time whet Buckley's appetite for contrarianism, Bond juxtaposes "the pacification program in Vietnam with the poverty program in America." He also tells the mainly prowar audience that the "Vietnamese militia" symbolizes "local [American] police officers" and the "village bombing" with today's "riot control," illustrated by four thousand armed national guardsmen currently stalking the streets of Nashville. Not through, Bond starts prognosticating: "Next we will see in America the resettlement of Negroes in villages. In fact, it has already begun . . . in villages (ghettos) in the cities."[106]

Buckley, in his own "seat of special anxiety and turmoil" of praising Dr. King's fight against discrimination, disagrees strongly with Bond: "To imply that our rulers take sadistic pleasure in ghettoizing the Negro . . . depriving him . . . [or] that the administration has no conscience . . . is a contumely." Pushing back against the notion of the United States as aggressor, Buckley tells Bond and the crowd, "To accuse the United States of waging the most aggressive war of the twentieth century shows a lack of judgment."[107]

Buckley's current anxiety is understandable. Even though the audience, on the surface, is predominantly White and Southern, the majority are college students who, because of King's death, feel the need to express sympathy toward Bond's point of view. It's Bond who garners strong applause after his statements (or accusations, in Buckley's eyes). Buckley will later say to an older group of listeners that the young audience is wishing to "atone for the crime against Martin Luther King . . . by offering its body, prostrate, in expiation. Its own innocent, virginal body, unflexed, to the scourges of Julian Bond."[108]

Buckley fixates on the demographic in front of him, and he asks the audience directly to raise their hands to this question: *Do you think you are representative of America?* He specifies himself. Are there rich men, poor men, old, and young? Are there "Southerners, Easterners,

Westerners, Midwesterners? Catholics, Protestants, Jews? College graduates, high school dropouts?" The audience leans toward a yes. (Bond, if given the chance, may have asked how many Black people were in the audience.) Buckley, the skilled Yale debater, has them in the palm of his hand. His next question floors the audience. Now, Buckley directs, "Raise your hands, those of you who consider yourselves implicated in the assassination of Martin Luther King?"[109]

He waits . . . but no hands are raised. Perhaps some are hung up on the word "implicate," or perhaps some are not alert to the question. Regardless, Buckley takes from this public challenge that none of the six thousand audience members before him blame themselves for King's death. To Buckley, the grief many White Americans are feeling is more a general reflection of a nation's grief. Or, in Buckley's words, a "community which in fact considers itself aggrieved."[110] The conservative author has quite often disagreed with Dr. King, most notably about the Vietnam War, but he does still see a man who loved America dearly, and, like John F. Kennedy, did nothing to deserve being killed.

An American Troubadour's Blues

At around 9:00 PM in Chicago's Orchestra Hall, a twenty-seven-year-old folk singer named Phil Ochs takes the stage. He's tall and lanky, with "black tousled hair, a shy smile," and "an easy manner." He's wearing green Levis and a "blue khaki shirt unbuttoned at the neck." As he takes the stage, his eyes lock onto the hundreds in the audience. It is an empathetic look, as if showing everyone how aware he is of the ongoing riots less than a mile away. As Ochs stands in front of the microphone, he greets the crowd kindly. "Hello, brave souls."[111]

Ochs isn't feeling well. Perhaps it's because of a demanding tour schedule made worse by the news of Dr. King's death, but after performing one song, Ochs asks the audience to give him a little time and heads offstage. The news of King's assassination has devastated Ochs, and as the young crowd of doves waits, many of whom are wearing buttons supporting Eugene McCarthy, several people throw handwritten note requests onto the stage. When Ochs returns, he picks up many of the notes and decides to sit down for the remainder of his performance.

"I don't know if I have the strength," he says, reading several of the requests.

The auditorium isn't quite full, so Orchestra Hall management decides to turn the lights on in front and invite the audience to move closer to the stage. One journalist is thrilled, saying that the move creates an "intimate . . . special one-to-one thing."[112]

Somehow, perhaps through the crowd's support, Ochs finishes his set, and the audience needs his words to help release the tension of the day. One song, "Changes," has a beautiful melody that seems to capture the essence of today's melancholy:

> The world's spinning madly, it drifts in the dark
> Swings through a hollow of haze,
> A race around the stars, a journey through
> The universe ablaze with changes.

Ochs saves the best for last, a nine-minute epic about Kennedy's assassination titled "Crucifixion," with some believing it to be even more meaningful than Dylan's 1965 "Desolation Row." The song's lyrics now carry new resonance, with one verse in particular pushing its way into the darkness of the day:

> But ignorance is everywhere and people have their way;
> Success is an enemy to the losers of the day.
> In the shadows of the churches, who knows what they pray?
> For blood is the language of the band.

It is an exhausting song for Ochs to play while under the weather, but at the end he's given a standing ovation. When he walks off, the audience demands an encore. Ochs obliges, and dedicates his last song "in memory of Dr. King," a man Ochs had played for back during the protests near the UN Secretariat Building in April 1967.[113]

The song he chooses is known only to those in attendance, but for at least one flick of time, Ochs has managed to bring light to a dark place.

7

SATURDAY, APRIL 6, 1968

The Beginning of the End

Bobby Seale and seventeen-year-old Bobby Hutton (hat) at the Oakland
Police Department, May 23, 1967. *Photo by Ron Riesterer.*

"Violence creates many more social problems than it solves. . . . If [black people] succumb to the temptation of using violence in their struggle, unborn generations will be the recipients of a long and desolate night of bitterness, and our chief legacy to the future will be an endless reign of meaningless chaos. Violence isn't the way."

—Rev. Martin Luther King Jr.[1]

It Ends with a Panther

"A panther never attacks anyone, but when he is pushed into a corner . . . like the brothers were last night, he has one thing to do: to defend himself. . . . Our brother Martin Luther King exhausted all means of nonviolence."

—Bobby Seale, April 7 1968[2]

It's around half past seven in West Oakland, California. The sun has set and the Black Panther's minister of information, Eldridge Cleaver, wants to ambush a few "racist pig cops," and give them a sampling of the same behavior Black people have been subjected to for years. In the living room, a group of nine Black Panthers have come together.[3] On the table and floor rest a collection of weapons, "rifles, carbines, shotguns, handguns . . . all kinds of ammunition."[4]

The young men pick their guns and thirty-three-year-old Cleaver, as "captain," tells the group they're driving to Berkeley in three cars. They listen to him. Cleaver has a commanding presence and the experience to back it up. Cleaver has spent the last six years in prisons such as San Quentin on counts of rape and assault. He's used the time in jail to reshape his beliefs, and just recently published a bestselling memoir called *Soul on Ice*. Most of the young men around him are between the ages of seventeen and twenty-three, including treasurer Lil' Bobby J. Hutton, one of the first to join the Black Panther Party for Self-Defense in 1966. As of April 1968, there are three authoritative figures in the group—Bobby Seale, Huey Newton, and Eldridge Cleaver. With Seale absent and Newton in jail, it's Cleaver pushing his own agenda tonight. While Seale respects Cleaver, he knows Eldridge is looking to wage war, and "doing stuff that I didn't want him to do."[5]

The trio of cars heads over to Berkeley and spots a police car. Cleaver wants this to go just right. He's hoping "white radicals" will voice their support and join in a massive uprising. The crew of nine get out of their cars, looking to provoke the officers into a gunfight, but something about this doesn't feel quite right. Cleaver tells everyone to get back into their cars. They head back toward the McClymonds neighborhood of West Oakland. At around 9:00 PM, Cleaver pulls his white Ford over near the intersection of Twenty-Eighth and Union Streets. His car, a donation to the Black Panther Party, stands out with Florida license plates.[6]

Cleaver leans for a moment against the driver's-side door. As he does, two police officers in a patrol car, Nolan Darnell and Richard Jensen, slow down and see Cleaver. The officers stop and open their doors. It's already dark, as Cleaver runs around to the other side and crouches behind the back side of his car. With his crew ready to fire, Cleaver gives the order. Suddenly, bullets are "coming from every angle." Windows are broken, and officer Jensen is cut multiple times. Officer Darnell tries to get out of the car but is shot in the shoulder and decides to stay in the car. As soon as the barrage of bullets pauses, he radios, "940-B: Officer Needs Help."[7]

Instead of climbing back into their cars, the crew runs. Some jump fences and hide in backyards, but eight make their way into a nearby house, 1218 Twenty-Eighth Street. In a matter of minutes, police cars have arrived and surround the front of the house. The Black Panthers fire a few rounds through windows and the police fire back. The house's actual residents begin to shout and manage to escape without being hurt. The firing continues as more police arrive. There are at least thirty policemen clustered around cars in the front of the house.[8]

Inside, Eldridge Cleaver has been shot in the foot, and the Panthers in the house defend themselves. Floodlights are brought in, and the police toss teargas through the windows. Cleaver and Lil' Bobby Hutton make their way to the basement.

Meanwhile, a crowd of over a hundred watch from a distance, but the police are able to wave them off. Someone lights a police car on fire as the bullets make their way into nearby vehicles and come close to hitting the now-scattered crowd.

As the teargas burns their eyes, the Panthers know they must surrender. In the basement, Cleaver tells Bobby Hutton to strip his clothes off so that when they come out the police will know they're unarmed. Hutton chooses not to. The Panthers shout their surrender, and after ninety minutes of intermittent gunfire, the shooting stops.

Cleaver, stripped to just his boxers, and fully clothed Hutton climb out a lower side basement window and roll on the ground. Several officers are less than five feet away, guns aimed. Several move up "a walkway beside the house to get to them."[9]

Cleaver and Hutton are being shoved by the police with their hands up as they walk in front of the house. One police officer, Gwynne Peirson, standing next to a telephone across the street, sees one of the lead police officers shove Hutton hard enough that he stumbles and nearly falls to the ground. For just a moment, Hutton brings his hands down to stop from falling, but the police fire around ten shots in near unison. Five hit Hutton, killing him. One bullet lands "in his head, two in the back of his thighs, one in the lower back, and one in his arm."[10]

Days go by as two sides of the story are released to the press. The Oakland Police Department say that Lil' Bobby Hutton was trying to run away, while the Black Panthers emphasize that Hutton had surrendered and had his hands up, murdered under floodlights. The OPD make sure to spotlight the wounds the police officers suffered (always at least two, sometimes four). The Black Panthers say that Lil' Bobby was executed and shot five times in the head.

But it's not until Gwynne Peirson's eyewitness account in 1971, a full three years later, that events are clarified. After twenty-two years with the OPD, Peirson, who is Black, retires in 1970 and completes his master's degree in criminology in 1971. His master's thesis is an account of that night Lil' Bobby Hutton was murdered. He tells the *San Francisco Examiner* that he was never asked by either the Black Panthers or the OPD to testify for the grand jury back in April 1968. When he did provide his statement of what occurred to the OPD, a stenographer wrote down what he said, but Peirson's account was never typed up.[11]

One fact, however, cannot be altered: a group of police officers fired multiple times at an unarmed, surrendering teenager from a distance of ten feet or less.

LBJ Holds the Fort

A soldier stands by a mounted .50-caliber machine gun resting on the steps of the Capitol Building. He and other "stationed soldiers" have been ordered to stand guard near each White House gate entrance as smoke continues to billow from DC's Fourteenth and U Streets. With roadblocks around the White House, the building resembles a fortress preparing for battle.[12]

Early in the morning, with Lady Bird and Luci back in Texas, Johnson has Saturday and Sunday to meet with Gen. William Westmoreland (the meeting he was supposed to have in Honolulu) and put together an expedited Fair Housing Act. Calls are made to trusted colleagues and civil rights advisers, such as Black journalist Louis A. Martin. But when Martin brings his car up to a gate, the soldiers check his trunk and finds golf clubs. He's also casually dressed. They consider reporting him. . . . *A Black man wearing casual clothes and playing golf? We might have a looter.* Eventually the soldiers are told to let him through, but not before disrespecting Martin, considered by politicians to be the "godfather of black politics."[13]

There is an edge to the day, as if each action is more scrutinized than ever. When Johnson attempts to track down Mississippi senator John Stennis, known for his prosegregation stance, the president finds out that Stennis has "taken a little trip through [DC]. Just to get a feel for things." Johnson decides not to ask what he means exactly and, after half-joking that he was about to get the FBI to search for him, asks that he join him in the meeting with General Westmoreland.[14]

Calls pour in as Westmoreland briefs him on the situation in Vietnam. Mayor Richard Daley, fearing that the Chicago violence will soon to be too widespread for his police force to handle, talks to the president in a state of panic. The first words out of the mayor's mouth as soon as he has Johnson on the line are "Mr. President . . . we're in trouble and we need some help." It's a short three-minute call, and

Daley first asks for three thousand more national guardsmen. Johnson disagrees. "Better make it five." Later on in the day, around two o'clock, West Virginia senator Robert Byrd calls in wondering why martial law hasn't been put in place for the DC area, opining that "looters should be shot [in the leg] if they are adults."[15]

Inanities aside, Saturday is a juggling act for President Johnson. When it comes to General Westmoreland, LBJ wants to know the precise current situation in Vietnam as he continues his 90 percent bombing halt, but just as much he needs to see how he feels about keeping the general in command of a war they appear to be losing, now that the Tet Offensive has reached the general American public via the evening news.

At the same time, Johnson needs to maintain communication with mayors in cities with riots currently in progress. But his raison d'être is assuring the passage of the Fair Housing Act, a bill he has been fighting to push through Congress since 1966. But in this rare, chaotic moment, Johnson has the circumstances necessary to guarantee its passage. For starters, thanks to his March 31 announcement, his presidency sits in the neutral zone, meaning there is a better chance that his opponents won't say that he is pushing a certain agenda to assist his own party. With the disturbances and violence in DC and Chicago being played over the television, Johnson knows how swiftly the "riots could turn normal compassion into bitterness, anger, and retaliation." In this way, the longer they wait to pass legislation in honor of King, the more it will seem a reaction to the riots and not a gesture of goodwill toward King's nonviolent (and vastly preferred) methods of diplomacy.[16]

Still, there will be opponents regardless of any favorable situation, and Johnson, as well as his key fair-housing adviser, civil rights activist and NAACP lobbyist Clarence Mitchell, has heard all their arguments over the years: "Open housing is forced housing." "A man's home is his castle." And, perhaps the strongest of them all, "A man's got a constitutional right to sell to whomever he wants."[17]

But, as Johnson may say, nowhere in the constitution does it say that a man can discriminate against a potential buyer because of his race. The Fair Housing Act is intended to be "a broad ban against racial discrimination in the sale and rental of housing and apartments." On this Saturday afternoon, however, Johnson is worried about foreseeing any potential obstacles from his opponents in Congress. Knowing time is of the essence, he decides to go ahead and make the bill "vanilla" enough to please enough congressmen.

Later on, his speechwriter and good Texan friend Horace Busby walks up to the president and takes a look at the list of issues he wishes to address. The president, in full honesty, believes the bill won't "begin to touch our problem."[18]

Busby studies his longtime friend and sees a man weary of it all. "Until we all get to be a whole lot smarter," Johnson says, in a state of melancholic reflection, "I guess the country will just have to go with what it has already."

Busby has confidence that Johnson doesn't really believe he is leaving the country with "what it has already" and chooses to leave his friend "alone at the end of the week which ended his political life."[19]

Trapped Within the Amber of Patriarchy

"For the longest time, way before I married Martin, I had believed that women should allow our essence and presence to shine, rather than letting ourselves be buried or shunted to the sidelines."

—Coretta Scott King[20]

November 26, 1942. It was Thanksgiving night in "backwoods" Heiberger, Alabama, and fifteen-year-old Coretta Scott and her older sister Edythe were out late practicing with the Lincoln High School choir. Her mother, Bernice McMurry, and father, Obadiah Scott, were about to head to bed after a long day of cooking and washing dishes when they smelled smoke. They didn't have a phone, and the closest town, Marion, was twelve miles away and not exactly open armed when it came to a Black family in need of help.[21]

The fire roared quickly through the Scott's "simple and plain" home, and Mr. and Mrs. Scott only had enough time to rescue Coretta's twelve-year-old brother, Obie, and collapse onto the front lawn. They watched as the fire raged, burning "clothes, family albums, . . . furniture." By the time Coretta and Edythe arrived, the home had been completely destroyed. In tears, Coretta thought about their "prized Victrola" and how she'd lost her recording of Bessie Smith's "Nobody Knows You When You're Down and Out."

At the moment, the Scotts were down and out, and nobody knew who set the fire, but the family didn't have to rack their brains too long to assume a few White men in town. Such was life for the Scotts in 1942 Alabama. The fading shadows of 1857's *Dred Scott v. Sandford* were made darker after the Civil War, when Reconstruction teased Coretta's grandparents with the right to vote, only to be obstructed by outlandish poll taxes, literacy tests (if you couldn't read or write, you'd need to own a certain amount of property), and the creation of the "grandfather clause," which meant that if illiterate or undereducated White male voters couldn't pass the new tests, they were still allowed to vote because they *used* to be able to vote.

To Coretta's family it was foolish, but then in 1896 came the pro-segregation *Plessy v. Ferguson* decision, "engraving inequality in stone." And if the Scotts had any problem with this, or if, say, her father's lumber business stood in the way of a White male competitor, well, the darkest of shadows were cast in the form of a lynching or a home burned to the ground.

Obadiah Scott had lived with these shadows all his life, and he was not about to let his family despair over their setback. Shortly after the fire, he brought his wife and three children together and asked them to stay strong. "We don't have time to cry." Obadiah told them that it will be OK—they'll start again. Yes, he could go into Marion and tell the police that his home had burned to the ground, but this is the same city where a proud "Marion schoolteacher" first designed the Confederate flag and uniform, and where Coretta would walk past WHITES ONLY signs and buy an old sandwich or ice cream ("usually vanilla") only at the back door of a store; so support seemed iffy at best.[22]

No, Coretta's father did what he'd always done—he went back to work. As they moved in with their grandparents, Obadiah Scott spent his days "hauling lumber, cutting hair, and selling scrap iron" to make back what they'd lost. As he did, Coretta committed herself to her dream of earning a complete education *away* from the limitations of her current surroundings. Her mother's determination helped too: "You are just as good as anyone else. You get an education. Then you won't have to be kicked around."

But at night, when her father was late coming home, Coretta trembled with concern that somebody would soon knock on their door "to tell us our dad had been killed."[23]

———————

Twenty-five and a half years later, it's 6:00 PM inside Ebenezer Baptist Church, and Rev. Bernard Lee, Ralph Abernathy, and Coretta Scott King walk toward a table filled with microphones. The table has been placed directly under the center stage pulpit, where Dr. King had so often preached to congregations about the ills of society and his nonviolent strategy.

Reverend Lee directs Coretta to the center seat, and Ralph sits to her left. The view from Coretta's eyes doesn't match a church service. Instead, video cameras, photographers, and reporters swarm the front pews. Forty-eight hours after the murder of her husband, Coretta has a few words she'd like to share with the media and the nation.

After Reverend Lee apologizes for "the lateness" of the press conference, he turns the media's attention over to Abernathy, who declares this moment as "one of the darkest hours in the history of black people in this nation." As he speaks, the pain in his eyes becomes palpable. He has lost his "closest friend and dearest associate."

Still, today is Coretta's moment, and Abernathy attempts an odd-sounding introduction. "We no longer have with us Martin Luther King . . . but we do have with us his very charming [*Coretta's eyes dart up*] and beautiful and loving wife who has come this evening to join with me in saying to this nation . . . that even though you may have been able to stop the heartbeat of Martin Luther King . . . you certainly will never be able to stop the search for freedom, dignity, and equality here in this country. It gives me a great deal of pleasure to present to you my very dear sister, Mrs. Martin Luther King Jr."

Coretta has grown used to this kind of introduction—standard in its time. She is "charming" but not "brilliant," and, again commonplace, she is not Coretta, but rather the *Mrs.* behind the name of a greater man. In this profound moment of grief, however, she doesn't give it much concern. Rather, she knows that she needs to address the "join with me" part of Ralph's statement and show that she supports his new position as the leader of the Southern Christian Leadership Conference.

"My husband always said that if anything happened to him he would like for Ralph Abernathy to take his place in the struggle." She says that Ralph "is like a brother to me" and that Dr. King had always felt that Ralph "could express and interpret his views on nonviolence better than anyone else and would know how he would want things to be carried on."[24]

She says this with a degree of conviction, but anyone who actually knows Coretta Scott King as an individual knows she has plans of her own. After her respectful nod of appreciation to Ralph and the SCLC, she tells the press that "the most important thing is that my husband's work will be carried forward."

She ends the press conference with a few lines worthy of one of her husband's sermons. "On the day want is abolished, on the day wars are no more, on that day I know my husband will rest in a long-deserved peace."[25]

Coretta Scott King has come a long way from that Thanksgiving night fire, and she has seen firsthand the progress made through her husband's methods. Similar to her father, she saw in her husband an ability to remain restrained yet in total command of a situation. For the next thirty-seven years she will draw upon that same resolve to help cement her husband's legacy, differentiating herself in the process.

Gas Leaks, Gunpowder, and Hope in Richmond

"The community grieves for those who lost their lives, and for the families of those who died."

—Richmond mayor Byron E. Klute[26]

About two hundred miles southeast of the University of Notre Dame rests the quiet city of Richmond, Indiana—population forty-four thousand. On a mild, sunny Saturday afternoon, the downtown area is active as local residents complete some Easter shopping at their favorite stores. Some wait in line at the State Theater to purchase one-dollar tickets (children pay fifty cents) for the 1:30 matinee of *Stay Away, Joe* starring Elvis Presley as an American Indian returning to his reservation. A few women choose to go get their hair done over at Violet's House of Beauty or stroll around the corner to Virginia's Beauty Shop while men head over to Birck's Hardware for some tools. Couples may spend the afternoon dreaming of a new living room at the Holthouse Furniture Store, or pick up a few odds and ends at Vigran's Variety Store.[27]

In the middle of these stores stands Marting Arms, a ninety-two-foot-long, eighteen-foot-wide establishment that runs along South Sixth Street, its storefront situated on the corner of Main Street. Built in 1935, the building that Marting Arms uses is a "two-story concrete block . . . with a brick facade." Inside, customers will find "guns, ammunition, loading components for reloading small arms ammunition, and sporting equipment." The owners, thirty-nine-year-old Donald Marting and his wife, Louise, also provide gunpowder that they sell wholesale to gun clubs across Wayne County, which use it for hunting and skeet shooting.[28]

For months at least, the demand for gunpowder has been high, with Marting often temporarily breaking the law by keeping more than a hundred pounds of gunpowder on the store's concrete floor basement. This was the case on March 19, when the Richmond Fire Prevention Department inspectors discovered "35 to 50 three-pound cans of smokeless gunpowder" in the basement. After being ordered to remove the gunpowder, Marting told the inspectors that it was all part of a "shipment that was to go out that day."[29]

At the start of April, a gas odor had been reported by several customers shopping at Marting Arms. Donald Marting, unsure of the source of the odor, opened windows and doors to allow the fumes to escape. On April 3, the Federal Bureau of Mines completed a citywide inspection of pipelines and found "55 leaks . . . seven of them creating hazardous conditions."[30]

Meanwhile, orders for gunpowder continued, and Marting Arms attempted to fulfill them. On January 21 a large order for 2,103 pounds was shipped to the store, then 628 for February, 25 for March, 80 on April 2, and 60 on April 3. Since inspectors had seen recently a maximum of 150 pounds of smokeless gunpowder, as of April 6, Marting Arms could well have had between 500 and 2,000 pounds of smokeless gunpowder stored in its basement.[31]

At 1:47 PM, Mrs. Taraneh Mohanes is in her car with her baby daughter and mother. They are stopped at a stoplight and are the third car in line. She glances at the Marting Arms storefront and hears a noise come from the basement of the store. Then she sees the foundations of the store expand, "like a bubble rising." Seconds later, a violent explosion starting from the basement blows apart "every brick in the first floor . . . each flew separately." Soon the second floor collapses, and Mrs. Mohanes sees "a body come out of the second-floor window."

The force of the blast blows the cars in front of her a dozen feet away. With walls coming down around her, she tells her mother and daughter to get out of the car quickly. They do, with "my little girl under her coat." Within seconds she impulsively flicks her car keys to a nearby male bystander and runs down Main Street, "looking death in the face." Later she wonders why her car wasn't blown away from the blast and believes it's only because her windows were down, the car rising "in the air" then falling back down.[32]

At 1:47 PM, after a Tom and Jerry short, a young packed crowd at the State Theater watches the epic opening credits of *Stay Away, Joe* play across the screen as Elvis sings, "Far too long / Have I stayed apart / From this land that I love / and divide my heart" as they fly past panoramic views of valleys, canyons, and rock hills. A minute later, the explosion blocks away at Marting Arms is loud enough to briefly muffle Elvis's voice, and strong enough to shake the balcony and give the "west wall a gaping gap." Bricks and dust begin to fall, and the patrons, mainly young adults and children, run out of the theater. When they're outside, they can see a short distance away the increasing smoke, beginning to eerily resemble a small mushroom cloud.[33]

Moments earlier, back on the first floor of Marting Arms, two best friends, Greg Oler, twenty-one, and Jack Bales, eighteen, move through the selection of firearms and decide to take a look at a few bow and arrow sets. Standing "side by side," the first explosion causes the rear to shatter and fall in on them. Seconds pass, and what follows next is a burst that detonates the ceiling above them. A beam thuds against them both, leaving Bales pinned underneath. Oler, however, is hit hardest and his lifeless body tossed fifty feet away. Bales, somehow still alive, manages to escape the beam as the sound of firing ammunition continues under the gun-filled rubble.[34]

Within an hour, the expanding flames destroy ten businesses and damage dozens of others. A thick cloud of grayish-black smoke consumes the downtown area, and as local residents help others climb out of the rubble, pay phones and business phones ring continuously—family members calling from their homes. To survivors and rescuers, the buzzed ringing is haunting amid the backdrop of roaring fire, smoke, and minor electrical explosions. Rescue teams attempting to locate bodies are often tricked by mannequins that have flown out of storefront windows and appear trapped beneath rubble.[35]

With the downtown slowly being consumed by a fire spreading east and west, the Richmond community sets aside prior conflicts and helps where they can. Nine young Black middle and high school students, only yesterday "chewing out" an officer for a "misdeed," and perhaps offended by a shocking political cartoon of Martin Luther King Jr. holding a gun that was published on April 4 (and apologized for on April 7), try to help the dozens of trapped residents and assist firefighters who attempt to put out fires with high-powered hoses. As over a dozen cities across the country fight fires of their own making, local residents are moved to see Black and White people uniting in a common cause. The mayor sees this and is touched, later saying that "in time of crisis throughout our country, following the death of Martin Luther King Jr., the Negroes of our community responded as did everyone else to help ease the disaster."[36]

After many hours, the fire is contained, but downtown Richmond is nearly destroyed, and thirty-nine bodies are recovered. Two bodies are never found—David Lee Gibbs, eighteen, and Donald Marting. There is never a clear conclusion as to how the explosion first occurred. One

theory, first offered in print by the *Muncie Star Press* through an anony-
mous Richmond official, believes it may have started from a spark in
the basement. It's known by many shoppers that Mr. Marting had a
shooting range where customers could test out a purchase. Mr. Marting
also had stored both smokeless and black gunpowder in the basement.
According to the *Muncie Star Press*, black powder is more explosive and
burns quickly: "A spark from static electricity, from a gun discharge, or
from any other source might have ignited the black powder."

It's never written this way, but a horrific image soon emerges.
David Lee Gibbs, perhaps on a break from stocking shelves at Vigran's
across the street, headed over to Marting Arms and asked Mr. Marting
if he could try out a gun. They walked down into the basement and
Mr. Marting set up his bullet trap, as he had done many times for customers ever since moving into the building in 1964. With the basement
air heavy with natural gas from a nearby underground leak due to a
neglected pipe, Gibbs aimed and fired the gun. Did he miss and hit a
nearby pipe? Was the basement air already thick with natural gas? One
will never know, but within milliseconds the two men were engulfed
in flames from the combination of gas and ignited black powder. The
flames soon reached the other hundreds of pounds of stored gunpowder,
triggering an explosion very similar to just *one* of the thousands of
bombs dropped by pilots over Vietnam as a part of the currently on-
hold Operation Rolling Thunder.[37]

A Moment of Silence Followed by Fundraising

As downtown Richmond deals with the fallout of the massive explosion,
South Bend is relatively quiet. On campus, the literary festival holds its
final event, a symposium, in the Center for Continuing Education building, the same location where Dow president Herbert Doan had spoken
amid protest several days earlier.[38]

This event is far more peaceful. With *Chicago News* literary editor
Van Allen Bradley as moderator, four authors (Hicks, Ellison, Heller,
and Vonnegut) sit behind a table to discuss "the role of literature in
our time."[39]

Before the discussion starts, John Mroz asks Van Allen Bradley and the other authors if he can read Wright Morris's letter. There is no resistance—Heller and Vonnegut are not as close to Morris as the others, but Ellison, for years a big fan, is always keen to hear Morris's perspective. And Hicks and Morris go way back, first corresponding in 1942. Hicks has always enjoyed Morris's humor, calling him "one of the best talkers [Dorothy and I] have ever encountered, remarkably well informed in literary matters, and completely serious about his work, but a great man for laughter."[40]

No one has read the letter except Mroz. As Mroz reads it aloud, the select audience of around 150 literary festival patrons listens to the quiet words of an author in pain for his country.

Dear John:

On Sunday evening Mr. Hicks spoke on the subject of a bad time, and how we're in one, and he was rightfully and appreciatively applauded. On Monday afternoon I talked about fiction and fact, how they increasingly overlap, and how difficult it is to choose, if we must, between them, and for these remarks I was applauded. Monday evening Mr. Mailer aroused our beleaguered sense of justice and entertained us with his own inimitable brand of fiction, and for this he was roundly and understandably applauded. Tuesday night we saw his film, *Beyond the Law*—where we *all* are, in our fashion—and Mr. Mailer, his performance, and the film were applauded. On Wednesday night Mr. William Buckley, perspiring under the klieg lights, exhorted the young to maintain sound bearings (as he wittily disposed of various unsound ones) and for this, naturally, he too was applauded. Then on Thursday afternoon Senator Robert Kennedy, aware of our confusion, our despondency, and our pressing need for guidance, asked for our personal help to deal with these problems and for this, and other matters, he was wildly applauded. On Thursday evening, while I was dunking an ice cube, and others amongst us were scanning the menu, a man long tired of talk, out to speak louder than words, attempted to settle in an explosive instant an issue that words had proved powerless to settle—and we know, in the secret chambers of our hearts, that he, too, in many places, was being applauded. I could go on: how well we all know that the talk goes on and on. Is there, then, nothing we will not applaud? Is there nothing that applause does not give either the lie or an answer? I know of one thing only—or I believe I know it. This one thing is SILENCE.

Is it possible, then, that SILENCE is alone equal to our situation?—to the world *out there*? If so, who is equal to silence. Not me. As you are all well prepared to testify, I have been the most inexhaustible talker. Where silence is golden, alas, I have the ring of brass. I have, that is, until now.

But how am I to be silent without being rude? For a lecturer, a talker, the means are lacking—just as the means for the voice of my rage are lacking. I want to cry havoc—but that too proves to be just so many words. It is less expressive than the moment of silence between the event and the whine of the sirens.

Since I am not equal to silence, but anxious to avoid rudeness, or involve others in my own private and public discomfort, I am left, it seems to me, with no other recourse than inconspicuous and silent leave-taking, memorably and affectionately grateful—speaking also for my wife—for a hospitality so generous and comprehensive it is equally inadequate to talk about it, or repay you with words.

I do not believe, John Mroz, that you or your colleagues, or the numberless young men and women who have made our visit such a pleasure, will misunderstand this vow of silence or the sentiments and not a little of the torment that have brought me to it. In your large and not too soon to be concluded rebellion it is my own small contribution, and may add to your voice.[41]

Affectionately and sincerely yours,
Wright Morris

After Mroz reads Morris's letter, there is not much left to say. Still, the four try their best, especially Heller, who attempts to address the "reality is a crutch" topic head-on. The lighthearted counterculture saying had started to appear as buttons, bumper stickers, and graffiti on walls as early as 1966, but Heller chooses to alter one of the words. "I'm not so sure reality is a crutch," he says to the audience. "I think it's ailment. An incurable one."[42]

As Hicks will later write, although the symposium is far from any kind of intellectual "triumph . . . all of us, speakers and students alike," feel "that something important had happened in the course of the week." Amid the "confusion and disaster the Festival offered glimmers of hope."[43]

The symposium and closing reception ends around 4:00 PM, and Heller and Vonnegut have a flight to catch. They've decided to fly back together to New York City, but before their late afternoon departure, they ask a few members of the sophomore committee to drive them over to the Ludwick home on 730 Park Avenue for a private fundraising party for Eugene McCarthy. They have already promised to attend, and their remarks have been published in the *South Bend Tribune*. Vonnegut even promised he would campaign around his hometown of Indianapolis, but that doesn't appear to be the case.[44]

Still, the two men wish to at least make a presence at the Ludwick's. With several sophomore committee members in tow, as well as a few interested Notre Dame professors, the two authors make their way through the living room and chat with guests. By the entrance door there is a large bowl casually being filled with one-, five-, and ten-dollar bills. In the middle are snacks to be nibbled on and wine. Dr. Harry Ludwick, a South Bend coroner who in four months will find himself in the middle of the raucous, bloody protests at the August Democratic National Convention, and his wife, Norma, an actress in community theater, ask a Notre Dame professor to properly introduce the two writers to the crowd. After a polite applause, a bit more mingling occurs: "Hi, Mr. Heller, I just loved *Catch-22* . . . what a hoot!" "Oh, I'm so sorry, Mr. Vonnegut, my son has a copy of *Cat's Cradle*. I'll get around to it. You must be so proud."[45]

The two men grab drinks, but the sophomores are starting to panic. Their schedule meticulously organized by John Mroz, they don't want the writers to miss their flights. One professor admires from a distance as a sophomore grabs the sleeve of Mr. Heller. "We've *really* got to go, sir."

Norma Ludwick notices the urgency and decides to make a moment out of it. She calls the attention of the guests and asks that Heller and

Vonnegut perhaps say something about the current political situation before their departure. Before Heller starts, Ludwick *ahems* toward the bowl. Heller, with the nervous sophomores looking on, mentions the "virtues" of Eugene McCarthy and how he can possibly end the war in Vietnam. Heller rambles a bit, unsure of how to close, but is still given some applause.

Vonnegut is next, and he begins playacting as if he's searching for his wallet. As he looks, he says to the crowd with that straight-faced delivery, "They say that Buddha, in his final address to his followers, spoke not a word. His address consisted entirely of him standing before them in silence, holding aloft a lotus flower for them to contemplate." *Ah, what's this . . .* Vonnegut pulls out his wallet and removes a twenty-dollar bill. He holds it exultantly in the air and walks toward the bowl. "Is this the treasurer?" He drops the twenty in the bowl as the audience loses it.

Heller trails behind, shaking his head. "Son of a bitch upstaged me again."[46]

———————

On April 7, a travel-weary Heller plops down by his typewriter in his New York City apartment, "after flying back from South Bend to Chicago with Ralph Ellison and reading the papers . . . worrying that Chicago was on fire" from the MLK riots. He's had quite a week, as have many, but he musters enough energy to fire off a letter of thanks to the sophomore committee at Notre Dame. He tells the "Gentlemen" that his week on campus was "a satisfying and stimulating experience for me in every respect, and I especially enjoyed meeting so many [people] who were so deeply interested in and respectful toward one of my favorite novels—my own."[47]

A few months later, his play *We Bombed in New Haven* is released in print. Critics deem it an "extension" of the antiwar material found in *Catch-22* and a "grimly humorous vision of war's reality." With its publication, Heller is labeled "a moral comedian . . . who can thrust a satirical blade into our psyches and provoke pathetic laughter."[48]

Heller's writing career never finds a way to escape the public's love and loyalty to *Catch-22*, but he doesn't lose too much sleep over it. After his death in December 1999, his lifelong friend and fellow satirist Kurt Vonnegut writes a poem/tribute of their friendship:

> JOE HELLER
> True story, Word of Honor:
> Joseph Heller, an important and funny writer
> now dead,
> and I were at a party given by a billionaire
> on Shelter Island.
> I said, "Joe, how does it make you feel
> to know that our host only yesterday
> may have made more money
> than your novel 'Catch-22'
> has earned in its entire history?"
> And Joe said, "I've got something he can never have."
> And I said, "What on earth could that be, Joe?"
> And Joe said, "The knowledge that I've got enough."
> Not bad! Rest in peace![49]

Catch-22 (1961) and *Slaughterhouse-Five* (1969), antiwar to their funny bone, stand as bookends in sixties literature, and thanks to the innocent dream of a nineteen-year-old sophomore, the authors and World War II veterans were able to become friends and bond over this miraculous, chaotic, and tragic stuff we call life in America.

EPILOGUE

How John Mroz Turned Out

Fall 1968: John Mroz at the podium introducing
Timothy Leary, who sits in a blue knit outfit
and barefoot. *Photo courtesy of Karen Linehan-Mroz.*

*"I definitely see the Literary Festival as an annual event
at Notre Dame. We have a nationwide reputation now.
A number of authors have already expressed a willingness to come next year, even before this year's festival
started. . . . The important thing now is starting the
work."*

—John Mroz, April 10, 1968,
Notre Dame Observer

The 1968 Notre Dame Sophomore Literary Festival was by all accounts a
total success, and John Mroz's student life was changed. The one author
whose festival experience Mroz may have been concerned about, Ralph
Ellison, owing to the sensitive circumstances he was up against, wrote
Mroz a personal message that accompanied an autographed photo and
dispelled any concerns: "For John Mroz, who was responsible for one
of the most pleasant and inspiring visits I've ever made to a university."
Mroz also stayed in touch with Wright Morris, who wrote to Mroz that
"some time will [have to] pass before our spinning hearts and heads have
sorted out the impressions of the Festival, and whether we want J. Mroz
Buckley or Norman Mailer Heller for President."[1]

But similar to millions of other supporters, Mroz was devastated
upon hearing of the June 5 assassination of Robert Kennedy at the
Ambassador Hotel in Los Angeles. He confessed how torn up he was
in a letter to the Morrises. Wright Morris, perhaps once again vowing
a time of silence, didn't reply, but his wife, Josephine, did in August
1968: "We were thoroughly broken hearted—and I was completely shat-
tered—by the death of Robert Kennedy. I am glad you mentioned it in
your letter—to know that this pain is not just a matter of a few days,
this loss will be with us always."

Mroz continued to push the boundaries of what could be done at
Notre Dame, heading up the Student Union Academic Commission
(bigger budget, more events). He handed off the literary festival chairman position to friend James E. Metzger, but not before Mroz once
again tried to reconnect with Ray Bradbury and Robert Penn Warren
to see if they'd attend the 1969 festival. (They didn't.)[2]

In October 1968, with his "think big" philosophy guiding him, and deeper pockets to pull from, Mroz helped to organize a successful debate between former Harvard professor and LSD advocate Timothy Leary ("Drugs are a way to God") and psychologist and researcher Dr. Sidney Cohen ("Don't kid yourself"). Mroz knew in order to compete with the colossal giant of Notre Dame football in the fall, he needed to provide events that had the potency to generate a spike of attention. At the same time, he hoped to give students a chance to hear both sides of an issue escalating in popularity.[3]

Not all of Mroz's events went so smoothly, and in February 1969 one of them led to one of the first violent police-student incidents in Notre Dame campus history. While leading the Student Union Academic Commission, Mroz and other members decided to attempt what they titled a "Pornography and Censorship Conference." Mroz and the committee convinced Beat poet Allen Ginsberg to open the conference with a "profane" talk and reading, and later watched *Lady Godiva*, "an off-off-Broadway parody of porn and politics."

Where the trouble came from, however, was their controversial screening of two adult films, *Kodak Ghost Poems* and *Flaming Creatures*, the latter of which had been "declared pornographic by the Supreme Court." On February 7, "plainclothes agents equipped with Mace" interrupted the showing of *Kodak Ghost Poems* and confiscated the film, but not before "spraying the eyes of as many as 15" students and assaulting a St. Mary's student named Kathy Cecil, "who had the film under her coat" to protect it from being taken. The four police officers tore it away from her body and ran off as they were pegged with snowballs. A few incensed students were fast enough to attempt to lie down in front of the car to stop them from driving off, but the officers were able to maneuver around their bodies and pull away.[4]

After a nearly victorious campaign for student body president, Mroz graduated from Notre Dame in 1970 with honed entrepreneurial skills. In graduate school at Northeastern University, he met the love of his life, Karen Linehan, and they married in 1972. At the beginning of their marriage, Mroz made it very clear to Karen that he was someone who would always seek to accomplish big projects, but he asked her to help "mute his excesses and kick the pedestal out from under him when" his ego became too large for the room he's in.[5]

Adulthood suited the dreamer well. Mroz would become a father of three, and as the '70s played themselves out, he spent years mastering the geopolitics in the Middle East, eventually publishing, at the age of thirty-two, *Beyond Security: Private Perceptions Among Arabs and Israelis*, a two-hundred-page analysis that included one-on-one interviews Mroz conducted in various locations across the Middle East.

By this time, he had moved his way up the ranks of the International Peace Academy, an institute offering extensive training in peacekeeping methods and negotiating skills, to become the director of Middle East Studies. But in 1981, when Mroz sat down with businessman and philanthropist Ira D. Wallach, the rest of his life was laid out in front of him.

Wallach, like Mroz a figurative member of the Think Big club, had money and wanted to put it in the hands of people who knew how to bring people and different perspectives together. By this point, Wallach was in his seventies, and as he looked at John, an everlasting battery in his early thirties, he asked the younger man to think as big as he could: make this world a safer place for my grandchildren, he told him.

From this moment, Mroz dreamed up the biggest event of his life—the creation of his own organization—the Institute for East-West Security Studies, later to be called the EastWest Institute (EWI). Wallach and Mroz hammered out the specifics, and Wallach agreed to provide $1 million each year to the institute for the first five years. Thirteen years after bringing together some of the finest literary talent in the country onto the Notre Dame campus, Mroz would now bring together some of the most powerful business leaders and politicians to help broker peace.[6]

Mroz eventually met privately over fifty times with the Palestinian Liberation Organization's leader Yasser Arafat, acting as an unofficial and unpaid go-between for the Reagan administration. With the EWI not yet globally known, he used his position at the International Peace Academy to secure meetings with top officials. "If I could get Arab recognition of Israel," the thirty-six-year-old said to the *New York Times*, "there's nothing I could do that would be more important in my life."[7]

The EastWest Institute kept its bridge-building ways for forty years, even surviving Mroz's passing in August 2014. For Karen, John's death was a devastating loss, salved only by the reaction of so many around the country who would miss his inspiration and boundless energy. Upon hearing the news, Condoleezza Rice wrote to Karen that John was "a dear friend and mentor to me," while Henry Kissinger wrote that John had always been "a dedicated fighter for the cause of freedom." His legacy will continue in the form of the John Edwin Mroz Global Leadership Institute at the College of Charleston.[8]

As for Notre Dame's Sophomore Literary Festival, it, too, holds a significant place in the university's history. For the next four decades the festival would remain more or less within the same framework that Mroz concocted in 1968. But over time, as the nation shifts its interests more and more toward the mediums of film, television, and music for its storytelling, popularity in authors wanes, and the rich tradition of the weeklong festival—bringing to campus writers such as Joyce Carol Oates, Nikki Giovanni, John Irving, Tom Wolfe, Ishmael Reed, Tim O'Brien, and hundreds of others—has entered a state of flux, picked up every so often by anyone looking, as young John Mroz once did, to make something out of nothing.[9]

Or $2.72.

ACKNOWLEDGMENTS

I first jumped into storytelling while sitting inside a Catholic church service near Vero Beach, Florida. I was seventeen and down visiting my father, a church music director, when the priest started in on a lengthy homily. It was an early morning service, and the priest's mellow voice echoed off the broad walls as a gentle sun illuminated the top edges of the pews. Within a minute, I could feel myself nodding off. Sitting near the choir at the time, I didn't want others to see the son of the choir director doing the ol' head bob, so I tried to stay awake. I grabbed the paper program and turned it over to the backside. There was just a bit of blank space at the bottom, so I thought I would start a "things to do" list. Instead—well, I'll never be able to fully explain it—I had an idea for a story. A small town in middle America in the 1870s, the population half Native American and half White American. There would be fights every day, and the only way they'd have peace is through the invention of baseball. I called it Bobby Wagner. Such a superficially classic American name, isn't it? I thought so . . .

The idea became a short story, then a feature-length screenplay, then a table leg. I moved on to another idea, and another, until I started to escape to the corner of the second-floor library at Catawba College. I became an English major, and through classes I learned of the legendary post-war novelists of my time—Mailer, Vonnegut, Heller, Ellison (no Morris, sadly)—and attempted to write the Great American Novel. For the next fifteen years, I lived and breathed fiction, reading for inspiration biographies of Vonnegut, Heller, and Mailer and hoping to catch a break.

Oh, I have a few publications out there. Small plunks in the lake, I call them. If you Google my name, you may find on page seven or eight my story about a smashed piece of gum, or people killing themselves by jumping into a Japanese volcano. All told, after fifteen years of writing, I managed fifteen publications. Total monetary compensation? $375. That's a monthly take home of nearly $2.72 per month. John Mroz would probably tell me, "You can work with that."

One day, after another round of me hitting my head against the edge of a wooden desk, my wife asked me a simple question: *What have you always enjoyed reading?* An easy answer, right? Fiction . . . Yes, I . . . I . . .

I'd stopped enjoying fiction. For many years I enjoyed it, but at some point (I'm not sure when), I found myself daydreaming around biography aisles, pathetically scouring books detailing the life of a famous writer. *How did they make it? How did . . .*

At the age of thirty-two, I realized I've always loved biography and American history.

My wife's question kept me from giving myself a mental concussion. Soon I started a book about famous historical figures in their early twenties, and out of that came a passion for Martin Luther King Jr. and my first book, *The Seminarian: Martin Luther King Jr. Comes of Age* (thanks again to Yuval Taylor and Devon Freeny of Chicago Review Press).

As for this book, the idea started small and in the deadness of night. Sometimes, while unable to sleep, I look through the hundreds of document files on my computer and think about what an immense waste of time so many of them were. Fiction story after fiction story . . . just rubbish. *Oh, and look at this one . . . You were trying to be Vonnegut . . . poser.*

I'd been working on *The Seminarian* night and day, so you could say the question I posed was somewhat natural: *Did Kurt Vonnegut ever meet Martin Luther King Jr.? That'd be odd.* Although they never met, I was eventually led toward the 1992 *Playboy* interview completed by Carole Mallory called "The Kurt and Joe Show." Mallory (through the interview help of Norman Mailer, no less) managed to get the two writers to reminisce about their first meeting at Notre Dame, when King was assassinated. Vonnegut then went ahead and told his somewhat accurate zinger of Heller being put on the spot after the announcement, and that clinched it for me. *I'm going to write an article about this someday.*

It remained "an article" for quite some time. When I decided to complete a four-thousand-word article about the literary festival for the fiftieth anniversary (and in support of my first book's release) I decided to search for a few of the festival attendees to interview. John Mroz was at the top of the list. I soon found that he had passed and attempted to contact his wife, Karen. We spoke via email, then by Skype, and after an hour or so of conversation, Karen told me of all the letters John had kept of the authors attending the '68 festival, not to mention describing the incredible story of putting together such an event with little to no money.

I was floored. Simply put, without the kindness and generosity of Karen Linehan-Mroz, this would not have become the book it is today. With a slow and respectful bow, I thank her dearly.

What really hooked me, however, was James McKenzie's story of hearing Joseph Heller speak the night of April 4. I found McKenzie's retelling of that night in a comment on a blog post from the summer of 2010. The emotional absurdity of that moment with Heller seems to me to reflect the absurd reality of the times. For his comment, and our follow-up correspondence, I am deeply appreciative.

Still, if it had all stopped there, then this study would have just been a long-form article. But there was still plenty left to discover. Elizabeth Hogan and Joseph R. Smith at the University of Notre Dame Archives were immensely helpful when it came to digitizing the photo negatives from the event and allowing me to search for documents related to the 1968 literary festival during my visit to the Notre Dame campus in May 2018. In addition, researcher Nicole Potter helped me with records in the Granville Hicks Collection at Syracuse University, and Kira Jones helped with the Ralph McGill papers at Emory University. A big thank-you to them all.

The greatest joy during these last few years working on the book has been in talking with the people who were involved in some way with the

1968 literary festival. I tried to track down each of the fourteen members of the sophomore committee but fell a bit short of that goal. Still, it was extremely illuminating and entertaining talking and corresponding with George Ovitt, Marty Kress, Tito Trevino, Dean Hagen, Tom Schatz, William Locke, and Joseph L. Brown, all of whom had vivid memories of the week that was. Dr. Richard Bizot's sharp memory was a great help in putting together the events of the festival, especially Norman Mailer's premiere and the fundraising efforts of Joseph Heller. Father Ernest Bartell helped illuminate how students were feeling in the late 1960s and told me how back then there didn't seem to be a middle ground, much like today. For his time and wisdom, a deep bow of thanks.

Barney Gallagher was the first to share with me the original Notre Dame Sophomore Literary Festival program, and Phil Kukielski shared with me his memory of Joseph Heller speaking to his English class. Professors John Matthias and Peter Michelson's memories guided me toward a sharper portrait of the students and their behavior during the week. Michelson's essay in the summer 1998 *Notre Dame Review*, "The Day They Maced Our Lady," is great reading for anyone who wishes to relive that time in Notre Dame history. John Matthias's memories of the night Ralph Ellison spoke, and the after-party, were extremely helpful. I can't thank these men enough.

Further gratitude for sharing their time and memories to Fritz Hoefer (bookstore basketball!), Richard Moran (perhaps Vonnegut was a bit drunk at his talk), Jim Metzger (who replaced John Mroz as the SLF chairman in 1969, another wonderful event), and Edward Suzuki (designer of the front page of the 1968 SLF program), who helped me understand just what exactly were the benefits in building a geodesic dome such as the Stepan Center. Thank you, thank you, and thank you.

Through these interviews, the University of Notre Dame Archives, and local newspaper databases (buy a local paper!), the bedrock for the book was formed. I knew I could draw on my prior research of King's final week and LBJ's announcement—in addition to standout events like the horrendous Richmond explosion, the Chicago riots, and the tragic execution of Bobby Hutton—to start weaving together a rich, day-by-day tapestry of life within the microcosm of South Bend, Indiana, during that fateful week. I know this is vague, but I'd like to thank all local newspaper journalists doing their job right now. We need you now more than ever.

After having done my research, I still needed help in crafting a professional proposal. For that I thank my literary agent, Jane Dystel. She, along with Miriam Goderich and the Dystel Agency team, helped immensely with the focus of the book. "People want to read about people," they said to me. So true. . . .

Speaking of people, I would like to thank copyeditor Miki Gallasch as well as the entire Chicago Review Press team for how much they helped with this book. Jerome Pohlen, Devon Freeny, and Benjamin Krapohl all did such a great job in shaping and refining this narrative.

On a personal note, I'd like to thank David Garrow, Simon Park, and Arthur O'Keefe for being great friends and helping me keep the shadows at bay.

And, as always, my wife, Yuka. To paraphrase and reinterpret F. Scott Fitzgerald: *so we beat on, boats against the current, our love the engine that moves us through the maddening waters of time.*

NOTES

Prologue: How to Create a
Festival with Only $2.72

1. DeCicco, *SLF Album*, 6.

2. Hutchens, "One Thing," 21–22.

3. Karen Linehan-Mroz, interview with the author, May 1, 2017.

4. Linehan-Mroz, interview with the author.

5. "Johnson Urges Draft Lottery, Taking of 19-Year-Olds First," *Courier-Post* (UPI article), March 6, 1967, 1.

6. Martin Kress, interview with the author, June 16, 2017.

7. Hutchens, "One Thing," 21–22.

8. Hutchens, 21–22.

9. Hutchens, 21–22.

10. This exchange was an AP article published in dozens of newspapers across the country. I went with: "Bobby, LBJ, Spar on Vietnam Issue," *Detroit Free Press*, March 3, 1967, 2.

11. Quote found in a transcript of a question-and-answer session immediately after MLK's April 4, 1967, "Beyond Vietnam" speech.

12. Bill Zimmerman is the protester, from Ken Burns and Lynn Novick's documentary *The Vietnam War*, ep. 4, at 93 min. Information about the march's New York route was in *Daily Journal* (Vineland, NJ), April 12, 1967, 14.

13. Burns and Novick, *Vietnam War*, ep. 4, at 93 min., Bill Zimmerman commentary.

14. Morris, *Bill of Rites*, 7.

15. Hutchens, "One Thing," 21–22. Here are a few of the other writers Mroz contacted in late 1967, their shortened "best wishes" replies quoted on page 5 of the official 1968 Sophomore Literary Festival Program: John Barth, Saul Bellow, Bernard Malamud, Vern Sneider, and John Hawkes. Barth later came to the Notre Dame literary festival in 1969 and 1980, Hawkes in 1971. Linda DeCicco, *SLF Album: An Informal History of Notre Dame's Sophomore Literary Festival, 1967–1996.*

16. George Ovitt Jr., interview with the author, October 9, 2017.

17. DeCicco, *SLF Album*, 7.

18. DeCicco, 7.

19. Letter from Ray Bradbury to John Mroz, July 24, 1967.

20. Letter from Robert Penn Warren to John Mroz, August 1, 1967.

21. William C. Locke, "Literary Festival Chairman: John Mroz" (interview), *Notre Dame Scholastic* 109, no. 16 (March 15, 1968): 22–23. Locke was also a member of the 1968 sophomore festival committee.

22. Hutchens, "One Thing," 21–22. In another article, Joseph Haas, writing for the *Chicago Daily News*, states that they had $3.22 in the account. Either way, two quarters won't get you any writer. Well, maybe me.

23. DeCicco, *SLF Album*, 6.

24. Hutchens, "One Thing," 21–22.

25. Hutchens, 21–22. I also heard about flyers and other methods of collecting money through interviews with several of the sophomore committee members, such as George Ovitt, Tito Trevino, and Marty Kress, among others.

26. William Pannill, "Author Rejects Black Separatism," *Detroit Free Press*, October 5, 1967, p. 4-A. Ellison said this in front of four thousand people at the University of Michigan's Hill Auditorium on October 4, 1967. Ellison was thought by some then as "a man 10 years behind the times" and was determined to push back from the "one side or the other" mentality: "There is also an American Negro tradition which teaches one to deflect racial provocations and to master and contain pain. It is a tradition which abhors as obscene any trading on one's anguish for gains and sympathy." Mike McGrady, "Writer Ellison's Lonely Stand," *Oakland Tribune*, November 7, 1967, 1.

27. Kress, interview with the author, June 16, 2017.

28. From the Granville Hicks Papers, box 46. The letter is dated November 17, 1967, on SLF letterhead, https://library.syr.edu/digital/guides/h/hicks_g.htm; printed here courtesy of Syracuse University Archives.

29. Ralph Blumenthal, "Wright Morris, a Novelist of the Nebraska Prairie, Dies at 88," *New York Times*, April 29, 1988, https://www.nytimes.com/1998/04/29/arts/wright-morris-a-novelist-of-the-nebraska-prairie-dies-at-88.html.

30. Morris used the same "grubby, disinterested" line that Mroz used in the Hicks letter.

31. George Ovitt Jr., interview and correspondence with the author, October 9, 2017.

32. Wright Morris, letter to John E. Mroz, December 4, 1967.

33. Locke, "John Mroz," *Notre Dame Scholastic* 109, no. 16 (March 1968): 22–23, https://studylib.net/doc/8686049/notre-dame-scholastic—vol.-109—no.-16—.

34. Locke, 22–23. For the Ellison quote, see Laura Kelly, "Words, Words, Words," *Notre Dame Observer*, February 4, 2002, 10.

35. *Notre Dame Observer*, January 11, 1968, 3. By this point, Mroz had not yet booked the Stepan Center for Norman Mailer's film, since he mentioned Washington Hall as the location for a "world premiere . . . to be announced soon."

36. Details here can be found in the original 1968 'Minds and Motivations' Notre Dame Sophomore Literary Festival program. Included is the lengthy list of patrons.

37. Hutchens, "One Thing," 21–22.

38. Kress, interview with the author, June 16, 2017.

39. Scanned letter of Joseph Heller to John Mroz, reprinted here from Karen Linehan-Mroz, who owns the original.

40. *Notre Dame Observer*, "Hunter Urges LBJ to Run," March 18, 1968. The student organizer for LBJ was Notre Dame freshman Richard Hunter.

41. Laura Kelly, "Words, Words, Words," *Notre Dame Observer*, February 4, 2002, 10.

42. Franklin D. Schurz, ed., "The Week That Was," *South Bend Tribune*, April 7, 1968.

1. Sunday, March 31, 1968:
A White Flag of Celebration

1. From Bernard Malamud's 1967 National Book Award–winning acceptance speech for his novel *The Fixer*, as cited in Granville Hicks's March 31, 1968, speech at Notre Dame.

2. Quote taken from a February 13, 1968, letter of protest by a woman named Eleanor Harbinson, and sent to the Washington National Cathedral. Accessed here via the WNC website: https://cathedral.org/wp-content /uploads/2018/01/1968-letter-protesting-King-invite.pdf.

3. "Remaining Awake Through a Great Revolution," sermon by Rev. Martin Luther King Jr., accessed December 2018, https://kinginstitute.stanford.edu /king-papers/publications/knock-midnight-inspiration-great-sermons -reverend-martin-luther-king-jr-10; also available in *A Knock at Midnight: Inspiration from the Greatest Sermons of Reverend Martin Luther King Jr.*, ed. Pete Holloran and Clayborne Carson (New York: Warner, 2000), 201–224.

4. King, "Remaining Awake"; *"discouraged"*: Garrow, *Bearing the Cross*, 618.

5. King, "Remaining Awake."

6. WNC press conference, Q and A transcript, March 31, 1968.

7. Coretta King, *My Life with Martin*, 314.

8. Quotes taken from Busby, *Thirty-First of March*, 176.

9. Busby, 178-180.

10. Douglas Brinkley, *Cronkite* (New York: HarperCollins, 2012), 638. Brinkley concedes that the reaction could have been overdramatized, as Bill Moyers has Johnson magnanimously switching off the television set, then speaking the sentence. Perhaps he did, but no question did Johnson's burden feel heavier after Cronkite's much-watched report.

11. Busby, *Thirty-First of March*, 192.

12. Busby, 194.

13. Busby, 205.

14. Busby, 211.

15. March 31, 1968, speech by Granville Hicks at the University of Notre Dame. Original speech is part of the Granville Hicks collection at Syracuse University.

16. Hicks, *Part of the Truth*, 23.

17. Hicks, 34.

18. Hicks kept Mroz's hourly-schedule itinerary, and it can be viewed with his archives at Syracuse University, box 46.

19. "Social. Candidate Condemns Whites and 'White Power,'" *Notre Dame Observer*, April 1, 1968, 2.

20. "Social. Candidate Condemns," 2.

21. Hicks, *Part of the Truth*, 119.

22. Hicks, 102.

23. From his March 31, 1968, keynote address.

24. Ovitt, interview and correspondence with the author, October 9, 2017. What Ovitt told me generally echoes what I gathered from most of the other interviewees, all of whom in some way helped with the literary festival.

25. *Notre Dame Observer*, March 18, 1968. Sketch is on p. 3 and signed W. Maloney, with the caption "Et Tu Bobby."

26. Granville Hicks, "A Bad Time" keynote address to the Sophomore Literary Festival, March 31, 1968. From the Granville Hicks Papers at the Syracuse University Archives.

27. Tito Trevino, interview with the author, March 14, 2018.

28. Granville Hicks, "The Sophomores at Notre Dame," *Saturday Review*, May 4, 1968, 19.

29. Lady Bird Johnson, *A White House Diary* (New York: Holt, Rinehart and Winston, 1970), 646.

30. "Bay Area Campuses Jump with Joy," *San Francisco Examiner*, April 1, 1968, 9.

31. "Crowds March After Hearing LBJ Decision," *South Bend Tribune*, April 1, 1968.

32. "True Greatness," *Emporia Gazette*, April 1, 1968, 1.

33. Chris Plumb, "McCarthy Describes Efforts by Intellectuals," *Waukesha Daily Freeman*, April 1, 1968, 3.

34. "A Different Choice Now—McCarthy," *Akron Beacon Journal*, April 1, 1968, 4.

35. "McCarthy Calls Move Surprise; Kennedy Mum," *Decatur Herald*, April 1, 1968, 1.

36. "Nixon's View: Can Johnson Pick Successor?," *Journal News*, April 1, 1968, 4.

37. The hour-by-hour SLF schedule in box 46 in the Granville Hicks Archives at Syracuse University.

38. This line of thought was consistent with what I learned in interviews with other members of the sophomore committee, as well as Father Ernest Bartell, a Notre Dame professor who often sat and listened with many undergraduates struggling to understand their own moral stance.

39. Chris Jarabek, "They Were There," *Notre Dame Observer*, March 29, 1968, 5.

40. P. J. Schroeder, "Administration Suspends Four for Parietal Rules Violation," *Notre Dame Observer*, March 27, 1968, 1.

41. Phil Ault, "The Men Who Draft Your Sons," *South Bend Tribune*, April 1, 1968, 4–6. For anyone researching the Vietnam draft system prelottery, Ault's report here is a good place to start.

42. "Hesburgh Reverse Stand but Parietal Rules Enforced!" *Notre Dame Observer*, April 1, 1968, 1. "You May Live" sketch is on p. 4.

43. Ault, "Men Who Draft Your Sons," 4–6. The number forty-eight thousand is listed by Col. William L. Shaw in "Selective Service Litigation and the 1967 Statute," *Military Law Review* 48 (1970): 39, https://www.loc.gov/rr/frd/Military_Law/Military_Law_Review/pdf-files/277877~1.pdf.

44. Ault, 4–6.

45. Ault, 4–6. I stayed local with my selective service analysis, my focus mainly in St. Joseph County, Indiana. I imagine there are many who have different stories to share.

2. Monday, April 1, 1968: The Loner and the Noisemaker

1. Busby, *Thirty-First of March*, 226–228.

2. Busby, 226–228.

3. Luci Baines Johnson interview on NPR: https://www.npr.org/sections/itsallpolitics/2014/04/10/301414624/luci-baines-johnson-vietnam-war-lanced-lbjs-gut-every-night.

4. Busby, *Thirty-First of March*, 228.

5. "Address to the National Association of Broadcasters," April 1, 1968, accessed December 2018, Miller Center, University of Virginia, https://millercenter .org/the-presidency/presidential-speeches/april-1–1968-address-national -association-broadcasters.

6. "Address to the National Association."

7. "Address to the National Association."

8. Garrow, *Bearing the Cross*, 524. Originally from "The Parable of the Good Samaritan," a sermon delivered at Ebenezer Baptist Church on August 28, 1966. A cassette recording can be found at Stanford University's Martin Luther King Jr. Papers Project.

9. Etta Horn, minutes from SCLC meeting, April 1, 1968. Original located at the Marquette University Archives, box 43, filed under SCLC DC.

10. Horn, SCLC meeting. Walker passed away in Feb. 2018. Barry Amundson, "National Native American leader from ND dies at 88," *West Fargo Pioneer*, Feb. 16, 2018

11. Horn, SCLC meeting. The minutes taker quotes Young like this: "Dr. King attacked the war; they attacked him. Now, about one year after (cites political developments of a night ago: President Johnson's announcement that he will not seek nor accept nomination as Democratic presidential candidate.)"

12. Horn, SCLC meeting.

13. "George Wallace: Settin' the Woods on Fire," *The American Experience*, PBS, April 23–24, 2000, available on YouTube, 25:00, https://www.youtube.com /watch?v=wLkCY0f73iE.

14. Don F. Wasson, "Wallace Says LBJ's Move Won't Affect Candidacy," *Montgomery Advertiser*, April 2, 1968, 12.

15. Wasson, 12.

16. "George Wallace: Settin' the Woods on Fire." See also Dan T. Carter, *The Politics of Rage: George Wallace, the Origins of New Conservatism, and the Transformation of American Politics* (Baton Rouge: Louisiana State University Press, 2000).

17. "Settin' the Woods on Fire."

18. "How to Build a Credibility Gap," *Alabama Journal*, April 3, 1968, 4.

19. "Credibility Gap," 4.

20. "S.F. State 'Squatters' Told to Quit," *San Francisco Examiner*, March 29, 1968, 1.

21. "Campus Commemorates 1968 Student-Led Strike," SF State News, accessed December 2018, http://www.sfsu.edu/news/2008/fall/8.html.

22. "Professor Urges Revolution in U.S. Education," *Colorado Springs Gazette-Telegraph*, November 15, 1968, 1 and 6.

23. Jackson J. Benson, *Haunted: The Strange and Profound Art of Wright Morris* (self published, Xlibris, 2013), ch. 8.

24. Morris, *Bill of Rites*, 60

25. Morris, *Loneliness*, 3. This edition, published by Black Sparrow Press, contains both *The Works of Love* and *The Huge Season*. Highly recommended if you can find it.

26. Benson, *Haunted*.

27. Morris, *Bill of Rites*, 105 and 128.

28. Morris, 105 and 128.

29. Patricia Koval, "Politics Draws Mailer Invective," *South Bend Tribune*, April 2, 1968.

30. Hicks, "Sophomores at Notre Dame," 19.

31. Ovitt, correspondence with the author, October 9, 2017. In 1970, a *New York Times Book Review* critic will call Morris "the least well-known and most widely unappreciated important writer alive in this country."

32. Morris, *Bill of Rites*, 77.

33. Lennon, *A Double Life*, 40 and 74.

34. Lennon, 95.

35. Lennon, 2.

36. W. G. Rogers, "Author of the Week," *Daily Record*, May 1, 1948, 4.

37. Lennon, *A Double Life*, 2; "ever in my life" is in Lennon's notes.

38. Lennon, 3; "small voice" is from Mailer's sister's memory, one which she writes she'll "never forget the sound of because it so totally captured the feeling that none of this was quite real."

39. Locke, "John Mroz," 22.

40. Kelly, "Words, Words, Words," 10.

41. Hicks, "Sophomores at Notre Dame," 19–20. Also, Patricia Koval, "Literary Festival a Swinging Affair," *South Bend Tribune*, May 5, 1968.

42. Jack Altman, "Mailer's Life-Style Is One of Hyperbole," *Indianapolis News*, April 10, 1968, 11; and Joseph Haas, "Notre Dame Meets Norman Mailer," *Chicago Daily News*, April 6, 1968, panorama, 2.

43. Altman, "Mailer's Life-Style," 11.

44. Haas, "Notre Dame Meets Norman Mailer," panorama, 2.

45. Koval, "Politics Draws Mailer Invective."

46. Koval.

47. Mailer, *Armies of the Night*, 288.

48. Granville Hicks, "Lark in the Race for Presidency," *Saturday Review*, September 16, 1967, 39.

49. Hicks, "Sophomores at Notre Dame," 19–20.

50. Haas, "Notre Dame Meets Norman Mailer," 2.

51. Altman, "Mailer's Life-Style," 11.

3. Tuesday, April 2, 1968: A World Premiere in Middle America

1. Joseph A. Califano Jr., *The Triumph and Tragedy of Lyndon Johnson: The White House Years* (New York: Simon & Schuster, 1991).

2. "Hanoi Press Says U.S. Hasn't Halted Raids Unconditionally," *Los Angeles Times* (morning ed.), April 3, 1968, front page.

3. "Johnson's Sincerity on Peace Reasserted," *Los Angeles Times* (morning ed.), April 3, 1968, 13.

4. Coretta King, *My Life with Martin*, 216.

5. King, 107 and 211.

6. King, 212.

7. Dexter King, *Growing Up King: An Intimate Memoir* (New York: Warner, 2003), 45; *"dispirited"*: Garrow, *Bearing the Cross*, 619.

8. From the campaign documentary *A Time to Begin—Nixon in New Hampshire 1968*, Richard Nixon Foundation, available on YouTube, accessed November 17, 2018, https://www.youtube.com/watch?v=9aiGt2_4xy4.

9. Bob Webb, "Nixon Proposes U.S.-Soviet Talks on Vietnam, Other Trouble Spots," *Cincinnati Enquirer*, April 3, 1968, 1. Also, for the "hawks and doves" quote, see the "Cincinnati News Briefs," *Cincinnati Enquirer*, April 3, 1968, 42. The councilman was John J. Gilligan.

10. Webb, "Nixon Proposes," 1.

11. *A Time to Begin*, Richard Nixon Foundation.

12. *A Time to Begin*.

13. Norman Mailer, *Miami and the Siege of Chicago*: An Informal History of the Republican and Democratic Conventions of 1968 (New York: New American Library, 1968).

14. From the 1968 Notre Dame Sophomore Literary Festival program, "Minds and Motivations," 10.

15. Clifford Terry, "From Split Ends to Book Ends: Notre Dame and Normal Norman," *Chicago Tribune*, April 14, 1968, 14.

16. Haas, "Notre Dame Meets Norman Mailer," panorama, 2–4.

17. Haas, 2–4. Author correspondence August 19, 2017, with Richard Bizot helped to fix the mistake in Joseph Haas article stating that the boy was the son of a student. . . . Bizot was a young professor at the time.

18. Haas, 2–4.

19. Terry, "Split Ends to Book Ends," 14.

20. Hutchens, "One Thing," 22.

21. Hutchens, 22.

22. Hutchens, 22; also Haas, "Notre Dame Meets Norman Mailer," panorama, 2–4.

23. Haas, 2–4.

24. Hicks, "Sophomores at Notre Dame," 19–20.

25. Clifford Terry, "Mailer Tries it Again," *Chicago Tribune*, April 4, 1968, 11; Patricia Koval, "Popcorn Is Only Item Missing at Premiere of Mailer Film," *South Bend Tribune*, April 3, 1968; Haas, "Notre Dame Meets Norman Mailer," panorama, 2–4.

26. Haas, "Notre Dame Meets Norman Mailer," panorama, 2–4; and Terry, "Split Ends to Book Ends," 14.

27. Correspondence with Richard Bizot, who wrote a short piece titled "Mailer at Notre Dame" and sent it to me August 21, 2017.

28. Hicks, "Sophomores at Notre Dame," 19–20.

29. Information about the band was given to me by former Notre Dame professor (and party attendee) Richard Bizot, whose wife, Joyce, would eventually manage the band and help it to perform in national competition, losing one battle to Kool and the Gang.

30. Haas, "Notre Dame Meets Norman Mailer," panorama, 2–4

31. DeCicco, *SLF Album*, 9.

32. Terry, "Split Ends to Book Ends," 14.

33. DeCicco, *SLF Album*, 6.

4. Wednesday, April 3, 1968: A Hawk and a Dove Soar Below a Mountaintop

1. The full text of the Hanoi statement can be found in many newspapers on April 4, 1968. I used "Here's Text of Hanoi's Offer to Talk with U.S.," *Cincinnati Enquirer*, 16.

2. "Text of Hanoi's Offer."

3. "LBJ Briefs HHH, RFK on Viet," *Arizona Republic*, April 4, 1968, 1.

4. Lyndon B. Johnson, press conference, April 3, 1968, available online via Miller Center, University of Virginia, accessed August 7, 2018, https://millercenter .org/the-presidency/presidential-speeches/april-3-1968-press-conference.

5. Johnson, press conference, April 3, 1968.

6. McCarthy, *Year of the People*, 17.

7. McCarthy, 17.

8. McCarthy, 18.

9. "Probe Urged of CIA's Foreign Policy Role," *Philadelphia Inquirer*, January 25, 1966, 2.

10. AP article in "15 Dem Senators Urge Extension of Bombing Lull," *Akron Beacon Journal*, 2.

11. Barry Goldwater, *Los Angeles Times*, "A Dangerous Principle," May 15, 1966, G-7.

12. Ronald Steel, *Chicago Tribune*, "From McCarthy of Minnesota, Cautious Dissent," November 19, 1967, 5.

13. Rowland Evans and Robert Novak, "Stage Set for Battle at ADA Meeting over Anti-LBJ Activities of Official," *Daily Press*, September 18, 1967, 4.

14. George Gallup, "RFK Wins Handily Against Johnson," October 1, 1967, *Minneapolis Star Tribune*, 1.

15. Thomas J. Knock, *The Rise of the Prairie Statesman: The Life and Times of George McGovern* (Princeton, NJ: Princeton University Press, 2016), 372.

16. Saul Friedman and Philip Meyer, "From One Side Comes John Galbraith, from the Other Side, Gen. Gavin," *Detroit Free Press*, October 15, 1967, B-1.

17. Knock, *Prairie Statesman*, 373–374.

18. William H. Chafe, *Never Stop Running: Allard Lowenstein and American Liberal Activism* (New York: Basic, 1993), 271.

19. Chafe, 271.

20. Knock, *Prairie Statesman*, 374.

21. William F. Buckley Jr., "Pro-Kennedy Tint on McCarthy Path," *Star Press*, November 19, 1967, 4.

22. Max Lerner, "On McCarthy," *Gazette* (Montreal, Canada), April 1, 1968, 6.

23. Mary McGrory, "A Success for McCarthy: Closing the Generation Gap," *Boston Globe*, March 5, 1968, 34.

24. King's McCarthy endorsement is in McCarthy, *Year of the People*, 159. His comment on both candidates was printed in the *Journal Times* (Racine, WI) under the headline "King Urges Backing RFK or McCarthy," March 18, 1968, 6.

25. *Shadow bout . . . Daily Telegram*: "Luster Taken Off Primary by LBJ Move," April 1, 1968, 1. Results of Wisconsin Primary in "McCarthy: 57%; Nixon: 80%," *Journal Times*, April 3, 1968.

26. "McCarthy Address Airport Crowd Says Indiana 'Next Great Test,'" *Notre Dame Observer*, April 5, 1968, 3.

27. Joel Connelly, "The Politics of Hope," *Notre Dame Observer*, April 8, 1968, 6.

28. Thomas Jewell, "McCarthy Focuses on Economics," *South Bend Tribune*, April 3, 1968, 29.

29. Jack Colwell, "Peace Hopes 'Closest in Two Years,'" *South Bend Tribune* (evening), April 3, 1968, 1

30. Colwell, 26.

31. "McCarthy Address Airport Crowd Says Indiana," 3.

32. Connelly, "Politics of Hope"; "gold outflow" in Jewell, "McCarthy Focuses on Economics."

33. Connelly; Jewell.

34. Dave Hope, "McCarthy in Eastbay for Rally," *Oakland Tribune*, April 4, 1968, 2.

35. "Arena Crowd Wild About Gene," *Hartford Courant*, April 4, 1968, 51

36. Tom Ehrbar, "Dow Protest Draws Admin. Reaction, Doan Speech Closed to Demonstrators," *Notre Dame Observer*, April 5, 1968, 1.

37. Through the *New York Times* service, reprinted by *Daily Oklahoman* ("Napalm Plant Draws Fire," April 17, 1966, 93).

38. Roger Birdsell, "Notre Dame Locks Out Protesters,'" *South Bend Tribune*, April 4, 1968, 29.

39. Napalm figures: "U.S. Criticized for Napalm Plant," *Daily Oklahoman*, April 17, 1966, 94. The contract for the napalm was for six months, starting May 1, and was being formulated at the Dow Chemical plant in Torrance, California.

40. "U.S. Criticized for Napalm Plant." Kim Phuc Phan Thi's excellent memoir *Fire Road* (she was the naked "Napalm Girl" in that devastating 1972 photo) helped me to understand the effect of napalm on human skin.

41. "Officials Arrest 16 UW Students," *Oshkosh Northwestern*, February 23, 1967, 16. The article shows a list of seventeen students who were arrested.

42. "76 Hurt in UW Rioting'; Campus Strike Results," *Wisconsin State Journal*, October 19, 1967, 1. This moment was also covered in a well-done PBS documentary, *Two Days in October*.

43. "Protesters Locked Out," *South Bend Tribune*, April 3, 1968, front page.

44. Jack Lavelle, "The President of Dow Chemical Is Just Like Your Father," *Notre Dame Observer*, April 5, 1968, 6.

45. Lavelle, 6.

46. "The President of Dow Chemical Company on: Napalm in Vietnam," *Scholastic*, April 5, 1968, 18.

47. Jeremiah V. Murphy, "Common Mobbed; 235 Turn in Draft Cards," *Boston Globe*, April 4, 1968, 2.

48. James C. Young, "32 Clergymen Assist Draft-Card 'Turn-In' at Viet War Protest," *Philadelphia Inquirer*, April 4, 1968, 4.

49. Howard Zinn, *You Can't Be Neutral on a Moving Train: A Personal History of Our Times* (Boston: Beacon, 2002), 132.

50. Zinn, 133.

51. Murphy, "Common Mobbed."

52. Patricia Koval, "Buckley Tells N.D. Audience of Student Responsibility," *South Bend Tribune*, April 4, 1968, 18. Nixon gave his "Great Silent Majority" speech on November 3, 1969. "Nixon's 'Great Silent Majority,'" *The American Experience*, PBS, YouTube video, accessed September 2018, https://www.youtube.com/watch?v=Hqz0i83Jqxg.

53. William F. Buckley Jr., "Mission Statement," *National Review*, November 19, 1955; also, William F. Buckley Jr. "On the Right: Hate LBJ," *New Castle News*, April 3, 1968.

54. As advertised in the *Pittsburgh Post-Gazette*, April 3, 1968, 39. For a recording of Hentoff's debate with Buckley: "Black Power," *Firing Line with William F. Buckley Jr.*, March 7, 1967, accessed February 20, 2020, from the Hoover Institution Library & Archives, https://digitalcollections.hoover.org/objects/5983. One comment made by Mr. Hentoff stands out: "All cultures that interact, and this is the case in this country, become tainted, one against the other. . . . Before there is going to be any reconciliation between the races in this country, there's going to be a great deal more of tension . . . a great deal of expression and anger. I think this is inevitable."

55. "Mr. Conservative Stresses Student Responsibility," *Notre Dame Observer*, April 5, 1968, 3.

56. Patricia Koval, "Buckley Tells N.D. Audience," 18.

57. Koval, 18.

58. The UND student was Richard Moran, whom the author corresponded with in late August 2017; George Ovitt was from correspondence dated October 9, 2017.

59. Coretta King, *My Life with Martin*, 314.

60. As quoted in Garrow, *Bearing the Cross*, 619.

61. Dorothy F. Cotton, interview with Joseph Rosenbloom, February 18, 2013; quoted in *Redemption: Martin Luther King Jr.'s Last 31 Hours.*

62. Cotton, interview with Rosenbloom.

63. Also in *Redemption*, story from Rosenbloom interview with Andrew Young, October 12, 2012.

64. Ralph Abernathy, *And the Walls Came Tumbling Down* (New York: Harper & Row, 1989), 428.

65. Rosenbloom, *Redemption*, 25

66. "New Curbs in War Urged," *Baltimore Sun*, April 4, 1968, A4.

67. Rosenbloom, *Redemption*, 55.

68. John Burl Smith, as told to Ruth Hopkins, "I Met with Martin Luther King Minutes Before He Was Murdered," Narratively: Hidden History, April 4, 2017, https://narratively.com/the-secret-life-of-a-professional-statue/. Smith says that King handed Cabbage and him a promissory note for $10,000 after talking to the National Council of Churches but says that this took place on the afternoon of April 4.

69. Rosenbloom, *Redemption*, 48.

70. Rosenbloom, *Redemption*, 70.

71. Keith Miller, *Martin Luther King's Biblical Epic* (Jackson: University of Mississippi Press, 2011), 12.

72. Rosenbloom, *Redemption,* 105.

73. Full text of the speech can be found in Clayborne Carson, ed., *A Call to Conscience: The Landmark Speeches of Martin Luther King Jr.* (New York: Warner, 2001), 207–223.

74. Carson, 222–223. I inserted my own audience reaction tags after listening to the audio of the speech, so there will be slight variations between the two.

75. Coretta King, *My Life with Martin*, 316.

5. Thursday, April 4, 1968: The Death of a King and the Life of a Millionaire

1. Robert F. Kennedy, "Remarks to the Cleveland City Club, April 5, 1968," John F. Kennedy Presidential Library and Museum, https://www.jfklibrary.org/learn /about-jfk/the-kennedy-family/robert-f-kennedy/robert-f-kennedy -speeches/remarks-to-the-cleveland-city-club-april-5-1968.

2. "King Must Be Dissuaded," *Orlando Sentinel* (main ed.), April 4, 1968, 22

3. Norman Scott, "It's Time to Act," *McKinney Weekly Democrat-Gazette*, April 4, 1968, 1

4. "Time to Take Real Look at Dr. King," *Daily Capital News*, April 4, 1968; Maj. Gen. T. A. Lane, "Memphis Riot Repeats King Tactic," *Jefferson City Post-Tribune*, April 4, 1968, 4.

5. *Eyes on the Prize* (TV series), part 10, "The Promised Land," at thirty-eight minutes, Andrew Young interview.

6. Rosenbloom, *Redemption*, 155–156.

7. Rosenbloom, 154.

8. Hampton Sides, *Hellhound on His Trail* (New York: Anchor, 2010), 150.

9. As quoted in Arthur M. Schlesinger Jr., *Robert Kennedy and His Times* (New Yorker: Mariner, 2002), 921. The quote is from a comment former president Eisenhower made to Robert Cutler on March 26, 1968, later published in the *New York Post* on March 21, 1975.

10. "Drive, Talk Planned by Kennedy: Bulletin," *South Bend Tribune* (evening), April 4, 1968, 1.

11. David Iliff, "Hundreds Welcome Bob Kennedy to Muncie Airport," *Muncie Star Press*, April 5, 1968, 3.

12. Jack Colwell, "RFK Visit Rekindles Magic," *South Bend Tribune*, April 5, 1968, 40.

13. Norton Kay, "Teens Pull for Bobby—Yank Him from Car," *Chicago American*, April 4, 1968. Copy of article found at the University of Notre Dame Archives. The *Chicago American* later became *Chicago Today*.

14. Thomas Jewell, "RFK Visits Elderly at County Home," *South Bend Tribune*, April 5, 1968, 23. The woman's name is Pearl Klein.

15. Jack Colwell, "Crowds Greet Kennedy Here," *South Bend Tribune*, April 4, 1968, 11.

16. Ovitt, correspondence with the author, December 18, 2017. Branigin used this kind of rhetoric from the beginning of the campaign. To find these two words, see Jep Cadou Jr., "Branigin Plea to GOP: Cross Over, Support Me," *Indianapolis Star*, April 20, 1968, 1 and 15.

17. Ovitt, correspondence with the author; Granville Hicks, *Saturday Review*, May 4, 1968.

18. Hutchens, "One Thing," 22.

19. To read his Notre Dame speech, see Robert Kennedy, *Unfulfilled Promise: The Speeches and Notes from the Last Campaign of Robert F. Kennedy, March 16, 1968 to June 5, 1968* (San Diego: M. J. Aguirre, 1986), 177–182.

20. Joel Connelly, "Kennedy Kicks Off Ind. Campaign with Stepan Center Speech," *Notre Dame Observer*, April 5, 1968, 1

21. To create this schedule, I used Arthur Schlesinger's biography *Robert Kennedy and His Times*, Ray E. Boomhower's *Robert F. Kennedy and the 1968 Indiana Primary*, and a variety of local newspapers, such as the *Muncie Star Press*, *South Bend Tribune*, the *Indianapolis Star*, and the *Rushville Republican*, the last of which provided a generalized schedule: "Bobby Visits Indiana Today," April 4, 1968, p. 1.

22. Joel Connelly, "Kennedy Kicks off Ind. Campaign with Stepan Center Speech," *Notre Dame Observer*, April 5, 1968, p. 1.

23. *RFK: His Words for Our Times*, part 4, "Child Poverty and Hunger: University of Notre Dame," (New York: William Morrow, 2018), 354.

24. Jack Colwell, "RFK Visit Rekindles 'Magic,'" *South Bend Tribune*, April 5, 1968, 40

25. "King's Death Stirs Bobby's Talk of JFK," *Elwood Call-Leader*, April 5, 1968, 1 and 8.

26. Jewell, "RFK Visits Elderly at County Home," 23.

27. Jewell, 23.

28. Jewell, 23.

29. Colwell, "RFK Visit Rekindles," 23.

30. David Iliff, "Hundreds Welcome Bob Kennedy to Muncie Airport," *Muncie Star Press*, April 5, 1968, 3; Floyd Creech, "Packed Gym Roars Welcome for Bobby's Campus Visit," *Muncie Evening Press*, April 5, 1968, 5.

31. Brian Usher, "Kennedy Gets Frenzied Greeting from Students," *Muncie Star*, April 5, 1968, 1

32. Shirley Hayes, "Ethel Weary but Willing on Campaign Jaunt Here," *Muncie Star*, April 5, 1968, 1.

33. Brian Usher, "Kennedy Gets Frenzied Greeting," 1 and 3.

34. Larry Shores, "RFK Raps Food Program," *Muncie Star*, April 5, 1968, 1 and 3.

35. Brian Usher, "Kennedy Gets Frenzied Greeting," 1 and 3.

36. Dexter King, *Growing Up King*, 47–48.

37. King, 47–48.

38. Maya Angelou, *A Song Flung Up to Heaven* (New York: Random House, 2002), 177.

39. Angelou, 188–189.

40. Angelou, 193.

41. James Baldwin, "Malcolm and Martin," *Esquire* 77, no. 4 (April 1972); reprinted in *Portable Malcolm X Reader*, ed. Manning Marable and Garrett Felber (New York: Penguin, 2013), 485–508.

42. Baldwin, "Malcom and Martin"; reprinted in Marable and Felber, 485–508.

43. Rev. Samuel McKinney, interview with the author, December 12, 2014.

44. Patricia Koval, "Writer Heller Wears McCarthy Button," *South Bend Tribune*, April 5, 1968.

45. Kress, interview with the author, June 16, 2017.

46. Phil Kukielski, correspondence with the author, September 18, 2017.

47. Kukielski, correspondence with the author.

48. James R., "The Day I Met Kurt Vonnegut," *In Progress* (blog), April 18, 2013, http://harv8.blogspot.com/2013/04/the-day-i-met-kurt-vonnegut.html. This may be UND alum James or Jim Ruzicka.

49. Tito Trevino, correspondence with the author, March 14, 2018.

50. Trevino, correspondence with the author.

51. Patricia Koval (now writing under the name Kate Alcott), correspondence with the author, July 31, 2018.

52. See Playboy interview with Vonnegut and Heller. For the "stunned" quote, see Koval, "Literary Festival a Swinging Affair."

53. James McKenzie, correspondence with the author, April 12, 2017. McKenzie originally responded to a post via *Notre Dame Magazine*'s website—a letter to the editor in the summer of 2010. McKenzie's "a silence I regret" remark was an important spark for me in the early stages of writing this book.

54. Tom Schatz, interview with the author, January 5, 2019.

55. Patricia Koval, "Writer Heller Wears McCarthy Button," *South Bend Tribune*, April 5, 1968.

56. Joseph Heller, *Catch-22* (New York: Simon & Schuster: 1961), 437.

57. "Sharp Sense of Humor Shown by 'Catch-22' Author," *South Bend Tribune*, May 5, 1968, 218.

58. McKenzie, correspondence with the author, April 12, 2017; *Notre Dame Magazine* letter to editor, summer 2010.

59. Schlesinger, *Robert Kennedy and His Times*, 939.

60. Boomhower, *Robert F. Kennedy and the 1968 Indiana Primary*, 62.

61. Boomhower, 63–64.

62. Boomhower, 63–64. Also see Witcover, *85 Days*, 112.

63. An article that goes into further detail about the Kennedys and Greek myth is Daniel Mendelsohn's "J.F.K., Tragedy, Myth," *New Yorker*, November 22, 2013. For Lewis quote, see Boomhower, 65.

64. Robert Kennedy, statement on assassination of Martin Luther King, Jr., Indianapolis, Indiana, April 4, 1968, accessed December 2018 from the John F. Kennedy Presidential Museum and Library website, https://www.jfklibrary .org/learn/about-jfk/the-kennedy-family/robert-f-kennedy/robert-f-kennedy -speeches/statement-on-assassination-of-martin-luther-king-jr-indianapolis -indiana-april-4-1968.

65. "RFK Asks Negroes to Reject Revenge," *South Bend Tribune*, April 5, 1968, section 2, 40.

66. Schlesinger, *Robert Kennedy and His Times*, 941.

67. AP, "Cooke Installed as New York Archbishop," *Evening Sun* (Baltimore, MD), April 4, 1968, 4.

68. Califano, *Triumph and Tragedy*, 272. Confirmation of standing ovation in *Evening Sun* article, "Cooke Installed as New York Archbishop."

69. "Johnson Confers with Thant," *Honolulu-Star Bulletin*, April 4, 1968, 4.

70. Lyndon B. Johnson, "Statement by the President on the Assassination of Dr. Martin Luther King, Jr.," April 4, 1968, The American Presidency Project, https://www.presidency.ucsb.edu/node/238016.

71. Lady Bird Johnson, *White House Diary*, 648.

72. "Minneapolis Man Charged with Murder in Shooting," *Minneapolis Star Tribune*, April 6, 1968, 19.

73. "Minneapolis Man Charged"; see also Marianne Combs, "The Night Uncle Clarence Went Out and Killed a White Man," Minnesota Public Radio, April 4, 2018, https://www.mprnews.org/story/2018/04/04/the-night-uncle -clarence-went-out-to-kill-a-white-man.

74. "Minneapolis Man Charged." One other article helped provide a few other details. Erica Rivera, "Composer Grapples with 1960's Killing," *Minneapolis Star Tribune*, April 2, 2018, http://e.startribune.com/Olive/ODN/Star Tribune/shared/ShowArticle.aspx?doc=MST%2F2018%2F04%2F02&entity =Ar03100&sk=10EFBBF4&mode=text.

75. Stokely Carmichael, *Ready for Revolution: The Life and Legacy of Stokely Carmichael (Kwame Ture)* (New York: Scribner, 2003), 656.

76. Risen, *Nation on Fire*, 47. Also see Ben W. Gilbert, *Ten Blocks from the White House: Anatomy of the Washington Riots of 1968* (New York: Praeger, 1968), 16.

77. Carmichael, *Ready for Revolution*, 656.

78. Robert W. Lucas. "Divisiveness Feared by LBJ Is Real Threat," *Star-Gazette*, April 4, 1968, 6.

79. Carmichael, *Ready for Revolution*, 656.

80. Stokely Carmichael, interview with Judy Richardson, November 7, 1988, Eyes on the Prize project, Washington University, accessed August 2018, http://digital .wustl.edu/e/eii/eiiweb/car5427.0967.029stokleycarmichael.html.

81. Carmichael, *Ready for Revolution*, 659.

82. Jim Rankin, "A Marching Song," *Atlanta Constitution*, April 6, 1968, 4. "Bill" Rankin has worked for the *Atlanta Journal-Constitution* since 1989.

83. Rankin, 4.

6. Friday, April 5, 1968: The Fallout of a Nation

1. Burns and Novick, *Vietnam War*, ep. 6, "Things Fall Apart," at the twenty-minute mark.

2. David Harker, "Harker: The Last Full Measure of Devotion," *Lynchburg News & Advance*, May 28, 2017. Harker was a POW with Kushner at the same camp.

3. Ken Willis, "POW Survived Five Years in Hell," *Dayton Beach News Journal*, July 4, 2010.

4. Hal Kushner, "The POW Experience with Dr. Hal Kushner" speech, The Vietnam War at 50 symposium, Virginia Military Institute, uploaded September 24, 2018, accessed October 2018, https://www.youtube.com/watch?v=yxisuX8HPyQ&t=338s.

5. Kushner.

6. Burns and Novick, *Vietnam War*, ep. 6.

7. Burns and Novick.

8. Charles Jackson, "'Violent Retaliation Is Out,' Students Plan a King Fund," *Atlanta Constitution*, April 6, 1968, 1

9. Ralph McGill, "A Free Man Is Killed by White Slaves," *Atlanta Constitution*, April 5, 1968, 1.

10. Theo Lippman, "McGill and Patterson: Journalists for Justice," *Virginia Quarterly Review* (Autumn 2003): accessed August 25, 2018, https://www.vqronline.org/essay/mcgill-and-patterson-journalists-justice.

11. Contrary to what this man has written, Wallace in fact called King's death a "senseless, regrettable and tragic act . . . [and] another example of the breakdown of law and order in this country, which must be stopped . . . it is my hope that whoever is guilty of this act will be speedily apprehended." *Montgomery Advertiser*, "Wallace, Many Other Alabamians Decry the Assassination of King," April 5, 1968, pg. 1.

12. The original is kept in the Ralph McGill Papers at Emory University's Stuart A. Rose Manuscript, Archives & Rare Book Library, box 18, folder 7.

13. Rebecca Burns, *Burial for a King* (New York: Scribner, 2011), 45–46; also Ralph McGill, "Evil Played into His Hands," *Atlanta Constitution*, April 6, 1968, 1.

14. Sara Schulman, "April 4, 1968," found in the Ralph McGill Papers at Emory University's Stuart A. Rose Manuscript, Archives & Rare Book Library, box 18, folder 7. Thanks to researcher Kira Jones for helping me with this.

15. Jane Evinger, "UH Negro Students Shout Hate," *Honolulu Advertiser*, April 6, 1968, 1.

16. Evinger, 4.

17. "March Leaflet," *UC-San Diego Indicator* 3, no. 1 (April 1968): 8.

18. "Profs Discuss Assassination," *UC-San Diego Indicator* 3, no. 1 (April 1968): 2.

19. AP, "Arrests Follow Display by UM students," *Montana Standard*, April 6, 1968, 1.

20. At this point in the newspaper's history, there is the morning edition, *Daily Capital News*, and the *Jefferson City Post-Tribune*. The article referred to here is from *Daily Capital News*, "Intended Peaceful March Erupts into Fracas at Newspaper Plant," April 6, 1968, 1 and 6.

21. "Intended Peaceful March Erupts," 1 and 6. This conflict in Jefferson City is located less than a mile from where King's assassin spent seven years in jail.

22. AP Archives notes a time stamp of 4:00 PM, found here: http://www.aparchive.com/metadata/youtube/61d894631db5c1587f776d70149dc306.

23. Transcribed from audio accessed from "SNCC (Carmichael & Sellers) on the Day After MLK was shot," uploaded by "thepostarchive" on March 8, 2017, https://www.youtube.com/watch?v=8QnAEik_Y78; and from clips on the AP Archive website, accessed October 10, 2020, http://www.aparchive.com/metadata/youtube/61d894631db5c1587f776d70149dc306.

24. *CBS Evening News*, April 5, 1968, https://www.youtube.com/watch?v=g_YuKGxQbZE.

25. Juan Williams, *Thurgood Marshall: American Revolutionary*, Random House, 1998, 341.

26. Williams, 341. Williams used Johnson's notes from the meeting.

27. Califano, *Triumph and Tragedy*, 276

28. Califano, 277–279. For King's real estate quote, see the 2018 HBO documentary *King in the Wilderness*, Peter Kunhardt, director, around the thirty-three minute mark. King spoke on August 4, 1966.

29. As quoted by Gary Rivlin, "The Night Chicago Burned," *Chicago Reader*, August 25, 1988.

30. Robert Wiedrich, "Genesis of a Riot: Police Recount Its Escalation," *Chicago Tribune*, April 14, 1968.

31. Wiedrich.

32. Rivlin, "Night Chicago Burned."

33. "$9 Million Loss in Chicago Riots," *Mt. Vernon Register News*, April 13, 1968, 2.

34. Wiedrich, "Genesis of a Riot."

35. Steve Bogira, "They Were There: 16 First-Person Accounts of the Rioting," *Chicago Reader*, August 25, 1988.

36. "Obituaries, Holloway," *Alton Evening Telegraph*, April 10, 1968, 21.

37. Jon Anderson, with on-the-ground reporting by Joel Havemann and Ben Heineman Jr., "The 9 Who Died: Stories Behind the Riot Statistics," *Chicago Sun-Times*, April 15, 1968.

38. Anderson, with Havemann and Heineman.

39. Anderson, with Havemann and Heineman.

40. Anderson, with Havemann and Heineman.

41. Bogira, "They Were There."

42. "Probe in Deaths of 4 in Rioting Continues," *Chicago Tribune*, August 7, 1968, 18

43. A *Chicago Sun-Times* journalist, Ben Heineman Jr., would eventually uncover a connection between the four deaths but ended up having trouble publishing the story. His most comprehensive report was included in the April 15, 1968, article "Story Behind Riot Toll: The Nine Who Died." The case, despite an August commission report stating "especially disturbing" connections with police using unlawful force, was never pursued further. Heineman heard reports about an unmarked police car, a blue Chevy, called the "killer squad." Heineman would later write in 1968 for the *Chicago Journalism Review*: "What matters is that four men were killed—killed needlessly by men who may still be

dangerous—and the newspaper, the only independent institution with enough power to unravel the extent of police involvement, did not give its full efforts to the case." See also Christopher Chandler, "Shoot to Kill . . . Shoot to Maim," *Chicago Reader*, April 4, 2002.

44. Wiedrich, "Genesis of a Riot."

45. Bogira, "They Were There."

46. Bogira.

47. Roger Birdsell, "4,000 March Toward Courthouse," *South Bend Tribune*, April 5, 1968, 1 and 16.

48. Birdsell, 16.

49. Hicks, "Sophomores at Notre Dame," 20.

50. Charles J. Shields, *And So It Goes—Kurt Vonnegut: A Life* (New York: Henry Holt, 2011), 50–78.

51. Shields, 50–78.

52. Shields, 75.

53. Dan Wakefield, ed. *Kurt Vonnegut: Letters* (New York: Random House, 2012), 11.

54. Wakefield, 144–146. Also "Crash Baffles Jersey Central," *Morning News*, September 16, 1958, 6.

55. Wakefield, 146.

56. Wakefield, 146; Shields, *So It Goes*, 146.

57. From the 1968 Notre Dame Literary Festival program, "Minds and Motivations," 13.

58. Kurt Vonnegut, *Cat's Cradle* (New York: Dial Press, 2010), 5.

59. Richard Bizot, correspondence with the author, August 18, 2017.

60. Wakefield, *Kurt Vonnegut: Letters*, 138.

61. March 18, 1968, letter courtesy of the Indiana University Lilly Library, found in the folder "Kurt Vonnegut Letters to Sam Stewart: 1962–1968."

62. "Reveal Plans for McCarthy," *South Bend Tribune*, April 5, 1968.

63. Patricia Koval, "Face 'Violence Facts,' Writer Urges U.S.," *South Bend Tribune*, April 5, 1968.

64. "Sharp Sense of Humor Shown by 'Catch-22' Author," *South Bend Tribune*, May 5, 1968, 218.

65. William Locke, correspondence with the author, May 27, 2017.

66. Koval, "Face 'Violence Facts.'"

67. Vonnegut will deliver this same kind of chalkboard lecture, on and off, for the next thirty-seven years. Several of the festival attendees mentioned Cinderella and the chalkboard storytelling techniques. This passage is taken from this video, but he would have reused many of the same anecdotes: https://www .youtube.com/watch?v=oP3c1h8v2ZQ&t=191s.

68. Hicks, "Sophomores at Notre Dame," 19–22.

69. Trevino, interview with the author, March 14, 2018.

70. Kurt Vonnegut, *Slaughterhouse-Five* (New York: Dell, 1969). Kennedy was shot at the Ambassador Hotel in Los Angeles, California, right after midnight on June 5, 1968. He died at the hospital twenty-five hours later, on June 6, two months after Dr. King's death.

71. Andre Dubus, *Meditations from a Movable Chair* (New York: Random House 1999), 47.

72. Dubus, 48.

73. Dubus, 48.

74. For more about Ralph Ellison's full life, see Arnold Rampersad's *Ralph Ellison: A Biography* (New York: Vintage, 2008).

75. John Callahan, introduction to Ralph Ellison and Albert Murray, *Trading Twelves: The Selected Letters of Ralph Ellison and Albert Murray*, ed. John Callahan (New York: Vintage, 2010), xii.

76. Ellison and Murray, *Trading Twelves*, part 2, "Rome, Casablanca, and New York: 1955–1958," 116.

77. Ellison and Murray, 117. The letter is a scathing takedown of Faulkner, all the more surprising since Ellison had greatly respected the Mississippi author. After reading Faulkner's letter to *Life* magazine, Ellison was incensed: "He thinks that Negroes exist simply to give ironic overtone to the viciousness of white folks, when he should know very well that we're trying hard as hell to free ourselves; thoroughly and completely, so that when we got the crackers off our back we can discover what we (Moses) really are and what we really wish to preserve out of the experience that made us."

78. Rampersad, *Ralph Ellison*, 49.

79. Ellison and Murray, *Trading Twelves*, part 3, "Los Angeles and New York: 1958–1960," 196.

80. "King, Leaders Unveil 'Operation Dialogue,' New Rights Weapon," *Pittsburgh Courier*, February 13, 1965, 5.

81. Rampersad, *Ralph Ellison*, ch. 16.

82. Ralph Ellison, "The Myth of the Flawed White Southerner," *The Collected Essays of Ralph Ellison*, ed. John Callahan (New York: Modern Library, 2003), 561.

83. James Beaumont, *Des Moines Register*, "King Warns of Starting World War," October 30, 1967, 1 and 3; Willie Morris, *New York Days* (New York: Back Bay Books, 1993), 275–280.

84. Morris, 275–280.

85. Beaumont, "King Warns," 1.

86. Rampersad, *Ralph Ellison*, ch. 17.

87. Hicks, "Sophomores at Notre Dame," 19–22.

88. Trevino, interview with the author, March 14, 2018.

89. Hicks, "Sophomores at Notre Dame," 19–22.

90. Koval, "Face 'Violence Facts.'"

91. Koval.

92. See both Hicks, "Sophomores at Notre Dame," and Koval, "Face 'Violence Facts.'"

93. Koval.

94. Granville Hicks quote is from Robert O'Meally, ed., *New Essays on Invisible Man*, (Cambridge: Cambridge University Press, 1988), 6.

95. Wright Morris, "A Tale From Underground," *New York Times*, April 13, 1952, http://movies2.nytimes.com/library/books/072098ellison-invisible.html.

96. From "Quick Evaluations on the Talent in the Room" (1959), in *Mind of an Outlaw: Collected Essays*, by Norman Mailer and ed. Phillip Sipiora (New York: Random House, 2014), 80.

97. Koval, "Face 'Violence Facts'"; *"potted academic lecture"*: John Matthias, correspondence with the author, October 15, 2017.

98. Author correspondence October 15, 2017, with John Matthias, a Notre Dame professor during the literary festival. "Literature goes on" is also credited to Matthias and published in DeCicco, *SLF Album*, 6.

99. John Matthias and Peter Michelson, correspondence with the author, October 20, 2017.

100. The date of the typed letter reads April 5, 1968, and a *South Bend Tribune* picture has Morris attending the Ellison talk. This reception, the "farewell" party, would be where Morris hands the letter. Through my correspondence with John Mroz's wife, Karen Linehan-Mroz, I was shown the original copy of the letter.

101. William F. Buckley Jr., *Let Us Talk of Many Things* (New York: Basic, 2008), 120–123. One of the reasons for the chancellor's fears stems from the rumor that King's assassin was headed for Nashville after fleeing Memphis.

102. Crowd number reported by John Hemphill, "Bond, Buckley, Debate Fate of Nonviolence," *Tennessean*, April 6, 1968, 1 and 7. Press release accessed through VU's library website: http://exhibits.library.vanderbilt.edu/Impact/impact1968.php.

103. "Bond, Horace Julian," Martin Luther King, Jr., Research and Education Institute, Stanford University, accessed October 30, 2018, https://kinginstitute.stanford.edu/encyclopedia/bond-horace-julian.

104. "Bond, Horace Julian."

105. Hemphill, *Tennessean*, "Bond, Buckley, Debate," 1 and 7.

106. Hemphill, 1 and 7.

107. Hemphill, 1 and 7. "Anxiety" is from Buckley, *Let Us Talk of Many Things*, 120–123. The speech quoted here is an address Buckley gave two weeks later, on April 19, 1968, at the American Society of Newspaper Editors Convention in Washington, DC, titled "Did You Kill Martin Luther King?"

108. Buckley, *Let Us Talk of Many Things*, 120–123.

109. Buckley, 120–123.

110. Buckley, 120–123.

111. Robb Baker, "Ochs Ill, but On with the Show," April 6/7, 1968, *Chicago Tribune*. Information from a screenshot hosted on Celebrating Phil Ochs (website), accessed November 2018, https://celebratingphilochs.com/april-5-1968-chicago-il-orchestra-hall-2/. Orchestra Hall is now under the umbrella of the Symphony Center.

112. Baker.

113. "Most of Marchers Were Students," *Ohio State Lantern*, April 17, 1967, 5, https://celebratingphilochs.files.wordpress.com/2015/08/april1967.png.

7. Saturday, April 6, 1968: The Beginning of the End

1. Martin Luther King Jr., "Loving Your Enemies: Sermon Delivered at Dexter Avenue Baptist Church," November 17, 1957; full text of sermon can be found in *The Papers of Martin Luther King Jr*, vol. 4, *Symbol of the Movement, January 1957–December 1958* (Berkeley: University of California Press, 2000), 315–323.

2. As quoted in Joshua Bloom and Waldo E. Martin Jr., *Black Against Empire: The History and Politics of the Black Panther Party* (Oakland: University of California Press, 2016), 119.

3. "Silence on Killing of Panther," *San Francisco Examiner*, April 8, 1968, 1.

4. Ed Montgomery, "Panthers Looked for Shooting," *San Francisco Examiner*, April 25, 1968, 1 and 5.

5. Bobby Seale, *Power to the People: The World of the Black Panthers*, 31.

6. *Examiner* reporting, April 8 and 25 articles.

7. Kate Coleman, "Souled Out," *New West*, May 19, 1980. 18–27, http://coleman truth.net/kate1.pdf.

8. *San Francisco Examiner*, April 25, 1968, 1 and 5.

9. Dexter Waugh, *San Francisco Examiner*, "New Version of How Hutton Slain," April 18, 1971, 1 and 20.

10. Waugh, 1 and 20. The police officer, Gwynne Peirson, was never called to make a grand jury testimony. He confessed to seeing Bobby Hutton shoved in the back and then shot in Dexter Waugh's article. Peirson wrote about the incident in his master's thesis, and only made it public after retiring from the Oakland Police Department. He'd been with the OPD for twenty-two years.

11. Waugh, 1 and 20.

12. Califano, *Triumph and Tragedy*, 281.

13. Califano, 281.

14. "Conversation with John Stennis, April 6, 1968," Secret White House Tapes, Miller Center (website), University of Virginia, accessed October 16,

2018, https://millercenter.org/the-presidency/secret-white-house-tapes/conversation-john-stennis-april-6-1968.

15. "Conversation with John Stennis."

16. Lyndon Johnson, *The Vantage Point: Perspectives of the Presidency, 1963–1969*, 176–179.

17. Johnson, 176–177.

18. Busby, *Thirty-First of March*, 243.

19. Busby, 243.

20. Coretta Scott King and Barbara Reynolds, *Coretta: My Life, My Love, My Legacy* (New York: Macmillan, 2017), 183.

21. King and Reynolds, 1–50

22. King and Reynolds, 1–50.

23. King and Reynolds, 1–50.

24. WSB-TV newsfilm clip of Coretta Scott King speaking at an April 6, 1968, press conference at Ebenezer Baptist Church, Atlanta, Georgia, WSB-TV newsfilm collection, Walter J. Brown Media Archives and Peabody Awards Collection, accessed October 21, 2018, from the Civil Rights Digital Library, http://crdl.usg.edu/cgi/crdl?format=_video&query=id%3Augabma_wsbn_53564&_cc=1.

25. WSB-TV newsfilm clip of Coretta Scott King.

26. "Mayor Expresses Sympathy to Relatives of Victims," *Palladium-Item*, April 7, 1968, 1.

27. "Local Board's Blast Report," *Palladium-Item*, May 29, 1968, 4. Film information in the April 3, 1968 edition, 21. "Mild and sunny" in April 7, 1968, 2.

28. "Local Board's Blast Report"; see also "Richmond Blast Is Factor in Planned Gunpowder Storage Rules," *Indianapolis Star*, May 23, 1968, 33.

29. "Illegal Storage of Gunpowder Cited in Richmond Explosion," *Indianapolis Star*, May 30, 1968, 49.

30. "Illegal Storage of Gunpowder." The mention of customers reporting a "gas odor" was from RTV6 The Indy Channel. Also very much worth viewing is a documentary entitled *1:47*, the exact time of the explosion.

31. "Illegal Storage of Gunpowder"; see also *Palladium-Item*, May 29, 1968, 4–5. *Palladium-Item* published a sketch of the Marting Arms basement.

32. "Like Looking Death in the Face" *Palladium-Item*, Eye-Witness of Disaster Recalls," April 10, 1968, 30

33. Ed Kaeuper, "Citizens Wish It Was a Dream—But It Was All Too True," *Palladium-Item*, April 7, 1968, 2.

34. Don Compton, "Only Marting's Store Survivor Describes Miraculous Escape," *Palladium-Item*, April 8, 1968, 4.

35. Staff Reporters, "Short-Circuited Auto Horns, Jangling Phones in Blasted Stores Jar Nerves," *Palladium-Item*, April 7, 1968, 8.

36. "Mayor Expresses Sympathy to Relatives of Victims," *Palladium-Item*, April 7, 1968, 1; also Kaeuper, "Citizens Wish," 2.

37. Bob Barnet, "Spark May Have Triggered Explosion at Richmond," *Muncie Star*, April 10, 1968, 1–2.

38. Location in the *Notre Dame Observer*, April 5, 1968, and also mentioned in the original festival program.

39. Quotes from Hicks, "Sophomores at Notre Dame," 19–22.

40. Hicks, *Part of the Truth*, 280.

41. Wright Morris, letter to John Mroz, April 5, 1968. A copy of this letter was given to me by Mroz's wife, Karen Linehan-Mroz. John Mroz passed away in 2014.

42. Koval, "Literary Festival a Swinging Affair."

43. Hicks, "Sophomores at Notre Dame," 19–22.

44. Address published in the *South Bend Tribune*, April 5, 1968, "Reveal Plans for McCarthy,"

45. Author correspondence with Richard Bizot, August 17, 2017, including details from his unpublished essay, "Vonnegut and Heller at Notre Dame." Bizot taught at Notre Dame for seven years before accepting a teaching position at the University of North Florida. The professor who introduced the authors was Peter Michelson, who told me of the event via correspondence on October 20, 2017.

46. Several of the sophomores and professors I talked with mentioned the fund-raiser story. The version I've put here is a combination of a few sophomore committee member comments, but primarily Richard Bizot's account, given on August 17, 2017, and Peter Michelson's, given October 20, 2017.

47. *"With Ralph Ellison"*: Carole Mallory, "The Kurt and Joe Show," *Playboy*, May 1992.

48. Mike Steele, "The Actors Get No Encores When Script Calls for War," *Minneapolis Star Tribune*, September 29, 1968, 8E.

49. Poem first appeared in a May 2005 edition of the *New Yorker*. Accessed October 19, 2020, https://www.brainpickings.org/2014/01/16/kurt-vonnegut-joe -heller-having-enough/.

Epilogue: How John Mroz Turned Out

1. Ellison comment is from the autographed photo, a scan of which was provided to me by John Mroz's wife, Karen Linehan-Mroz.

2. The 1969 Notre Dame Literary Festival was March 23–29, and the authors who attended were Leroi Jones (later Amiri Baraka), Sidney Carrio, George Plimpton (of *Beyond the Law* fame, among other accomplishments), Peter DeVries (meant to attend the 1968 festival but dropped out due to an illness), John Knowles, and John Barth. Neither Bradbury nor Warren would attend the festival.

3. "Leary: 'Drugs a Way to God' Cohen: 'Don't Kid Yourself,'" *Notre Dame Observer*, October 3, 1968, 1.

4. "Notre Dame Pornography Show Raided," *Chicago Tribune*, February 8, 1969, 5; Tara Hunt, "The Damndest Experience We Ever Had," *Notre Dame Magazine*, Spring 2015, 13, 15–16.

5. Linehan-Mroz, correspondence with the author, May 4, 2017.

6. Linehan-Mroz, correspondence with the author, April 28, 2017.

7. Bruce Weber, "John Edwin Mroz, an Envoy to Arafat, Dies at 66," *New York Times*, September 3, 2014, A21.

8. Condoleezza Rice, letter to Karen Linehan-Mroz, August 2014. Henry Kissinger, letter to John Mroz, August 14, 2014, one day before Mroz passed away. These letters are from Karen Linehan-Mroz's private collection.

9. Linda DeCicco's lovely book *SLF Album* lists all the authors who have attended the festival until 1996 (pp. 121–126).

SELECTED BIBLIOGRAPHY

Books

Boomhower, Ray E. *Robert Kennedy and the 1968 Indiana Primary*. Bloomington, IN: University Press, 2008.

Buckley, William F., Jr. *The Jeweler's Eye: A Book of Irresistible Political Reflections*. New York: Putnam, 1968.

Busby, Horace. *The Thirty-First of March: An Intimate Portrait of Lyndon Johnson's Final Days in Office*. New York: Farrar, Straus and Giroux, 2005.

Carmichael, Stokely. *Ready for Revolution: The Life and Struggles of Stokely Carmichael*. New York: Scribner, 2003.

DeCicco, Linda. *SLF Album: An Informal History of Notre Dame's Sophomore Literary Festival, 1967–1996*. Notre Dame, IN: University of Notre Dame Press, 1997.

Ellison, Ralph. *Invisible Man*. New York: Random House, 1952.

Garrow, David J. *Bearing the Cross: Martin Luther King Jr. and the Southern Christian Leadership Conference*. New York: HarperCollins, 1986.

Goodwin, Doris Kearns. *Lyndon Johnson and the American Dream*. New York: Harper & Row, 1976.

Heller, Joseph. *Catch-22*. New York: Simon & Schuster, 1961.

———. *We Bombed in New Haven*. New York: Knopf, 1968.

Hicks, Granville. *Part of the Truth*. New York: Harcourt, Brace & World, 1965.

———. *Small Town*. New York: Fordham University Press, 2004. First published 1946.

Johnson, Lyndon B. *The Vantage Point: Perspectives of the Presidency, 1963–1969*. New York, Holt, 1971.

Joseph, Peniel E. *Stokely: A Life*. New York: Perseus, 2014.

King, Coretta Scott. *My Life with Martin Luther King Jr.* New York: Holt, 1969.

Lennon, J. Michael. *Norman Mailer: A Double Life.* New York: Simon & Schuster, 2013.

Lynd, Alice. *We Won't Go: Personal Accounts of War Objectors.* Boston: Beacon Press, 1968.

Mailer, Norman. *The Armies of the Night: History as a Novel, the Novel as History.* New York: Plume, 1968.

———. *Why Are We in Vietnam.* New York: New American Library, 1967.

McCarthy, Eugene J. *The Year of the People.* New York: Doubleday, 1969.

Morris, Wright. *A Bill of Rites, A Bill of Wrongs, A Bill of Goods.* New York: NAL, 1968.

———. *The Loneliness of the Long Distance Writer.* Santa Rosa, CA: Black Sparrow Press, 1995.

Rampersad, Arnold. *Ralph Ellison.* New York: Random House, 2007.

Risen, Clay. *A Nation on Fire.* New York: Wiley, 2007.

Rosenbloom, Joseph. *Redemption: Martin Luther King Jr.'s Last 31 Hours.* Boston: Beacon Press, 2018.

Schumacher, Michael. *There But for Fortune: The Life of Phil Ochs.* New York: Hyperion, 1996.

Shields, Charles J. *And So It Goes: Kurt Vonnegut: A Life.* New York: Holt, 2011.

Vonnegut, Kurt. *Slaughterhouse-Five.* New York: Dell, 1969.

Wakefield, Dan, ed. *Kurt Vonnegut: Letters.* New York: Dell, 2012.

Witcover, Jules. *85 Days: The Last Campaign of Robert Kennedy.* New York: Putnam, 1969.

Local Newspapers

Muncie Star (29 March–10 April 1968)

Notre Dame Observer (29 March–10 April, 1968)

South Bend Tribune (29 March–10 April 1968)

Miscellaneous

1968 *Dome* (Notre Dame yearbook)

1968 Sophomore Literary Festival official program

Anderson, Jon, with Joel Havemann and Ben Heineman Jr. "The 9 Who Died: Stories Behind the Riot Statistics." *Chicago Sun-Times*, April 15, 1968.

Hicks, Granville. "The Sophomores at Notre Dame." May 4, 1968, *Saturday Review.*

Hutchens, John K. "One Thing and Another." May 4, 1968, *Saturday Review.*

Mailer, Norman. *Beyond the Law.* 1968. Film.

Perrusquia, Marc. "6:01: Martin Luther King Jr.'s Last 32 Hours." April 4, 2013, *Commercial Appeal.*

Interviews of Festival Attendees

Bartell, Father Ernest. August 16, 2017
Bizot, Richard. August 18, 2017
Brown, James L. October 29, 2017
Gallagher, Barney, August 5, 2017
Hagan, Dean. March 31, 2018
Hoefer, Fritz. August 22, 2017
Kress, Martin. June 16, 2017
Kukielski, Phil. September 18, 2017
Locke, William C. June 16, 2017
Linehan-Mroz, Karen, May 1, 2017
Matthias, John. October 15, 2017
McKenzie, James. 25 April, 2017
Metzger, Jim. May 8, 2017
Michelson, Peter. October 20, 2017
Moran, Richard. August 27, 2017
Ovitt, George, Jr. October 9, 2017
Schatz, Tom. January 5, 2019
Suzuki, Edward. March 4, 2018
Trevino, Tito. March 14, 2018

INDEX